Advance Acclaim for *Grand The*

"With brilliance and grace, suitable outrage ʒ throws open the Pentagon and its pervasive cultuₗ much as a century ago Lincoln Steffens exposed the disgrace of meat packing and more. As with Steffens' government and business predators, the rot and madness will no doubt go on, but after St. Clair's equally enduring work, we can never say we didn't know why it happened—or how it all smelled."

—Roger Morris, former National Security Council staffer, author of *Partners in Power: the Clintons and Their America*

"This book should become a text in political science and public administration courses at every university. It is an invaluable guide to understanding the institutionalized corruption built into US policy."

—Saul Landau, author of *Pre-Emptive Empire*

"Jeffrey St. Clair's stalwart and scathing indictment of the war criminals running this country should inspire readers to do all they can to cease complicity with this lawless crowd. *Grand Theft Pentagon* builds a case for U.S. people to stop collaborating with these rulers and their callous disregard for the non-rich and non-white."

—Kathy Kelly, 3-time Nobel Peace prize nominee, co-founder Voices in the Wilderness, author of *Other Lands Have Dreams*

"A gripping tale of how neoconservatives fabricated a pretext for war that financially benefited the Bush regime's backers to the detriment of our country."

—Paul Craig Roberts, former Assistant Secretary of the Treasury under Ronald Reagan, author of *The Tyranny of Good Intentions*.

"Jeffrey St. Clair is the Seymour Hersh of environmental journalism."

—Josh Frank, author of *Left Out!*

"Only by reading *Grand Theft Pentagon* will the reader know that it is the height of flattery to call it merely thievery. The Pentagon, Congress, defense corporations, and—to its undying shame—the mainstream press are not just helping each other steal our money, they are trashing our security and raping our liberty. Examine this must read book, and weep for your country."

—Winslow T. Wheeler, veteran National Security advisor to the US Senate, author of *The Wastrels of Defense*.

"In days of yore in London town the pickpocket, technically known as the "file," never worked alone. He or she was preceded by the "bulk," a belligerent fellow good at starting fights, the perfect condition for the file industriously to ply the trade. Daniel Defoe explained their maneuvers back then; Jeffrey St. Clair explains the shenanigans of the bulk and file nowadays. Lockheed, Halliburton, Bechtel play the file; Vietnam, Somalia, Kosovo, Gulf I and Gulf II the work of the bulk. St. Clair names them—the outsourcers, the stuntmen, the war profiteers, the arms dealers, the fat cats, executive fixers, and neo-cons. Alternatively, the file in smoother operating mode would team up with the "buttock," an expert at distracting the public by charms or promises of eternal salvation. Today's buttocks are perception managers, PR gurus, spin meisters, information warriors, psy-operators, fundamentalists, and con men. Certainly, stuff happens, as Donald "the File" Rumsfield said. St. Clair tells us how and why in phraseology worthy of Tom Paine, with an attitude that would bring a smile to Mark Twain, and with the scholarly exactitude of an actual criminal indictment.

It's a brilliant book for our hideous times—comic, reforming, rousing. Heave the rascals out, buttock, bulk, and file!"

—Peter Linebaugh, author of *The London Hanged* and an editor of *Albion's Fatal Tree*

"For anyone who enjoys serious muckraking, caustic humor, or elegant invective, *Grand Theft Pentagon* is a triple threat. Jeffrey St. Clair is both thorough and unsparing in this collection of essays that disinters the first casualty of war. This is an expose of double-dealing politics, malignant lies, craven media, and the revolving doors between Pentagon procurement offices and corporate boardrooms. It is also a grim description of the militarization of every molecule of American society. GTP should be purchased as a gift for every soldier serving in Southwest Asia right now... as one of the bases for building a new GI resistance. Troops will no longer find themselves willing to go outside the wire when they realize they work for sanguinary carnival barkers... vicious buffoons who are driving us all toward the abyss in a runaway train of unsustainable greed and savage self-delusion. Best argument I've seen in a while for re-education camps built on the toxic brownfields. Congressmen, defense CEOs, and Generals... go to the front line."

—Stan Goff, former Sgt in US Army's Delta Force, author of *Full-Spectrum Disorder*

"St. Clair is a muckraker par excellence. Muckraking tends to date quickly; old scandals are no longer scandalous. What makes St. Clair's work so compelling, and so likely to endure, is his focus on people, the villains and the very few heroes of the piece.

St. Clair does not caricature; he feels his subjects like a novelist. George Bush and Donald Rumsfeld come alive in all their creepiness, but when the curtain falls it is Bunnatine Greenhouse, the unsung Halliburton whistleblower, who gets center stage. St. Clair brings ample research and devastating argument to his attack on indecent powerbrokers. In the end, though, it is his humanity that illuminates the tale."

—Michael Neumann, professor of philosophy, Trent University, author of *The Case Against Israel*

"Jeffrey St. Clair's *Grand Theft Pentagon* is a brilliant account of how trillions of dollars go into the pockets of arms makers and how the Pentagon's preeminent claim on the budget has become a hugh trough for them. This is the best book on how the defense system really functions, who gains—and how we all lose thereby. Extremely well written and full of convincing cases and insights, this book should be read by everyone who wants to know how—and why—America operates.

—Gabriel Kolko, Distinguished Research Professor Emeritus at York University, author of *Another Century of War* and *Anatomy of a War*

"Bribery, kickbacks, no-bid contracts, selling war, selling torture, buying politicians, pervasive sleaze. It's all here in grim detail in Jeffrey St. Clair's powerful chronicle of the theft of the U.S. defense industry by rapacious war profiteers and the increasing militarization of U.S. policy an U.S. society. This is a sad tale of the financial, political, and moral corruption that now characterizes so much of America, left as well as right."

—Kathleen Christison, former CIA analyst, author of *Perceptions of Palestine*

"Jeffrey St. Clair's invaluable book is a vivid profile of the sordid deals brokered by warmonger politicians and war-profiteer corporations. With the skill of a high class barber he uncovers all the bald patches of the imperial administration."

—Tariq Ali, author of *Bush in Babylon*

Grand Theft Pentagon

Tales of Corruption and Profiteering
in the War on Terror

Jeffrey St. Clair

Common Courage Press   Monroe, Maine

Library of Congress Cataloging-in-Publication Data is available from publisher on request.
ISBN 1-56751-336-0 paper
ISBN 1-56751-337-9 hardcover

ISBN 13 9781567513363
ISBN 13 9781567513370

Common Courage Press
121 Red Barn Road
Monroe, ME 04951

207-525-0900
fax: 207-525-3068

www.commoncouragepress.com
info@commoncouragepress.com

First printing
Printed in Canada

For what can war, but endless war, still breed?

—John Milton

In politics, what begins in fear, usually ends in failure.

—Samuel Taylor Coleridge

For Kimberly

The gem of mutual peace emerging from the wild chaos of love.

—D.H. Lawrence

Contents

Opening Statement

Versailles on the Potomac

W ar profiteer. It used to be one of the dirtiest slurs in American politics, potent enough to sully the reputations of the rich and powerful. Now it's a calling card, something you might find highlighted in a defense contractor's corporate prospectus as a lure to attract investors looking for bulging profits and escalating dividends.

In the summer of 2000, the defense industry was mired in a prolonged slump, as was the US economy, which under the lash of its neo-liberal architects had become dependent on the financial engines of the munitions makers. Unhappily for the defense industry and its investor clash, the Soviet Union had disintegrated before their very eyes and the People's Republic of China, long considered the bogeyman state in waiting, had lustily embraced state capitalism instead of stepping up to the plate as a brawny military rival.

The big ticket items of the Cold War, from Stealth bombers to nuclear subs, from aircraft carriers to Star Wars, that had sustained the industry to the tune of tens of billions every year no longer had the slightest pretext for continued production, except as the most extravagant form of corporate welfare. Those weapons systems that weren't obsolete, such as the B-2 bomber and F-22 fighter, simply didn't work, such as Star Wars, remarketed as Ballistic Missile Defense.

To make matters more fraught for the weapons industry, the Pentagon was poised to put the finishing touches on its Quadrennial Defense Review, which sets procurement, budget and policy goals for the Defense Department. Of course, the Pentagon would never slash its own budget and, in fact, many anticipated that the QDR would call for increasing annual defense spending to something approaching 4 percent of the gross domestic product. However, it seemed likely that the generals would call for the termination of many of the multi-billion dollar relics of the Cold War in exchange for massive increases in spending on newer killing technologies geared for what has come to be known as "4th Generation Warfare."

Then 9/11 happened and all the anxieties of the weapons lobby were alleviated in the flames of one fateful morning. The QDR, once so threatening, was simply another fat white paper that came and went without leaving so much as a scratch on the old Imperial Guard.

As we reveal here, the Taliban offered Osama Bin Laden and his top associates to the Bush administration on several occasions after the attacks of 9/11. Bush refused. They wanted a prolonged and ever-escalating war, not a deftly executed police action and not justice for the families of those slain and maimed by Bin Laden's kamikazes.

Instead, thousands of Cruise missiles were ordered up and, just like that, Boeing and Lockheed were back in business. For months, cruise missiles, J-DAM bombs and CB-87 cluster munitions shredded the hamlets and hovels of Afghanistan, killing more than 3,500 civilians. But this was simply a bloody prelude to a more profound slaughter. For Afghanistan, in the immortal words of Donald Rumsfeld, wasn't a "target rich" environment. But Iraq certainly was. And only days after the 9/11 attacks, Rumsfeld and his neocon coterie of laptop bombardiers began plotting the war on Saddam and the domestic propaganda campaign for how to sell it to a psychologically shattered and anxiety-ridden American public. The civilian body count in Iraq would climb much higher, topping 40,000 by the summer of 2005. Overall, more than 100,000 people have perished in the war.

The Bush wars on Afghanistan and Iraq were misguided, counter-productive and illegal ventures, although entirely predictable outbursts of imperial vengeance. What is truly perverse is the fact that while one wing of the Pentagon was planning wars against a "faceless enemy" and a "rogue state", another wing was lobbying congress on behalf of the weapons companies to approve billions in funding for all of the baroque artifacts of the Cold War, from Star Wars to Stealth fighters. Congress was only too happy to help. From the fall of 2001 through the end of 2002, not a single funding request for a big-ticket item went denied, from unneeded aircraft carriers to unwanted Boeing tankers.

But in order to fund these bailouts to the defense lobby for making weapons for a war that no longer existed, Congress had to rob other budgetary accounts. And here's where it gets truly bizarre. Intent on satiating the cravings for pork from their political patrons, the leadership of the Defense Appropriations committees, led by Senator Ted Stevens, the Alaska Republican, paid for these costly and useless projects by reprogramming billions from the so-called Operations and Maintenance accounts, which were being used to fund the logistics work for the on-the-ground wars in Afghanistan and Iraq. Even the normally docile Office of Management and

Budget raised a warning, writing in a letter to Stevens dated December 6, 2002: "These [Operations and Maintenance] reductions would undermine DoD's ability to adequately fund training, operations, maintenance, supplies and other essentials. They would seriously damage the readiness of our armed forces and undermine their ability to execute current operations, including the war on terrorism."

That warning letter (and thousands of documents like it), largely ignored by the war-hungry US press, is the congressional equivalent of the Pentagon Papers for the Afghanistan and Iraq wars. In order to shell out billions for Star Wars and the F-22 fighter, Congress took money from accounts that would have improved the terrible logistical planning in Iraq and bought essential items for the protection of US combat troops, such as body armor and armored Humvees. The blood of many a soldier maimed or killed in Iraq is indelibly stained on the hands of Stevens and his colleagues who choose to put the welfare of Boeing and Lockheed above the grunts in the field.

The Pentagon has become a kind of government operated casino, doling out billions in contracts to the big-time spenders in American politics: General Dynamics, Boeing, Raytheon, Bechtel, Lockheed and, of course, the bete noir of the Bush administration, Halliburton.

The saga of Halliburton, however, is only a grotesque symbol for a cancer that has gone systemic, gnawing away at corporations, politicians, bureaucrats, the legions of lobbyists on K Street, media elites, Wall Street fund managers and military brass.

Weapons making (and the credit companies) are the last thriving sectors of the American economy. Of course, even defense work is being inexorably outsourced, as the story of Magnequench's relocation from Indiana to China details with a cruel absurdity that may even have caused Artaud to blink.

War and credit. The two enterprises go hand in hand. Recall Ezra Pound's declaration in the *Cantos:* "The purpose of war is to make debt." Bush inherited a $500 billion budget surplus. After his tax giveaways to corporations and millionaires and five years of war-making, the surplus has been transformed into a record deficit that forecloses opportunities for urgently social spending on health care, education, and development of alternative sources of energy that would alleviate the impulse to wage wars for oil.

It's an easy but fateful step from war and debt to corruption and profit.

Washington has become a dizzying maze of revolving doors; bribery and kickbacks, where even generals betray their loyalties to the grunts in exchange for fat checks and cushy jobs with Pentagon contractors. The deals that reprimed the Boeing bank accounts and steered no-bid contracts to companies as big as Halliburton and as obscure as the Chenega Native Corporation were greased by the dispensation of political cash and, in some cases, more personal gratuities.

While the politicians, CEOs and generals got rich, the death toll in Iraq mounted with a grim inexorability. On average each week brings the death of 14 American soldiers, with over a hundred more being maimed. By August 2005, nearly 1900 US troops had died in Iraq, 1650 of them perishing after Bush announced "Mission Accomplished" from the deck of the USS Lincoln. And for every US death more than 30 Iraqis die in bombings and ambushes, in losses that are unmourned and almost unmentioned outside their own ravaged nation.

In Afghanistan, the Taliban has quietly regained control of much of the countryside, with US troops and NGOs under almost daily attack. In the first six months of 2005, nearly as many US troops were killed in Afghanistan than died there in the first three years of the war combined. But few want to look back at a war we'd been told that was long since won.

As for Osama Bin Laden, the world's most wanted man, he remains at large, his ranks of suicidal automatons swelled by the thousands as a direct result of Bush's clumsy crusades, the cruel torture chambers of Gitmo, Bagram and Abu Ghraib and the casual and unrepentant slaughter of innocents. Bush's ineptly executed war on terror may at last be running out of gas, but the fundamentalist forces that gave rise to it are only gaining in potency and global reach. The blowback next time may be a terrible thing to behold.

Yes, the wars in Afghanistan and Iraq blew up in Bush's face, but his cronies are laughing all the way to their off-shore banks, as they race to deposit their blood-soaked billions before the public finally catches on to their vile con-game and rises up in the revolutionary spirit that once defined the nation to demand that justice be served.

The stories in this volume attempt to probe how this perverse state of play could have come to pass during one of the most fraught hours of the Republic, to explore why so few of these episodes were pursued by the mainstream media and to the expose the macabre mindset of those who prowl the halls of what my friend Chuck Spinney, defense analyst and Pentagon whistleblower, calls Versailles on the Potomac.

Now, onward to the palaces…

Oregon City, August 17, 2005

Part One

Capitalism's Last Utopia

The sinews of war are infinite money.

—Marcus Tullius Cicero

One

The Duke and the Enterprise

On the morning of July 1, 2005, FBI agents raided the palatial southern California home of the ultra-hawkish congressman Randy "Duke" Cunningham. With search warrants in hand, the feds rummaged through Cunningham's $2.55 million mansion in the exclusive conclave of Rancho Santa Fe, outside San Diego, looking for evidence linking the 8-term Republican to Mitchell Wade, the founder and CEO of MZM, Incorporated, one of the Pentagon's top 100 contractors.

At the same time the FBI was searching through Cunningham's desk drawers, vaults and computers in California, other agents were executing a raid on the DC offices of MZM. Later that afternoon, FBI agents also rifled through a 42-foot yacht named the "Duke-Stir," docked on the Potomac River, where Cunningham resides, rent free, when he is in Washington.

The investigators were hunting for evidence that Cunningham, a former fighter pilot in Vietnam who claims to have been the inspiration for the Tom Cruise role in the movie "Top Gun," may have accepted bribes from Wade in exchange for helping MZM land a bevy of defense and intelligence contracts from the federal government.

The corruption probe was prompted by the disclosure that in 2003 Wade had purchased the congressman's old four-bedroom house in San Diego for princely sum of $1.7 million. Wade soon put his new house on the red-hot San Diego real estate market, where it sat unsold for almost a year. He finally unloaded it for $950,000.

During that same period of time, the average prices of houses sold in San Diego County climbed by more than 25 percent and rarely stayed on the market for more than a few weeks. Yet, Wade took a $750,000 bath on the Cunningham deal. The federal agents wanted to know why.

The Duke denied any wrongdoing and could offer no explanation for the mysterious and sudden nosedive in the value of his old house. "My whole life I've lived above board," Cunningham pleaded. "I've never even smoked a marijuana cigarette."

The Duke may not have treated his lungs with ganja, but he did attend one of the most infamous orgies in Pentagon history, the 1991 Tailhook Symposium in Las Vegas, the annual gathering of Navy flyers, Pentagon bigwigs, congressional kingpins and defense contractors. Over the course of that September weekend at the Vegas Hilton, at least 83 women were stripped, forced to run a gauntlet of drunken, groping pilots, and sexually molested, with some being forced to "ride the butt rodeo", a Tailhook euphemism for having a pilot bite your buttocks until you can shake yourself free. One investigator blamed the Tailhook scandal on the "Top Gun mentality" of the pilots and their superiors. Bring back some memories, Duke?

One female Navy commander later speculated that part of the vicious nature of the 1991 Tailhook orgy stemmed from the increasing hostility of the military and its backers to the increasing presence of women in positions which had traditionally been the exclusive domain of men. "This was the woman that was making you, you know, change your ways," she said. "This was the woman that was threatening your livelihood. This was the woman that wanted to take your spot in that combat aircraft."

For years after the event, Cunningham, though, referred to the "alleged misconduct" at Tailhook, claiming that the Navy flyboys were just engaging in a little benign steam-venting. He has also tried to block efforts by Congress to curb sexual harassment in the military, rousing himself into passionate denunciations of such measures as "stinking of political correctness".

Cunningham claims that he had been trying to sell his San Diego house for some time. He said he told several people that his house was on the market and one day out of the blue he got a call from Wade, who, Cunningham claims, said, "Hey, I'll buy it!" The Duke said that the price of the house was established by a local real estate agency.

The problem is that the records don't exactly back up Cunningham's miraculous tale of his sudden enrichment. The congressman's house was sold without the aid of a realtor and it was never put on the Multiple Listings Service database of homes for sale. Moreover, Cunningham did not record his munificent windfall on his financial disclosure form, which every member of congress must file each year.

Duke Cunningham prefers to sleep not in the toney community of Potomac, Maryland, but on the Potomac River itself in a yacht. Perhaps Cunningham's preference for the fetid swamps and mosquito-clotted banks of the Potomac stems from his nostalgia for Nixon and the president's nightly sojourns from Great Falls to the Tidal Basin aboard the USS Sequoia.

In 1997, Cunningham purchased the 65-foot riverboat named the Kelly C from his pal Sonny Callahan, the former Republican congressman from

Alabama, for $200,000. The flat-bottomed yacht, which is not deemed sea-worthy enough to venture out into the Chesapeake never mind the Atlantic, only occasionally puttered up and down the river where observers on the Georgetown tow-path could observe the former Navy aviator at the helm, dressed up, according to one longtime resident of M Street, like Admiral Halsey. Dockworkers at the Glen Cove Marina derided the Kelly C as merely a "big party barge."

In 2002, the Duke sold the Kelly C to a Long Island tycoon named Ted Kontogiannis for $600,000, snagging a cool $400,000 profit, even though the condition of the yacht had deteriorated to the point where the congressman himself had to pilot the boat to the shipyards of Consolidated Yachts to undergo a lengthy list of repairs. When the Duke dropped off the boat, he handed the owner of the shipyards an autographed glossy photo of himself adorned in his flight jacket.

For his part, Kontogiannis says the acquisition of the Kelly C was "a steal", although he has never taken the boat out of its slip and, in fact, never registered the sale of the boat with the Coast Guard, whose registry of ships still records the yacht as being owned by the congressman.

At the time, Kontogiannis bought the Kelly C, he was experiencing, what he calls, "a little problem." In fact, Kontogiannis had just been convicted on kickback and bribery charges involving his role in a bid-rigging scheme over contracts with the New York public school system and he was looking for a pardon from the Bush administration. Kontogiannis admits that he asked Duke Cunningham for help in finding a way to persuade Bush to expunge his conviction. According to Kontogiannis, the Duke put the convict into contact with a DC law firm and recommended the names of a couple of lawyers to press his case. Eventually, Kontogiannis said he declined to pursue the pardon because it involved "too much aggravation."

But the tycoon's favors for the Duke didn't end with the purchase of the congressman's party barge. Kontogiannis's daughter and nephew, who own a New York mortgage company, floated the congressman two loans totaling $1.1 million for the purchase of his Rancho Santa Fe mansion. Cunningham paid off one of the loans with the bloated proceeds from the sale of the Kelly C.

In the wake of the disposition of his riverboat, the Duke was not forced to seek cover in the Mitch Snyder Memorial Homeless Shelter. Instead, he made a pinpoint landing onto the deck of yet another yacht, named coincidentally or not, the Duke-Stir, and owned by his old pal, Mitchell Wade, CEO of MZM, Inc. Wade invited the congressman to live rent-free on the Duke-Stir. Since it's a crime for members of congress to live rent free on someone else's property, Cunningham has evaded this troublesome legality by paying $13,000 a year in dock fees, far below the going rent in the more habitable quadrants of the Washington metro area.

Wade and his company also helped to finance Cunningham's political campaigns. According to records from the Center for Responsive Politics, MZM's political action committee donated $17,000 to Cunningham's coffers from 2000 through 2004. Wade personally twisted the arms of his employees to extract donations for Cunningham. "By the spring of '02, Mitch was twisting employees' arms to donate to his MZM PAC," one former MZM employee told the San Diego *Union-Tribune*. "We were called in and told basically either donate to the MZM PAC or we would be fired."

But what did Wade and his firm get in return for the largesse they've shown the Duke? MZM is one of those obscure enterprises started up by former Pentagon staffers and military officers to feed off the defense budget. Along with Wade, a former Pentagon staffer, all of the other corporate officers at MZM joined the company after successful careers in the military. MZM vice-president Joseph Romano was the former head of the Defense Intelligence Agency's technological assessment group. Another MZM vice president, James C. King, is a former Lt. General from the Army, who once headed the National Imagery and Mapping Agency. Yet another vice president, Wayne Hall, is a retired Army general who commanded a military intelligence unit during the 1991 Gulf War. The lone exception is Sue Hogan, MZM's vice president for governmental relations. In her former life, she served as a top staffer on the Senate Appropriation's Committee's subcommittee on defense spending.

Unlike many such revolving door operations, MZM struggled in its formative years, rarely pulling in more than $20 million in revenues in a single year. Then came 9/11, Bush's wars, and the fruitful relationship with the Duke. In 2002, thanks to a flood of Pentagon and CIA contracts, MZM's fortunes took a sudden turn for the better. By 2004, the small firm was hauling in more than $166 million in defense contracts a year.

What kind of contracts did the Duke help MZM obtain? The congressman took refuge behind a veil of secrecy. "They are very, very classified," Cunningham said.

The details of the MZM contracts remain obscure, but a review of the firm's annual report shows that the work ranges from digital mapping, private intelligence operatives and interpreters to the production of psy-ops materials and "collections of foreign language vocal signals."

Cunningham discounts the allegation that he was doing any special favors for Wade or MZM. "The way it works here is: I support a lot of credible defense programs for the Air Force, Navy, ship building, ship repair or intelligence," Cunningham explained. " And they say, you know, 'Duke, these are good programs. This is what I want you to do.'"

Wade had a somewhat more succinct and instructive view of the impact of his political dispensations. According to a former MZM employee, Wade explained that he focused his lobbying efforts on a handful of influential members of congress that he had bankrolled such as Cunningham: "The only people I want to work with are people I give checks to. I own them."

The remarkable aspect of the Cunningham affair is its essential banality. The casual dispensation of political graft is the rule in Washington and has been since the days of the robber barons. This is especially true when it comes to politicians, such as Cunningham, who are in a position to protect and advance the interests of the Pentagon's beefy portfolio of weapons contractors.

Cunningham was never considered a particularly adept politician. He was not a gifted orator like Robert Byrd. Not a slick operator like Trent Lott or Christopher Dodd. Not a master of the legislative parlor tricks in the mode of Pete Dominici or Ted Stevens. Indeed, Cunningham is a clumsy speaker burdened with a boorish personality. The Duke got by on implacable loyalty to his party and, more decisively, on blind obedience to his political patrons.

What political power he enjoyed came courtesy of the economic geography of his southern California district, which harbors a thicket of defense industry giants, from TRW and SAIC to Northrop Grumman and Titan, and military bases. Cunningham was a company man and DC is a new kind of company town. His guardianship of those weapons firms secured Cunningham a seat on the Defense Appropriations Subcommittee, one of the most powerful enclaves on the Hill. With that seat, Cunningham became a mini-potentate in Congress and dozens of defense contractors made the annual Haj to his office to lay riches at his feet and requests on his desk.

As such, the Duke's travails serve as an edifying symbol for how completely Congress has been captured, from top to bottom and left to right, by the coterie munitions makers and weapons merchants that underwrite and direct the American political system. Some veterans of the Hill simply refer to incessant feeding of the Pentagon beast as "the Enterprise", the axiomatic function of their existence in Washington.

The Enterprise pivots on the annual disbursement of the $500 billion defense budget. In an era of shriveling federal spending on domestic social programs, the defense budget remains the most reliable pork barrel in town. Even the thawing of the Cold War and the death of the Soviet Union did little to inhibit the pace of Pentagon spending.

Indeed in July 2000, Admiral Jay Johnson pronounced, as he stepped down from his post as the Navy's top officer, that national security requires a defense expenditure of 4 percent of the nation's Gross Domestic Product. It became known as the 4 Per Cent Solution. A couple of weeks later, General James Jones, Commandant of the Marine Corps, told *Defense Daily* to call for a "gradual ramp up" in defense spending "to about 4 to 4.5 percent of the US gross domestic product." Two days after Jones's comments, Gen. Gordon Sullivan, formerly Army Chief of Staff and now president of the 100,000-strong Association of the US Army, confirmed the Pentagon's floor demand: "We must prepare for the future of the security of our nation. We should set the marker at 4 percent."

But what does 4 percent actually mean in dollar terms? In 2002, the Office of Management and Budget projected GDP at $10.9 trillion rising to $13.9 trillion in 2007. Thus a military budget set at 4 percent of GDP in 2002 would amount to $438 billion, and in 2007 $558 billion. The combined spending of all putative foes of the United States-Russia, China and our old friends the rogue states, including Iran, Syria, Iraq, Libya, North Korea, Serbia, Cuba and Sudan-amounts to a little over $100 billion.

It is not well understood that though the number of ships, planes and troops available to guard the nation has declined sharply, the actual flow of dollars into the pockets of the Praetorians and their commercial partners has remained at cold war levels. It is true that in the immediate aftermath of the cold war, US military spending under George Bush I diminished slightly. Clinton reversed this trend with enough brio to allow Al Gore, speaking to the Veterans of Foreign Wars in the 1996 campaign, to declare that the Democratic bid to the Praetorians that year was far superior to that of the Republicans.

The spending spree hasn't abated since. But all that money did nothing to prevent the attacks of 9/11, in part because the prime arteries of that federal largesse where still pumping billions into the big ticket items of the Cold War arsenal such as Star Wars, Stealth bombers and fighters and Navy battle groups. After 9/11, these perverse spending habits simply got worse. All the old projects, designed to fight an enemy that no longer existed and useless against those who nearly destroyed the Pentagon itself, got funded almost without a question being asked.

During the peak of the Cold War and the Reagan arms build up, the annual Pentagon budget topped out at $453 billion (in 2004 dollars). In 2004, the Defense budget soared to over $500 billion—$47 billion more than the hey day of the Reaganites.

The peculiar consequence of the budgetary and appropriations process meant that there was not a dime to spare from the annual budget to fund the Afghanistan and Iraq wars. Those invasions, which may end up costing $1.5 trillion, according to a conservative estimate by the GAO, had to be financed off the books, through special appropriations, with little public debate and a wink-and-a-nod from the leadership of both parties. There is a calculated opacity to the war and defense appropriations process that is designed to frustrate outsiders.

That's because much of the real defense spending on the Hill happens after hours and is planted in the bewildering copse of congressional earmarks, obscure line items conference committee ad-ons and last minute riders that most members of congress don't even know how to interpret. And these covert add-ons have spiked since 9/11, rising from $4 billion a year in 2001 to $12 billion a year in 2005.

Unlike most agencies, the Pentagon is not bound by its budget. The more it spends, the more it gets. For example, the Pentagon told congress that the Iraq war would cost about $1.5 billion a month. It ended up costing between $5 and $8 billion a month, with no end in sight. The Pentagon has an apt catch-phrase for this bloody flood of spending. Its accountants call it the "burn rate."

The members of the Senate and House Armed Services and Defense Appropriations committees act as a kind of elite Praetorian Guard overseeing the interests of the Pentagon and its cadre of contractors. The prime prerequisite for induction into this legislative tribunal is a finely tuned solicitousness to the desires of the weapons industry. And the faithful are richly recompensed for their labors.

Let's begin with Duke Cunningham's political haul. The eight-term congressman has faced negligible opposition in a district that has been delicately gerrymandered to ensure the continuity of Republican stewardship. Even so, each year Cunningham amassed a staggering tranche of campaign slush without breaking a sweat and the overwhelming amount of that loot originates with weapons and aerospace companies.

In the 2004 congressional election, Cunningham's opponent raised less than $100,000. By contrast, Cunningham heaped up $771,822 and had another $200,000 in reserve that had gone unspent from his previous campaign. His top PAC contributors were all Pentagon contractors, led by Lockheed and Titan who chipped in $15,000 each, MZM with $12,000, General Dynamics contributed $11,000, while General Atomics, Northrop-Grumman and SAIC each pitched in $10,000.

Those corporate contributions are the financial unguents that lubricate the political machinery of the Hill. Between 1997 and 2004, the twenty largest Pentagon contractors lavished Washington's political elites with $33.6 million in campaign contributions. But this is just the icing on a very rich cake. Over the same period, those same companies invested $390 million in lobbying congress. The investment paid off handsomely, yielding those very weapons companies $558.8 billion in federal contracts.

It's fine to live on the dole of a defense company; just don't press the point by reposing for free on their yacht. That's the kind of exposure that might spoil the game for everyone. The profligacy of an individual member of congress must not be permitted to interfere with the grander profligacy of the munitions makers. In the end, the Duke was told that he should fall on his sword, like a true Praetorian, to protect the business of the Empire. In mid-July the congressman suddenly announced his retirement, saying he had decided to "conclude the public chapter of my life" and not seek re-election to a ninth term.

What Cunningham in his obduracy never realized was that he was just an interchangeable part, a legislative errand boy, fetching home pails of contracts every fall when the appropriations bills come due. No special talent required. Almost anyone could do it. In the end, the congressman, the FBI nipping at his heels, was expendable, so that the Enterprise might endure. The Pentagon and its contractors and numberless parasites have many substitutes available to shoulder the Duke's duties.

July, 2005

Two

Bush Was Offered Bin Laden But He Wanted a War

George Bush, the man whose prime re-election campaign plank was his ability to wage war on terror, could have had Osama bin Laden's head handed to him on a platter on his very first day in office, and the offer held good until February 2 of 2002. This is the charge leveled by an Afghan American who had been retained by the US government as an intermediary between the Taliban and both the Clinton and Bush administrations.

Kabir Mohammed is a 48-year-old businessman living in Houston, Texas. Born in Paktia province in southern Afghanistan, he's from the Jaji clan (from which also came Afghanistan's last king). Educated at St Louis University, he spent much of the 1980s supervising foreign relations for the Afghan mujahiddeen, where he developed extensive contacts with the US foreign policy establishment, also with senior members of the Taliban.

After the eviction of the Soviets, Mohammed returned to the United States to develop an export business with Afghanistan and became a US citizen. Figuring in his extensive dealings with the Taliban in the late 1990s was much investment of time and effort for a contract to develop the proposed oil pipeline through northern Afghanistan.

In a lengthy interview and in a memorandum supplied by his lawyer, Kabir Mohammed has given a detailed account and documentation to buttress his charge that the Bush administration could have had Osama bin Laden and his senior staff either delivered to the US or to allies as prisoners, or killed at their Afghan base. Portions of Mohammed's role have been the subject of a number of news reports, including a CBS news story by Alan Pizzey aired September 25, 2001. This is the first he has made public the full story.

By the end of 1999 US sanctions and near-world-wide political ostracism were costing the Taliban dearly and they had come to see Osama bin Laden and his training camps as, in Mohammed's words, "just a damn liability". Mohammed says the Taliban leadership had also been informed in the clearest possible terms by a US diplomat that if any US citizen was harmed as a consequence of an Al Qaeda action, the US would hold the Taliban responsible and target Mullah Omar and the Taliban leaders.

In the summer of 2000, on one of his regular trips to Afghanistan, Mohammed had a summit session with the Taliban high command in Kandahar. They asked him to arrange a meeting with appropriate officials in the European Union, to broker a way in which they could hand over Osama bin Laden. Mohammed recommended they send bin Laden to the World Criminal Court in the Hague.

Shortly thereafter, in August of 2000, Mohammed set up a meeting at the Sheraton hotel in Frankfurt between a delegation from the Taliban and Reiner Weiland of the EU. The Taliban envoys repeated the offer to deport bin Laden. Weiland told them he would take the proposal to Elmar Brok, foreign relations director for the European Union. According to Mohammed, Brok then informed the US Ambassador to Germany of the offer.

At this point the US State Department called Mohammed and said the government wanted to retain his services, even before his official period on the payroll, which lasted from November of 2000 to late September, 2001, by which time he tells us he had been paid $115,000.

On the morning of October 12, 2000, Mohammed was in Washington DC, preparing for an 11am meeting at the State Department, when he got a call from State, telling him to turn on the TV and then come right over. The USS Cole had just been bombed. Mohammed had a session with the head of State's South East Asia desk and with officials from the NSC. They told him the US was going to "bomb the hell out of Afghanistan". "Give me three weeks," Mohammed answered, "and I will deliver Osama to your doorstep." They gave him a month.

Mohammed went to Kandahar and communicated the news of imminent bombing to the Taliban. They asked him to set up a meeting with US officials to arrange the circumstances of their handover of Osama. On November 2, 2000, less than a week before the US election, Mohammed arranged a face-to-face meeting, in that same Sheraton hotel in Frankfurt, between Taliban leaders and a US government team.

After a rocky start on the first day of the Frankfurt session, Mohammed says the Taliban realized the gravity of US threats and outlined various ways bin Laden could be dealt with. He could be turned over to the EU, killed by the Taliban, or made available as a target for Cruise missiles. In the end, Mohammed says, the Taliban promised the "unconditional surrender of bin Laden". "We all agreed," Mohammed tells us, "the best way was to gather Osama and all his lieutenants in one location and the US would send one or two Cruise missiles."

Up to that time Osama had been living on the outskirts of Kandahar. At some time shortly after the Frankfurt meeting, the Taliban moved Osama and placed him and his retinue under house arrest at Daronta, thirty miles from Kabul.

In the wake of the 2000 election Mohammed traveled to Islamabad and met with William Milam, US ambassador to Pakistan and the person designated by the Clinton administration to deal with the Taliban on the fate of bin Laden. Milam told Mohammed that it was a done deal but that the actual bombing of bin Laden would have to be handled by the incoming Bush administration.

On November 23, 2000, Mohammed got a call from the NSC saying they wanted to put him officially on the payroll as the US government's contact man for the Taliban. He agreed. A few weeks later an official from the newly installed Bush National Security Council asked him to continue in the same role and shortly thereafter he was given a letter from the administration (Mohammed showed us a copy of this document), apologizing to the Taliban for not having dealt with bin Laden, explaining that the new government was still setting in, and asking for a meeting in February 2001.

The Bush administration sent Mohammed back, carrying kindred tidings of delay and regret to the Taliban three more times in 2001, the last in September after the 9/11 attack. Each time he was asked to communicate similar regrets about the failure to act on the plan agreed to in Frankfurt. This procrastination became a standing joke with the Taliban. Mohammed tells us, "They made an offer to me that if the US didn't have fuel for the Cruise missiles to attack Osama in Daronta, where he was under house arrest, they would pay for it."

Kabir Mohammed's final trip to Afghanistan on the US government payroll took place on September 3, 2001. On September 11 Mohammed acted as translator for some of the Taliban leadership in Kabul as they watched TV coverage of the attacks on the World Trade Center and the Pentagon. Four days later the US State Department asked Mohammed to set up a meeting with the Taliban. Mohammed says the Taliban were flown to Quetta in two C-130s. The US team issued three demands:

1. Immediate handover of bin Laden;

2. Extradition of foreigners in Al Qaeda who were wanted in their home countries;

3. Shut-down of bin Laden's bases and training camps.

Mohammed says the Taliban agreed to all three conditions.

This meeting in Quetta was reported in carefully vague terms by Pizzey on September 25, where Mohammed was mentioned by name. He tells us that the Bush administration was far more exercised by this story than by any other event in the whole delayed and ultimately abandoned schedule of killing Osama.

On October 18, Mohammed tells us, he was invited to the US embassy in Islamabad and told that "there was light at the end of the tunnel for him", which translated into an invitation to occupy the role later assigned to Karzai. Mohammed declined, saying he had no desire for the role of puppet and probable fall guy.

A few days later the Pizzey story was aired and Mohammed drew the ire of the Bush administration where he already had an enemy in the form of Zalmay Khalilzad, appointed on September 22 as the US special envoy to Afghanistan. After giving him a dressing down, US officials told Mohammed the game had changed, and he should tell the Taliban the new terms: surrender or be killed. Mohammed declined to be the bearer of this news and went off the US government payroll.

Towards the end of that same month of October, 2001 Mohammed was successfully negotiating with the Taliban for the release of hostage Heather Mercer (acting in a private capacity at the request of her father) when the Taliban once again said they would hand over Osama bin Laden unconditionally. Mohammed tells us he relayed the offer to David Donohue, the US consulate general in Islamabad. He was told, in his words, that "the train had moved". Shortly thereafter the US bombing of Afghanistan began.

In December Mohammed was in Pakistan following with wry amusement the assault on Osama bin Laden's supposed mountain redoubt in Tora Bora, in the mountains bordering Pakistan. At the time he said, he informed US embassy officials the attack was a waste of time. Taliban leaders had told him that Bin Laden was nowhere near Tora Bora but in Waziristan. Knowing that the US was monitoring his cell phone traffic, Osama had sent a decoy to Tora Bora.

From the documents he's supplied us and from his detailed account we regard Kabir Mohammed's story as credible and are glad to make public his story of the truly incredible failure of the Bush administration to accept the Taliban's offer to eliminate Bin Laden. As a consequence of this failure more than 3,000 Americans and thousands of Afghans died. Mohammed himself narrowly escaped death on two occasions when Al Qaeda, apprised of his role, tried to kill him. In Kabul in February, 2001, a bomb was detonated in his hotel. Later that year, in July, a hand grenade thrown in his room in a hotel in Kandahar failed to explode.

He told his story to the 9/11 Commission whose main concern, he tells us, was that he not divulge his testimony to anyone else, also to the 9/11 Families who were pursuing a lawsuit based on the assumption of US intelligence blunders by the FBI and CIA. He says his statements to the 9/11 commissions were not much use to the families since his judgment, was, and still remains, that it was not intelligence failures that allowed the 9/11 attacks, but the political negligence of the Bush administration.

With Alexander Cockburn
October 2004

Three

How to Sell a War

Iago: He thinks men honest
That do but seem to be so.

—Othello

The war on Iraq won't be remembered for how it was waged so much as for how it was sold. It was a propaganda war, a war of perception management, where loaded phrases, such as "weapons of mass destruction" and "rogue state," were hurled like precision weapons at the target audience: us.

To understand the Iraq war you don't need to consult generals, but reformed spin doctors or, even better, two of the most seasoned investigators into the dark arts of political propaganda, John Stauber and Sheldon Rampton.

Stauber and Rampton run PR Watch, the Madison, Wisconsin-based group that keeps tabs on the nefarious schemes of the global PR industry to sugarcoat useless, costly and dangerous products. They have also written three of the most important non-fiction books of the last decade. In 1995, they published *Toxic Sludge is Good For You*, a detailed expose of how the PR industry plots and executes campaigns to greenwash corporate malfeasance. This was followed by the prescient and disturbing *Mad Cow USA*. Last year, they produced *Trust Us We're Experts*, a grim and exacting account of the way scientists-for-hire are deployed to rationalize the risks of dangerous products and smear opponents as know-nothings and worrywarts.

Now comes their exquisitely timed *Weapons of Mass Deception: The Uses of Propaganda in Bush's War on Iraq*. Here Stauber and Rampton give us an immediate history, a real-time deconstruction of the mechanics of the Bush war machine. This lushly documented book is a chilling catalog of lies and deceptions, which shows the press contretemps over the Niger yellowcake forgeries to be but a minor distraction given the outlandish frauds pullulating daily from the White House and the Pentagon. The history Rampton and Stauber recounts is every bit as ground breaking as Chomsky and Herman's *Manufacturing Consent* and *War Without Mercy*, John Dower's riveting account of the vile uses of propaganda against Japan during World War II. *Weapons of Mass Deception* shreds the lies, and the motives behind them, as they were being told and describes the techniques of the cover-up as they were being spun.

Stauber and Rampton cut through the accumulated media fog to reveal how the war on Saddam was conceived and how the media battle plan developed and deployed. The identify the key players behind the scenes who stage-managed the countdown to war and follow their paper trails back through the murky corridors of Washington where politics, corporate spin and psy-ops spooks cohabit.

Most of their book was written well before the invasion of Iraq. Yet, the story it relates is only now being nibbled at by the mainstream press, which had done so much to promote the vaporous deceptions of the Bush administration. Stauber and Rampton expose the gaping holes in the Bush administration's war brief and shine an unforgiving light on the neo-con ministers, such as Paul Wolfowitz, Douglas Feith and Richard Perle, who concocted the war in the sebaceous quadrants of the White House and the Pentagon, over the objections of the senior analysts at the CIA and State Department.

The two journalists also trace in comic detail the picaresque journey of Tony Blair's plagiarized dossier on Iraq, from a grad student's website to a cut-and-paste job in the prime minister's bombastic speech to the House of Commons. Blair, stubborn and verbose, paid a price for his grandiose puffery. Bush, who looted whole passages from Blair's speech for his own clumsy presentations, has skated freely through the tempest. Why?

Stauber and Rampton offer the best explanation to date. Unlike Blair, the Bush team never wanted to present a legal case for war. They had no interest in making any of their allegations about Iraq hold up to a standard of proof. The real effort was aimed at amping up the mood for war by using the psychology of fear.

Facts were never important to the Bush team. They were disposable nuggets that could be discarded at will and replaced by whatever new rationale that played favorably with their polls and focus groups. The war was about weapons of mass destruction one week, al-Qaeda the next. When neither allegation could be substantiated on the ground, the fall back position became the mass graves (many from the Iran/Iraq war supported by the US) proving that Saddam was an evil thug who deserved to be toppled. The motto of the Bush pr machine was: Move on. Don't explain. Say anything to conceal the perfidy behind the real motives for war: big defense contracts to political patrons, control of Middle East oil, political revenge on the man who outlasted his father, running interference for Israel. Never look back. Accuse the questioners of harboring unpatriotic sensibilities. Eventually, even the cagey Wolfowitz admitted that the official case for war was made mainly to make the invasion palatable not to justify it.

The Bush claque of neo-con hawks viewed the Iraq war a product and, just like a new pair of Nikes, it required a roll-out campaign to soften up the consumers. Stauber and Rampton demonstrate in convincing and step-by-step detail how the same techniques (and often the same PR gurus) that have been used to hawk cigarettes, SUVs and nuclear waste dumps were deployed to retail the Iraq war.

To peddle the invasion, Donald Rumsfeld and Colin Powell and company recruited public relations gurus into top-level jobs at the Pentagon and the State Department. These spin meisters soon had more say over how the rationale for war on Iraq should be presented than intelligence agencies and career diplomats. If the intelligence didn't fit the script, it was either shaded, retooled or junked.

Take Charlotte Beers who Powell tapped as Undersecretary of State in the post-9/11 world. Beers wasn't a diplomat. She wasn't even a politician. She was the grand diva of spin, known on the business and gossip pages as "the queen of Madison Avenue." On the strength of two advertising campaigns, one for Uncle Ben's Rice and another for Head and Shoulder's dandruff shampoo, Beers rocketed to the top of the heap in the PR world, heading two giant PR houses Ogilvy and Mathers as well as J. Walter Thompson.

At the state department, Beers, who had met Powell in 1995 when they both served on the board of Gulf Airstream, worked at, in Powell's words, "the branding of US foreign policy." She extracted more than $500 million from congress for her Brand America campaign, which largely focused on beaming US propaganda into the Muslim world, much of it directed at teens.

"Public diplomacy is a vital new arm in what will combat terrorism over time," said Beers. "All of a sudden we are in this position of redefining who America is, not only for ourselves, but for the outside world." Note the rapt attention Beers pays to the manipulation of perception, as opposed, say, to alterations of US policy.

Old-fashioned diplomacy involves direct communication between representatives of nations, a conversational give and take, often fraught with deception (see April Glaspie), but an exchange none-the-less. Public diplomacy, as defined by Beers, is something else entirely. It's a one-way street, a unilateral broadcast of American propaganda directly to the public, domestic and international-a kind of informational carpet bombing.

The themes of her campaigns were as simplistic and flimsy as a Bush press conference. The American incursions into Afghanistan and Iraq were all about bringing the balm of "freedom" to oppressed peoples. Hence, the title of the US war: Operation Iraqi Freedom, where cruise missiles were depicted as instruments of liberation. Bush himself distilled the Beers equation to its bizarre essence: "This war is about peace."

Beers quietly resigned her post a few weeks before the first volley of tomahawk missiles battered Baghdad. From her point of view, the war itself was already won, the fireworks of shock and awe were all after play.

Over at the Pentagon, Donald Rumsfeld drafted Victoria "Torie" Clarke as his director of public affairs. Clarke knew the ropes inside the Beltway. Prior to becoming Rumsfeld's mouthpiece, she had commanded one of the world's great parlors for powerbrokers: Hill and Knowlton's DC office.

Almost immediately upon taking up her new gig Clarke convened regular meetings with a select group of Washington's top private PR specialists and lobbyists to develop a marketing plan for the Pentagon's forthcoming terror wars. The group was filled with heavy-hitters and was strikingly bi-partisan in composition. She called it the Rumsfeld Group and it included PR executive Sheila Tate, columnist Rich Galen, and Republican political consultant Charles Black.

The brain trust also boasted top Democratic fixer Tommy Boggs, brother of NPR's Cokie Roberts and son of the late Congressman Hale Boggs of Arkansas. At the very time Boggs was conferring with top Pentagon brass on how to frame the war on terror, he was also working feverishly for the royal family of Saudi Arabia. In 2002 alone, the Saudis paid his Qorvis PR firm $20.2 million to protect its interests in Washington. In the wake of hostile press coverage following the exposure of Saudi links to the 9/11 hijackers, the royal family needed all the well-placed help it could buy. They seem to have gotten their money's worth. Boggs' felicitous influence peddling may help to explain why the damning references to Saudi funding of al-Qaeda were redacted from the recent congressional report on the investigation into intelligence failures and 9/11.

According to the trade publication *PR Week*, the Rumsfeld Group sent "messaging advice" to the Pentagon. The group told Clarke and Rumsfeld that in order to get the American public to buy into the war on terrorism they needed to suggest a link to nation states, not just nebulous groups such as al-Qaeda. In other words, there needed to be a fixed target for the military campaigns, some distant place to drop cruise missiles and cluster bombs. They suggested the notion (already embedded in Rumsfeld's mind) of playing up the notion of so-called rogue states as the real masters of terrorism. Thus was born the Axis of Evil, which, of course, wasn't an "axis" at all, since two of the states, Iran and Iraq hated each other, and neither had anything at all to do with the third, North Korea.

Tens of millions in federal money were poured into private public relations and media firms working to craft and broadcast the Bush dictat that Saddam had to be taken out before the Iraqi dictator blew up the world by dropping chemical and nuclear bombs from long-range drones. Many of these pr executives and image consultants were old friends of the high priests in the Bush inner sanctum. Indeed they were veterans, like Cheney and Powell, of the previous war against Iraq, another engagement that was more spin that combat.

At the top of the list was John Rendon, head of the DC firm the Rendon Group. Rendon is one of Washington's heaviest hitters, a Beltway fixer who never let political affiliation stand in the way of an assignment. Rendon served as a media consultant for both Michael Dukakis and Jimmy Carter, as well as Reagan and George H.W. Bush. Whenever the Pentagon wanted to go to war, he offered his services at a price. During Desert Storm Rendon pulled in $100,000 a month from the Kuwaiti royal family. He followed this up with a $23 million contract from the CIA to produce anti-Saddam propaganda in the region.

As part of this CIA project, Rendon created and named the Iraqi National Congress and tapped his friend Ahmed Chalabi, the shady financier, to head the organization.

Shortly after 9/11, the Pentagon handed the Rendon Group another big assignment: public relations for the US bombing of Afghanistan. Rendon was also deeply involved in the planning and public relations for the preemptive war on Iraq, though both Rendon and the Pentagon refused to disclose the details of the group's work there.

But it's not hard to detect the manipulative hand of Rendon behind many of the Iraq war's signature events, including the toppling of the Saddam statue (by US troops and Chalabi associates) and videotape of jubilant Iraqis waving American flags as the Third Infantry rolled by them. Rendon had pulled off the same stunt in the first Gulf War, handing out American flags to Kuwaitis and herding the media to the orchestrated demonstration. "Where do you think they got those American flags?" clucked Rendon in 1991. "That was my assignment."

The Rendon Group may also have had played a role in pushing the phony intelligence that has now come back to haunt the Bush administration. In December of 2002, Robert Dreyfuss reported that the inner circle of the Bush White House preferred the intelligence coming from Chalabi and his associated to that being proffered by analysts at the CIA.

So Rendon and his circle represented a new kind of off-the-shelf psy-ops, the privatization of official propaganda. "I am not a national security strategist or a military tactician," said Rendon. "I am a politician, and a person who uses communication to meet public policy or corporate policy objectives. In fact, I am an information warrior and a perception manager."

What exactly, pray tell, is perception management? Well, the Pentagon defines it this way: "actions to convey and/or deny selected information and indicators to foreign audiences to influence their emotions, motives and objective reasoning."

In other words, lying about the intentions of the US government. In a rare display of public frankness, the Pentagon actually let slip its plan (developed by Rendon) to establish a high-level den inside the Department Defense for perception management. They called it the Office of Strategic Influence and among its many missions was to plant false stories in the press.

Nothing stirs the corporate media into outbursts of pious outrage like an official government memo bragging about how the media is manipulated for political objectives. So the *New York Times* and *Washington Post* threw indignant fits about the Office of Strategic Influence, the Pentagon shut down the operation and the press gloated with satisfaction on its victory. Yet, Rumsfeld told the Pentagon press corps that while he was killing the office, the same devious work would continue. "You can have the corpse," said Rumsfeld. "You can have the name. But I'm going to keep doing every single thing that needs to be done. And I have."

At a diplomatic level, despite the hired guns and the planted stories, this image war was lost. It failed to convince even America's most fervent allies and dependent client states that Iraq posed much of a threat. It failed to win the blessing of the UN and even NATO, a wholly-owned subsidiary of Washington. At the end of the day, the vaunted coalition of the willing consisted of Britain, Spain, Italy, Australia, and a cohort of former Soviet bloc nations. Even so the citizens of the nations that cast their lot with the US overwhelmingly opposed the war.

Domestically, it was a different story.

A population traumatized by terror threats and shattered economy became easy prey for the saturation bombing of the Bush message that Iraq was a terrorist state linked to al-Qaeda that was only minutes away from launching attacks on America with weapons of mass destruction.

Americans were the victims of an elaborate con job, pelted with a daily barrage of threat inflation, distortions, deceptions and lies. Not about tactics or strategy or war plans. But about justifications for war. The lies were aimed not at confusing Saddam's regime, but the American people. By the start of the war, 66 percent of Americans thought Saddam Hussein was behind 9/11 and 79 percent thought he was close to having a nuclear weapon.

Of course, the closest Saddam came to possessing a nuke was a rusting gas centrifuge buried for 13 years in the garden of Mahdi Obeidi, a retired Iraqi scientist. Iraq didn't have any weaponized chemical or biological weapons. In fact, it didn't even possess any SCUD missiles, despite erroneous reports fed by Pentagon pr flacks alleging that it had fired SCUDs into Kuwait.

This charade wouldn't have worked without a gullible or a complicit press corps. Victoria Clarke, who developed the Pentagon plan for embedded reports, put it succinctly a few weeks before the war began: "Media coverage of any future operation will to a large extent shape public perception."

During the Vietnam war, TV images of maimed GIs and napalmed villages suburbanized opposition to the war and helped hasten the US withdrawal. The Bush gang meant to turn the Vietnam phenomenon on its head by using TV as a force to propel the US into a war that no one really wanted.

What the Pentagon sought was a new kind of living room war, where instead of photos of mangled soldiers and dead Iraqi kids, they could control the images Americans viewed and to a large extent the content of the stories. By embedding reporters inside selected divisions, Clarke believed the Pentagon could count on the reporters to build relationships with the troops and to feel dependent on them for their own safety. It worked, naturally. One reporter for a national network trembled on camera that the US army functioned as "our protectors." The late David Bloom of NBC confessed on the air that he was willing to do "anything and everything they can ask of us."

When the Pentagon needed a heroic story, the press obliged. Jessica Lynch became the war's first instant celebrity. Here was a neo-gothic tale of a steely young woman wounded in a fierce battled, captured and tortured by ruthless enemies and dramatically saved from certain death by a team of selfless rescuers, knights in camo and nightvision goggles. Of course, nearly every detail of her heroic adventure proved to be as fictive and maudlin as any made-for-TV-movie. But the ordeal of Private Lynch, which dominated the news for more than a week, served its purpose: to distract attention from a stalled campaign that was beginning to look at lot riskier than the American public had been hoodwinked into believing.

The Lynch story was fed to the eager press by a Pentagon operation called Combat Camera, the Army network of photographers, videographers and editors that sends 800 photos and 25 video clips a day to the media. The editors at Combat Camera carefully culled the footage to present the Pentagon's montage of the war, eliding such unsettling images as collateral damage, cluster bombs, dead children and US soldiers, napalm strikes and disgruntled troops.

"A lot of our imagery will have a big impact on world opinion," predicted Lt. Jane Larogue, director of Combat Camera in Iraq. She was right. But as the hot war turned into an even hotter occupation, the Pentagon, despite airy rhetoric from occupation supremo Paul Bremer about installing democratic institutions such as a free press, moved to tighten its monopoly on the flow images out of Iraq. First, it tried to shut down Al Jazeera, the Arab news channel. Then the Pentagon intimated that it would like to see all foreign TV news crews banished from Baghdad.

Few newspapers fanned the hysteria about the threat posed by Saddam's weapons of mass destruction as sedulously as did the *Washington Post*. In the months leading up to the war, the *Post's* pro-war op-eds outnumbered the anti-war columns by a 3 to 1 margin.

Back in 1988, the *Post* felt much differently about Saddam and his weapons of mass destruction. When reports trickled out about the gassing of Iranian troops, the *Washington Post* editorial page shrugged off the massacres, calling the mass poisonings "a quirk of war."

The Bush team displayed a similar amnesia. When Iraq used chemical weapons in grisly attacks on Iran, the US government not only didn't object, it encouraged Saddam. Anything to punish Iran was the message coming from the White House. Donald Rumsfeld himself was sent as President Ronald Reagan's personal envoy to Baghdad. Rumsfeld conveyed the bold message that an Iraq defeat would be viewed as a "strategic setback for the United States." This sleazy alliance was sealed with a handshake caught on videotape. When CNN reporter Jamie McIntyre replayed the footage for Rumsfeld in the spring of 2003, the secretary of defense snapped, "Where'd you get that? Iraqi television?"

The current crop of Iraq hawks also saw Saddam much differently then. Take the writer Laurie Mylroie, sometime colleague of the *New York Times'* Judy Miller, who persists in peddling the ludicrous conspiracy that Iraq was behind the 1993 bombing of the World Trade Center.

How times have changed. In 1987, Mylroie felt downright cuddly toward Saddam. She penned an article for the *New Republic* titled Back Iraq: Time for a US Tilt in the Mideast, arguing that the US should publicly embrace Saddam's secular regime as a bulwark against the Islamic fundamentalists in Iran. The co-author of this mesmerizing weave of wonkery was none other than the minor demon himself, Daniel Pipes, perhaps the nation's most bellicose Islamophobe. "The American weapons that Iraq could make good use of include remotely scatterable and anti-personnel mines and counterartillery radar," wrote Mylroie and Pipes. "The United States might also consider upgrading intelligence it is supplying Baghdad."

In the roll-out for the war, Mylroie seemed to be everywhere hawking the invasion of Iraq. She would often appear on two or three different networks in the same day. How did the reporter manage this feat? She had help in the form of Eleana Benador, the media placement guru who runs Benador Associates. Born in Peru, Benador parlayed her skills as a linguist into a lucrative career as media relations whiz for the Washington foreign policy elite. She also oversees the Middle East Forum, a fanatically pro-Zionist white paper mill. Her clients include some of the nation's most fervid hawks, including Michael Ledeen, Charles Krauthammer, Al Haig, Max Boot, Daniel Pipes, Richard Perle and Judy Miller. During the Iraq war, Benador's assignment was to embed this squadron of pro-war zealots into the national media, on talk shows and op-ed pages.

Benador not only got them the gigs, she also crafted the message and made sure they all stayed on the same theme. "There are some things, you just have to state them in a different way, in a slightly different way," said Benador. "If not people get scared." Scared of the intentions of their own government.

It could have been different. All of the holes in the Bush administration's gossamer case for war detailed by Stauber and Rampton (and other independent journalists) were right there for the mainstream press to unearth and expose. Instead, the US press, just like the oil companies, cravenly sought to commercialize the Iraq war and profit from the invasions. They didn't want to deal with uncomfortable facts or present voices of dissent.

Nothing sums up this unctuous approach more brazenly than MSNBC's firing of liberal talk show host Phil Donahue on the eve of the war. The network replaced the Donahue show with a running segment called Countdown: Iraq, featuring the usual nightly coterie of retired generals, security flacks and other cheerleaders for invasion. The network's executives blamed the cancellation on sagging ratings. In fact, during its run Donahue's show attracted more viewers than any other program on the network. The real reason for the pre-emptive strike on Donahue was spelled out in an internal memo from anxious executives at NBC. Donahue, the memo said, offered "a difficult face for NBC in a time of war. He seems to delight in presenting guests who are anti-war, anti-Bush and skeptical of the administration's motives."

The memo warned that Donahue's show risked tarring MSNBC as an unpatriotic network, "a home for liberal anti-war agenda at the same time that our competitors are waving the flag at every opportunity." So, with scarcely a second thought, the honchos at MSNBC gave Donahue the boot and hoisted the battle flag.

It's war that sells.

There's a helluva caveat, of course. Once you buy it, the merchants of war accept no returns.

September 2003

Four

No Bid, No Sweat

How to Make It Big on Defense Contracts
Without Really Trying

During the 2004 presidential campaign, the no-bid contracts to rebuild Iraq's oil infrastructure awarded to Dick Cheney's old firm Halliburton seemed to be a more contentious issue than the war on Iraq itself. Halliburton's $2.3 billion contract was certainly a sweet deal, made even riper by the fact that Cheney continues to receive millions in deferred compensation from the company he once commanded. But Halliburton's Iraq deal, excoriated by the Democrats and the mainstream press, is a mere pittance compared to the loot that is being doled out every day in no-bid contracts by the Pentagon to its favorite retinue of arms manufacturers.

In the last six years, the Pentagon has outsourced more than $900 billion worth of work to corporations through defense-oriented contracts. Of that total, more than $360 billion—or roughly 45 percent—were handed out in no bid deals without the slightest bit of competition. So much for the bracing forces of the free market.

Most of this loot was awarded to the nation's five biggest contractors: Lockheed got $94 billion, Boeing won $82 billion, Raytheon received $40 billion and Northrop Grumman and General Dynamics each scored about $34 billion. These five companies alone hauled in $283 billion in no bid deals. This figure represents a third of all defense contracts and 15 percent of all defense spending.

This is the path to risk free profits. Lockheed, the Pentagon's largest contractor, pulled in more than 70 percent of its defense-based revenue courtesy of no bid contracts. And this figure doesn't include the billions Lockheed gets in from joint-venture deals with the Pentagon, such as its work on the Joint Strike Fighter or Missile Defense. General Dynamics also received more than half of its Pentagon revenue without having to place its bids up to competition with other contractors.

A spokesman for Lockheed defended the move toward no bid contracting by saying it's simply a more efficient way of doing business. "It's not cost-effective for the Defense Department to develop a second source of production," explained Thomas Greer, a Lockheed executive.

At the very time the Pentagon increased the number of no bid deals, it started to slash its own auditors who were charged with overseeing compliance with the contracts by the weapons companies. Instead of government auditors, the Pentagon is now outsourcing oversight and monitoring to private accounting firms, such as Booze, Allen Hamilton and Jefferson Solutions. Most of the contracts to monitor the performance of no bid contractors were themselves awarded through no bid deals.

"The fact is, from running interrogations at Abu Ghraib to writing the president's defense budget, contractors are playing an increasingly significant role in Pentagon policy," says Charles Lewis, director of the Center for Public Integrity, which issued a ground-breaking report on Pentagon contractors in the fall of 2004. "The Pentagon management of these outside vendors is uneven and inadequate."

The Center excavated and examined more than 2.2 million Defense Department contracts made between 1998 and 2004. The report focused on the 737 companies that got at least $100 million in Pentagon deals in that period. But this is just the tip of the iceberg. Each year, the Pentagon awards 11 million contracts to private firms, most without competition and only superficial oversight.

Billions in no bid deals are masked from public viewed. Over $8 billion in Pentagon funds went to unnamed companies working on unnamed projects as classified contractors.

In other cases, the Pentagon seems to have lost track of where the money is going. The Department of Defense account ledgers lumps more than $10 billion worth of no-bid deals into a catchall category called simply "Miscellaneous Items."

The no bid deals are offered for big and small contracts, the spectacular and the mundane. Northrop Grumman, for example, has won a no bid contract to build the next generation of aircraft carriers. This is hardly surprising, since Northrop is the only US company in the business of building aircraft carriers. But the Pentagon has handed out other contracts for the staples of military life, such as milk, cheese and eggs ($2.8 billion), fuel oil ($3.8 billion), janitorial services ($2.3 billion) and expert witnesses to defend itself against lawsuits ($219 million). By the way, the military's electric bill totaled $3.7 billion for the six-year period.

As the Center for Public Integrity report reveals, the trend toward outsourcing Pentagon work through no-bid contracts didn't start with the Iraq war or even the Bush administration. As with so many other corporate-friendly initiatives, the origins of the frenzy of no-bid Pentagon deals can be found in the Clinton administration and Al Gore's reinventing government project or REGO. Under REGO, the Pentagon was instructed to outsource even the most essential services, such as family housing for troops, health care services and payroll services. Now, the Pentagon doesn't even run its own Internet system. That job now falls to Lockheed.

Since the Pentagon enacted Gore's REGO reforms, some of the biggest profits are now being made through service oriented contracts, not the riskier big ticket contracts for missiles, jets and fighter planes. In 2004, Pentagon contracts for the service sector, such as health care, maintenance and food preparation, accounted for nearly 60 percent of all defense contract spending.

Of course, when Bush came to DC the defense contractor block invested heavily in his campaign war chest in order to keep their gravy train rolling. The 70 top Pentagon contractors channeled about $500,000 to the Bush reelection campaign, more than the companies gave to any other politician in the last decade.

One of the leading political spenders is Bechtel. The company was well rewarded for its investment. After Halliburton, Bechtel garnered the second biggest no-bid contract from the Iraq war, a $1 billion deal for re-constructing Iraq's utilities, schools, roads, bridges and airports.

"We do engage in a political process, as do most companies in the US," explained a Bechtel pr flack. "We have legitimate policy interests and positions on matters before Congress, and we express them in many ways, including support for elected officials who support those positions."

Of course, PAC contributions can't be counted on to solve all of your corporate problems. It helps to have special political ambassadors to carry your banner on the Hill or inside the corridors of the Pentagon. Bechtel employs two seasoned hands to shepherd its interests at the highest levels of the government: former Secretary of State George Schultz, who sits on Bechtel's board, and Jack Sheehan, the company's senior vice-president for petroleum and chemicals operations, who resides on the Defense Policy Board, which advises Donald Rumsfeld on matters of war and peace and defense spending.

Bechtel isn't the only firm to land a seat on this powerful war council. More than one-third of the Defense Policy Board's members work for defense contractors.

February 2005

Five

Contract Casino

The Pentagon isn't alone in handing out plump no-bid contracts to politically wired corporations. The new Department of Homeland Security, a collage of 22 sub-agencies sprawling across the federal bureaucracy, is sluicing billions into the coffers of a few favorite contractors and many of the deals have been awarded on the same no-bid basis that brought such amazing largesse to corporations doing business in Iraq and Afghanistan, such as Bechtel and Halliburton.

Over the past two years, about 30 percent of the Department of Homeland Security's contracts have been awarded on a non-competitive, no-bid basis. These contracts amount to about $2.5 billion, for services ranging from computer systems to the maintenance of airport scanning devices.

Among the top beneficiaries of these sweetheart deals are two companies with a track record of contract fraud and overbilling: Boeing and Integrated Coast Guard Systems, the latter being a joint venture between Lockheed-Martin and Northrop Grumman. Combined, the two weapons giants reaped more than $700 million in no bid contracts from the Department of Homeland Security. This is in spite of recent audits by the Department's Inspector General, Clark Kent Ervin, which accused both firms of overcharging. Indeed, in the past three years alone, Lockheed and Boeing had been forced to pay more than $250 million in fines for violations of their contracts with the Pentagon.

Integrated Coast Guard Systems was handed the huge contract to install new engines on the Coast Guard's fleet of HH-65 helicopters. A task that the Coast Guard was more than capable of handling on its own more promptly and for much less money. But Lockheed's lobbyists won the day and wrested the contract into their subsidiary. Almost immediately things began to go awry. First, the project proposal was delivered more than a month late. And when auditors began to look at the fine print of the proposal they discovered that it was larded with "$123 million worth of goods and services that the Coast Guard did not ask for."

While the auditors raised a red flag, the Coast Guard brass and the honchos at the Department of Homeland Security sped on with the deal, ignoring the warnings of their own inspector general. Of course, any contract with Lockheed should come under special scrutiny given their ripe record of overbilling, shoddy work and contract fraud. Most recently, Lockheed was cited for providing the Air Force with C-130J transport planes that didn't meet military standards, delaying troop and equipment deployments to Iraq and Afghanistan. Even so, Lockheed raked in $2.6 billion on the deal and stands to make another $5 billion on the planes.

Kent's report cited Boeing with bilking the new department out of more than $49 million last year on its contract to install bomb detection equipment in the nation's airports. For its part Boeing, which has witnessed several of its executives carted off to federal prison in recent months for illegal lobbying on Pentagon contracts, dismissed Kent's allegation, saying they deserved the money for doing a stellar job. "Nobody thought it could be done and we did it," brayed Boeing spokesman Fernando Vivanco.

Another huge no-bid contract went to scandal-plagued BearingPoint Technologies. The McLean, Virginia-based consulting firm was given a $229 million contract to install a new computer system at the Department of Homeland Security. The contract was awarded only months after the Department of Veterans Affairs dumped a BearingPoint $472 million computer system for its VA hospitals in Florida after it failed a 9-month test. Bizarrely, BearingPoint executives were paid a $200,000 incentive bonus for keeping the doomed project on schedule. Now, BearingPoint executives find themselves the subject of two investigations. "One deals with allegations involving criminal activity, the other one involves matters of civil litigation, basically involving money," said Jon Wooditch, a spokesman for the Veteran Affair's Department's inspector general.

The IG's initial report into the BearingPoint's hospital computer system discovered "serious deficiencies" in the system and cost overruns averaging $4 million a month. According to VA investigators, key documents related to the award could not be located, "nor could we determine on what basis VA made the award to BearingPoint over other offers."

In the winter of 2005, BearingPoint disclosed to its shareholders that it's also the subject of a federal grand jury investigation in California for improprieties on government contracts in that state from 1998.

One of the biggest of Department of Homeland Security contracts went to an obscure company called Chenega Technology Services Corp, which is owned by Alaskan natives from the small village of Chenega. Chenega is a coastal village accessible only by floatplane. In July of 2002, the Customs Service asked Lockheed and DynCorp to submit proposals for a $500 million project to upgrade and maintain the x-ray and gamma ray machines at the US's ports and border stations. But six months later the Customs Service issued a press release saying that the project would not be put up for competitive bidding. Instead, it was being awarded on a no-bid basis to Chenega Technology. The decision stunned executives at DynCorp, who figured they were front-runners for the deal. "I didn't even know how to spell their name," said Raymond Mintz, who had been hired by DynCorp to prepare its bid for the Customs contract.

Chenega officials may have been stunned as well. Their company had little experience with the high-tech scanning machines. In the end, Chenega contracted most of the actual work out to two other companies, SAIC, Inc. and American Science and Engineering Inc.

The deal was actually brokered by Senator Ted Stevens, the Alaska Republican, who inserted the deal into a legislative rider on the Defense Appropriations bill. Stevens chairs the mighty Senate Appropriations Committee.

Chenega, however, appears to be a native corporation in name only. Of its 2,300 employees, only 33 are Alaskan natives. The headquarters of the company is located not in Anchorage or Juneau, but in shiny glass building in toney Alexandria, Virginia, just down the road from the Pentagon.

Through the legislative magic of Ted Stevens, Alaska Native Corporations enjoy cushy loopholes when it comes to federal contracts. For one thing, they can continue to maintain their small business status even when they are bringing in millions in revenue. This special dispensation allows them to be exempt from the $3 million federal cap on no-bid service contracts that are in place for other minority small businesses.

By another legislative quirk, Alaska Native Corporations, such as Chenega, don't even have to be run by Native Americans. Moreover, they can subcontract out most of the work to non-Native firms without having to undergo the rigorous cost-benefit analysis required for other corporations.

Jeff Hueners, the chief operating officer of Chenega, called the company "an American success story that benefits from preferential laws based upon the trust relationship the United States Government has with its indigenous, aboriginal people."

Chenega's success has hinged on the post-911 spending spree. In 2001, Chenega only recorded $42 million in revenues. In 2004, Chenega's revenues exceeded $480 million.

One of Chenega's biggest contracts came after the start of the Iraq war when the Pentagon transferred most of its military police to hellholes like Abu Ghraib and other prisons and detention centers in Iraq. This left thousands of open positions for military police at DoD facilities in the US. Strangely, Chenega and Alutiiq, another Alaska Native Corporation, won the contracts to provide security forces for 40 US military installations, ranging from Ft. Bragg to West Point to the Anniston Chemical Weapons Depot in Alabama. The contracts were worth about $500 million. They were awarded to the two Native Corporations on a no bid basis, even though neither corporation had any experience in providing security services. The Pentagon made no public announcement about the awarding of the contracts.

The deal calls for Chenega and Alutiiq to provide 4,385 private security guards. But neither company will actually provide any workers. Instead, both native firms subcontracted the work out to private security companies. Chenega made a deal with Vance International, the Republican-connected outfit that was founded by Gerald Ford's son-in-law and which provided security for the Bush-Cheney election campaign in 2000. Alutiiq forged a similar deal with Wackenhut Services, the British-owned security corporation.

The Pentagon had originally put the security contracts up for open bidding. Both Wackenhut and Vance had submitted bids, but both were rejected. Then, through the suggestion of the Office of Senator Ted Stevens, the Pentagon decided to award the contracts on a no-bid basis to the two Alaskan Native Corporations, which had already formed their partnerships with Wackenhut and Vance.

"Alutiiq approached us, we got together, and they said, 'We want to do this; we need you to come help us with it,'" explained Jim Long, Wackenhut's CEO. "We split it up 51-49."

The 51-49 relationship is crucial to the deal, since under the Stevens loophole 51 percent of the money from the contract must go to the Native Corporation. It's a great deal for Wackenhut, since as a foreign-owned corporation with a shoddy record at other federal facilities they were unlikely to get any Pentagon contracts.

Wackenhut is a subsidiary of Group 4 Securicor. After 9/11, the company came under scrutiny for its mismanagement of security at several Department of Energy facilities, including serious breaches at the Oak Ridge

Nuclear Weapons plant in Tennessee.

As a subcontractor, however, Wackenhut not only avoids competitive bidding, but they also evade scrutiny of their work by the Pentagon. Neither the Pentagon nor the Department of Homeland Security has any legal recourse over the performance of Vance or Wackenhut. That responsibility is reserved for the native corporations.

The Pentagon sees this kind of subcontracting as the wave of the future. An internal Pentagon memo unearthed by the General Accounting Office spoke of "contract security guards as a viable manpower option." It's not hard to see why the Pentagon likes it. They can please powerful senators like Stevens and free up troops for duty in Iraq and Afghanistan. Indeed, Rumsfeld has said that he would like to permanently transfer as many as 320,000 Pentagon positions to private companies.

Many federal employees see this as a kind of union-busting. "It's not complicated what they're doing here," says Anne Wagner, a lawyer with the American Federal Government Employees Union. "They hook up with a corporation like Wackenhut, which runs the entire operation." Wackenhut then hires former soldiers at non-union wages and offers them few or no benefits.

In 2003, the union sued to halt the issuance of these kinds of no-bid deals, but lost when the US Supreme Court refused to hear the case.

The privatized workforce isn't taking home much money, but the corporations certainly are. In 2003 alone the Alaskan native corporations and their subcontractors brought in $12 billion dollars in federal contracts. But little of this money actually makes its way back to Alaskan Natives. In 2004, for example, Chenega Corporation, which brought in nearly a half billion in revenues, only distributed about $1 million to native shareholders and cultural and education programs for natives.

Back on those tribal lands in Alaska, poverty rates remain the highest in the nation and unemployment exceeds 40 percent. Not a single member of one of the Alaskan tribes works on any of the Alutiiq/Wackenhut or Chenega/Vance contracts.

March, 2005

Six

Torture Air, Incorporated

The gleaming and sleek Gulfstream V jet with the tail number N379P has racked up more international miles than most passenger jets. Since October 2001, this jet has been spotted in some of the world's most exotic and forbidding airports: Tashkent, Uzbekistan; Karachi, Pakistan; Baku, Azerbaijan; Baghdad, Iraq; and Rabat, Morocco.

It has also frequently landed at Dulles International, outside Washington, DC and enjoys clearance to land at US military air bases in Scotland, Cyprus and Frankfurt, Germany. Observers around the world have noticed men in hoods and chains being taken on and off the jet.

The plane is owned by a company called Bayard Marketing, based in Portland, Oregon. According to FAA records, Bayard's lone corporate officer is a man called, Leonard T. Bayard. There is no contact information available for Bayard. Indeed, there's no public record of Bayard at all. No residential address. No telephone numbers. Nothing.

In fact, Bayard Marketing is a dummy corporation and Leonard Bayard is a false identity. They were both created by the CIA to conceal an operation launched after the attacks of September 11, 2001 to kidnap suspected terrorists and transport them to foreign governments where they could be interrogated using methods outlawed in the United States—that is tortured and sometimes killed.

Bayard Marketing is one of five or six different front companies the CIA has used to hide its role in the clandestine rendition of suspected terrorists. In this case, the CIA's desire to keep the program a secret doesn't spring from a need to protect it from al-Qaeda or other hostile forces, but from public exposure. The rendition of captives for the purpose torture violates international and US law.

Unfortunately for the CIA, the jet and its human cargo have been something of an open secret since early 2002, when spotters at international airports began to take note of its regular arrivals and departures, usually at night, from military air bases from Jordan to Indonesia.

A notorious example. On September 26, 2002, Maher Arar, a Canadian engineer born in Syria, was arrested by US intelligence officials at John F. Kennedy Airport in New York as he was changing planes. Arar and his family were returning home to Canada from a vacation in Tunisia. Arar was held in a federal cell for 13 days while he was interrogated about a man US intelligence believed was linked to al-Qaeda. Arar told his captors that he had never met the man in question, although he had worked with his brother on a construction project.

Then one night two plainclothes officers came for Arar, placed a hood over his head, secured his hands with plastic cuffs and shackled his feet in leg irons. He was taken from the federal jail to the airport, where he was placed on the Gulfstream V jet. The plane flew to Washington, DC, then to Portland, Maine. It stopped once in Rome, then landed in Amman, Jordan. During the flight, Arar recalls that he heard the pilots and crew referring to themselves as members of the "Special Removal Unit."

Arar was held in a cell in Amman for 10 hours. He pleaded with his captors to release him or allow him to talk with a lawyer. They refused. He was placed in a van and driven across the border into Syria, where he was handed over to a secret police unit. He was taken to a dark underground cell and immediately his interrogators began to beat him with battery cables. The beatings went on, day after day.

A year later, Arar was released by the Syrians at the behest of the Canadian government. He was never charged with a crime. His detention, interrogation and torture had been ordered by the CIA. He has received no apology. Arar is one of at least 150 people the CIA has captured and taken to other countries in a covert program known as "extraordinary rendition."

While Arar ended up in Syria, other detainees have stayed in Jordan, where the CIA runs a "ghost prison" for the detention, interrogation and torture of some of the most senior members of al-Qaeda captured by US forces over the last three years. According to an article in the Israeli daily *Ha'aretz*, 11 top al-Qaeda operatives have been sent to the al-Jafr prison in Jordan's southern desert, where they have been interrogated and tortured. Among those being held in Jordan are Abu Zubaydah, Riduan Isamuddin and Khalid Sheikh Mohammed.

Khalid Sheik Mohammed, a suspected planner of the 9/11 attacks was captured in Pakistan in March 2003. Mohammed was reportedly taken to a US base in Afghanistan for his initial interrogation and then was sent to the prison in Jordan, where he was subjected to range of tortures, including the infamous "water-boarding" technique, where he was bound tightly with ropes to a piece of plywood and then dunked in ice cold water until he nearly drowned.

The water-boarding method was one of several varieties of torture approved by President Bush in an executive order issued in February 2002. Bush's order, which exempted the CIA from compliance with the rules of the Geneva Conventions, was extended seven months later by an August 2002 memorandum signed by Assistant Attorney General Jay S. Bybee. The Bybee Memo (largely written by his deputy John Yoo) called for the continuation of CIA interrogation methods, including rendition, and blessed as legal methods of physical and psychological inducement that inflicted discomfort "equivalent in intensity to the pain accompanying serious physical injury, such as organ failure, impairment of bodily function, or even death."

The prison in Jordan is only one of 24 secret detention and interrogation centers worldwide operated by the CIA. According to a report by Human Rights Watch, "at least half of these operate in total secrecy."

Originally, the Gulfstream V that flew Arar to Amman was owned by a company called Premier Executive Transport Services, Inc, a company based in Dedham, Massachusetts. An investigation by the *Washington Post's* reporter Dana Priest revealed that the corporate papers filed by Premier Executive included a list of executive officer and board members who, in Priest's words, "exist only on paper." The names, Bryan Dyess, Steven Kent, Timothy Sperling and Audrey Tailor, had been issued new Social Security numbers and included only Post Office box numbers for addresses.

The Post Offices are located in Arlington, Virginia, Oakton and Chevy Chase, Maryland and the District of Columbia. Over the past few years, those very same Post Office boxes have been registered to 325 other fictitious names, as well as a company called Executive Support OFC, another CIA front.

* * *

Of course, the Bush administration hasn't tried very hard to keep its torture-by-proxy program a secret. That's because the administration's torture lawyers, such as John Yoo, former deputy to Alberto Gonzales and now a law professor at Berkeley, argue that the administration is free to breach international and domestic laws in its pursuit of suspected terrorists. While working for the Bush administration, Yoo drafted a legal memo, which set the framework for the rendition program. He argued that the US was not bound by the Geneva Accords (or US prohibitions on torture) in its pursuit of al-Qaeda members or Taliban soldiers because Afghanistan was "a failed state" and therefore not subject to the protections of the anti-torture. The detainees were slotted into a newly created category called "illegal enemy combatants," a legal rubric which treated them as subhumans lacking all basic human rights.

"Why is it so hard for people to understand that there is a category of behavior not covered by the legal system?" Yoo brayed. "Historically, there were people so bad that they were not given protection of the laws. There were no specific provisions for their trial, or imprisonment. If you were an illegal combatant, you didn't deserve the protection of the laws of war."

Of course, in the absence of a trial, who is to determine if the people detained as "illegal combatants" are either "illegal" or even "combatants?"

Even more brazenly, Yoo contends that the Bush administration is free to ignore US laws against torture.

"Congress doesn't have the power to tie the hands of the President in regard to torture as an interrogation technique," said Yoo. "It's the core of the Commander-in-Chief function. Congress can't prevent the president from ordering torture."

Yoo snips that if Congress has a problem with Bush flouting its laws, the solution is simple: impeachment. He also argued that the US public had its shot at repudiating Bush's detention and torture program and instead endorsed it. "The issue is dying out," Yoo told the *New Yorker* magazine. "The war has had its referendum."

As in so many cases with the Bush administration, it appears that Dick Cheney himself gave the green light for the kidnapping and torture scenario. Displaying his signature gloss of evil pride, Cheney even dropped a public hint that the Bush administration was going to deal savagely with suspected terrorists. During an interview on Meet the Press, a week after the attacks on the World Trade Center and the Pentagon, Cheney said that the administration wasn't going to shackle itself to conventional methods in tracking down suspected terrorists. "A lot of what needs to be done here will have to be done quietly, without any discussion, using sources and methods that are available to our intelligence agencies, if we're going to be successful," Cheney said. "That's the world these folks operate in. And so it's going to be vital for us to use any means at our disposal, basically, to achieve our objective. We may have to work through, sort of, the dark side."

Welcome to the dark ages.

April 2005

Part Two

The Enablers

"I believe there are more instances of the abridgement of freedom of the people by gradual and silent encroachments of those in power than by violent and sudden usurpations."

—James Madison

Seven

High Plains Grifter

The Life and Crimes of George W. Bush

T he mad cowboys are on the loose. Pack only what you can carry. Liberate the animals. Leave the rest behind. The looters are hot on the trail. Only ruin stands in their wake. Not even women and children are safe. Especially not them. Run for the hills and don't look back. Don't ever look back.

So the story goes, anyway.

We find ourselves living out a scene in a bad Western. A movie filmed long after all the old plot lines have been exhausted, the grizzled character actors put out to pasture, the Indians slaughtered and confined to desert prisons, the cattle slotted into stinking feed lots, the scenic montane backdrops pulverized by strip mines. All that remains are the guns, bulked up beyond all comprehension, and the hangman and his gibbet. We've seen it all before. But there's no escape now. Someone's locked the exits. The film rolls on to the bitter end. Cue music: Toby Keith.

Perhaps only the Pasolini of *Salo: 120 Days of Sodom* could have done this celluloid scenario justice. Or the impish Mel Brooks, who gave us *Blazing Saddles* (one of the most instructive films on the true nature of American politics), if you understand the narrative as comedy, which is probably the most emetic way to embrace it. Both Pasolini and Brooks are masters of scatological cinema. And there's mounds of bullshit to dig through to get at the core of George W. Bush.

Because it's all an act, of course, a put on, a dress game. And not a very convincing one at that. Start from the beginning. George W. Bush wasn't born a cowboy. He entered the world in New Haven, Connecticut, hallowed hamlet of Yale. His bloodlines include two presidents and a US senator. The cowboy act came later, when he was famously re-birthed, with spurs on his boots, tea in his cup and the philosophical tracts of Jesus of Nazareth on his night table. Bush is a pure-blooded WASP, sired by a man who would later become the nation's chief spook, a man frequently called upon to clean up the messes left by apex crooks in his own political party, including his own entanglements (and those of his sons) with the more noirish aspects of life. His grandfather was a US senator and Wall Street lawyer, who shamelessly represented American corporations as they did business with the Nazi death machine. Old Prescott narrowly escaped charges of treason. But those were different times, when trading with the enemy was viewed as, at the very least, unseemly.

His mother, Barbara, is a bitter and grouchy gorgon, who must have frightened her own offspring as they first focused their filmy eyes onto her stern visage. She is a Pierce, a descendent of Franklin, the famously incompetent president, patron of Nathaniel Hawthorne and avowed racist, who joined in a bizarre cabal to overthrow Abraham Lincoln. (For more on this long neglected episode in American history check out Charles Higham's excellent recent book *Murdering Mr. Lincoln.*)

Understandably, George Sr. spent much of his time far away from Barbara Bush's icy boudoir, indulging in a discreet fling or two while earning his stripes as a master of the empire, leaving juvenile George to cower under the unstinting commands of his cruel mother, who his younger brother Jeb dubbed "the Enforcer." This woman's veins pulse with glacial melt. According to Neil Bush, his mother was devoted to corporal punishment and would "slap around" the Bush children. She was known in the family as "the one who instills fear." She still does...with a global reach.

How wicked is Barbara Bush? Well, she refused to attend her own mother's funeral. And the day after her five-year old daughter Robin died of leukemia Barbara Bush was in a jolly enough mood to spend the afternoon on the golf course. Revealingly, Mrs. Bush kept Robin's terminal illness a secret from young George, a stupid and cruel move that provided one of the early warps to his psyche.

Her loathsome demeanor hasn't lightened much over the years. Refresh your memory with this quote on Good Morning America, dismissing the escalating body count of American soldiers in Iraq. "Why should we hear about body bags and deaths and how many," the Presidential Mother snapped. "It's not relevant. So why should I waste my beautiful mind on something like that?"

Even Freud might have struggled with this case study. Imagine young George the Hysteric on Siggy's couch in the curtained room on Berggasse 19. The analysand doesn't enunciate; he mumbles and sputters in non-sequential sentence fragments. His quavering voice a whiny singsong. The fantasy has to be teased out. It's grueling work. But finally Freud puts it all together. This lad doesn't want to fuck his mother. Not this harridan.

Not this boy. He wants to kill her and chuckle in triumph over the corpse. Oh, dear. This doesn't fit the Oedipal Complex, per se. But it explains so much of George the Younger's subsequent behavior. (See his cold-blooded chuckling over the state murder of Karla Faye Tucker.)

Perhaps, Freud isn't the right shrink for Bush, after all. Maybe the president's pathology is better understood through the lens of Freud's most gifted and troubled protégé, Wilhelm Reich. (I commend to your attention Dr. Reich's neglected masterpiece *Listen, Little Man.*) Sadly, we cannot avail ourselves of psychological exegeses of either Freud or Reich. So Justin Frank, the disciple of Melanie Klein, will have to substitute. In the spirit of his mentor, Frank, author of *Bush on the Couch*, zeroes in on the crucial first five years of W's existence, where three factors loom over all others: an early trauma, an absent father and an abusive mother. It is a recipe for the making of a dissociated megalomaniac. Add in a learning disability (dyslexia) and a brain bruised by booze and coke and you have a pretty vivid portrait of the Bush psyche.

With this stern upbringing, is it really surprising that Bush evidenced early signs of sadism? As a teenager he jammed firecrackers in the orifices of frogs and snickered as he blew them to bits. A few years later, as president of the DKE frat house at Yale, Bush instituted branding on the ass-crack as an initiation ritual. Young pledges were seared with a red-hot wire clothes hanger. One victim complained to the New Haven police, who raided the frat house. The story was covered-up for several decades until it surfaced in Bush's first run for governor of Texas. He laughed at the allegations, writing the torture off as little more than "a cigarette burn." From Andover to Abu Ghraib.

In his teens, this man-child was shoved into a distant boarding school. It must have been a relief for him. The squirrelly adolescent with the pointy ears did just enough to get by. At Andover they called him "Bushtail." Ambition wasn't his thing. And he didn't have the athletic talent or thespian skills to do much more than play the role of class goof. So he went on to an undistinguished academic career, highlighted only by his ebullient performances as a cheerleader and a reputation for selling fake IDs. Even in his youth he was adept at forgery.

George the Younger crawled into Yale on a legacy admission, a courtesy to his father and grandfather. He was a remedial student at best, awarded a bevy of Cs, the lowest score possible for the legacy cohort. Repositories

like Andover and Yale know what to do with the dim children of the elite.
George nestled in his niche. No demands were made of him. He spent much
his time acquainting himself with a menu of designer intoxicants. He was
arrested twice. Once for petty theft. Once for public drunkenness. No one
cared.

When Vietnam loomed, Lil' George fled to New Haven from Houston
and the safe harbor of the Texas Air National Guard, then jokingly known as
Air Canada—a domestic safe-haven for the combat-averse children of the
political elite. It was a deftly executed dodge. His father pulled some strings.
Escape hatches opened. The scions of the ruling class, even the half-wits,
weren't meant to be eviscerated in the rice paddies of the Mekong—that's
why they freed the slaves.

But soon George grew bored of the weekend warrior routine. And who
among us wouldn't? He slunk off to Alabama, and promptly went AWOL
for a year and a half. Nobody seemed to miss him. He wasn't a crucial cog
in anyone's machine. George? George *Bush*??

How did the president-in-training fritter away those idle days?
Supposedly he was lending his expertise to the congressional campaign
of Winton "Red" Blount. But he apparently soon went AWOL from this
assignment as well. Other campaign staffers recall young George ambling
into the campaign office in the late afternoon, propping his cowboy booted
heals on a desk and recounting his nocturnal revels in the bars, strip joints
and waterbeds of Montgomery. The other staffers took to calling him the
"Texas Soufflé." As one recalled, "Bush was all puffed up and full of hot
air."

Precisely, how did he wile away those humid nights on the Gulf Coast?
According to the intrepid Larry Flynt, he spent part of his time impregnating
his girlfriend and, like a true southern gentleman, then escorting her to an
abortion clinic. Checkbook birth control, the tried and true method of the
ruling classes. A year later, according to Bush biographer J.H. Hatfield,
George W. got popped in Texas on cocaine possession charges. The old
man intervened once again; George diverted for six months of community
service a Project PULL in a black area of Houston and the incident was
scrubbed from the police blotter and court records. Today, Bush denies all
knowledge of those squalid indiscretions. Just two more lost weekends in
George's blurry book of days.

Speaking of cocaine, Bush, by many accounts, had more than a passing familiarity with the powder. Several acquaintances from his days at Yale tell us that Bush not only snorted cocaine, but sold it. Not by the spoonful, but by the ounce bag, a quantity that would land any black or Latino dealer in the pen for a decade. Young Bushtail had become the Snow Bird of New Haven.

Even the Bush family, so smugly self-conscious of its public image, didn't seem to care much. Jr. wasn't the star child. They just wanted him alive and out of jail. (The habitual drunk driving was already a nagging problem. On a December night in 1973, George came up from Houston to visit his family in DC. He took his younger brother Marvin out drinking in the bars of Georgetown. Returning home after midnight, Bush, drunk at the wheel, careened down the road, toppling garbage cans. When he pulled into the driveway, he was confronted by his father. Young Bush threatened to pummel his old man, mano-a-mano. Jeb intervened before young George could be humiliated by his father. A couple of years later, the drunk driving would later land him in the drunk tank of a Maine jail—his fourth arrest.) No need to plump up his resumé with medals or valedictory speeches. Anyway back then, the inside money was riding on Neil, who they said had a head for figures, or perhaps young Jeb, whose gregarious looks hid a real mean streak. (Neil, of course, came to ruin in the looting of the Silverado Savings and Loan (though he deftly avoided jail time), while Jeb proved his utility in Florida and amplified his presidential ambitions.)

By all accounts, the family elders saw George as a pathetic case, as goofy as a black lab. They got him out of the National Guard eight months early (or 20 months, if you insist on counting the Lost Year) and sent him off to Harvard Business School. He didn't have the grades to merit admission, but bloodlines are so much more important than GPA when it comes to prowling the halls at the Ivy League. The original affirmative action, immune from any judicial meddling. In Cambridge, he strutted around in his flight jacket and chewed tobacco in class. The sound of Bushtail spitting the sour juice into a cup punctuated many a lecture on the surplus value theory. At Harvard, one colleague quipped that Bush majored in advanced party planning and the arcana of money laundering. George met every expectation.

Then came the dark years. Booze, drugs, cavorting and bankruptcy in dreary west Texas. There he also met Laura Welch, the steamy librarian who had slain her own ex-boyfriend, by speeding through a stop sign and plowing broadside into his car with a lethal fury. (Rep. Bill Janklow got sentenced to 100 days in the pen for a similar crime; Laura wasn't even charged.) They mated, married, raised fun-loving twins. In 1978, George decided to run for congress. His opponent cast him as carpetbagger with an Ivy League education. It worked. And it didn't help his chances much that Bush apparently was drunk much of time. After one drunken stump speech, Laura gave him a tongue lashing on the ride home. Bush got so irate that he drove the car through the garage door. He lost big.

Eventually, Laura got George to quit the booze—though the librarian never got him to read. It wasn't a moral thing for her. Laura still imbibes herself, even around her husband. She smokes, too. Refreshingly, so do the Bush Twins, who have both been popped for underage drinking.

George was Laura's ticket out of the dusty doldrums of west Texas. She sobered him up and rode him hard all the way to Dallas, Austin and beyond. "Oh, that Welch girl," recalled a retired librarian in Midland. "She got around." Wink, wink.

If the son of a millionaire political powerbroker can't make it in Midland, Texas, he can't make it anywhere. George was set up in his own oil company in the heart of the Permian Basin. His two starter companies, Bush Exploration and Arbusto, promptly went bust, hemorrhaging millions of dollars. His father's cronies in a group called Spectrum 7 picked up the pieces. It flat lined too. A new group of saviors in the form of Harken Oil swooped in. Ditto. Yet in the end, George walked away from the wreckage of Harken Oil with a few million in his pocket. One of the investors in Harken was George Soros, who explained the bail out of Bush in frank terms. "We were buying political influence. That was it. Bush wasn't much of a businessman."

Among the retinue of rescuers in his hours of crisis was a Saudi construction conglomerate, headed by Mohammad bin Laden, sire of Osama. The ties that blind.

Flush with unearned cash, George and Laura hightailed it to Arlington, the Dallas suburb, soon to be the new home of the Texas Rangers, perennial also rans in the American League. Bush served as front man for a flotilla of investors, backed by the Bass brothers and other oil and real estate luminaries, who bought the Rangers and then bullied the city of Arlington into building a posh new stadium for the team with $200 million in public money, raised through a tax hike, for which Bush, the apostle of tax-cuts for the rich, sedulously lobbied. Here's a lesson in the art of political larceny. The super-rich always get their way. When taxes are raised, public money is sluiced upward to the politically connected. When taxes are cut, the money ends up in the same accounts. As William Burrough's hero Jack Black (the hobo writer, not the rotund actor) prophesied, you can't win.

The Rangers deal was never about building a competitive baseball team for the people of Dallas/Ft. Worth. No. The Bush group seduced the city into building a stadium with nearly all the proceeds going straight into their pockets. It was a high level grifter's game, right out of a novel by Jim Thompson, the grand master of Texas noir. Bush played his bit part as affable con man ably enough. Even though he only plunked down $600,000 of his own cash, he walked away from the deal with $14.7 million-a staggering swindle that made Hillary Clinton's windfalls in the cattle future's market look like chump change.

As team president, Bush printed up baseball cards with his photo on them in Ranger attire, indulging his life-long fetish for dress-up fantasies. He would hand out the Bush cards during home game. Invariably, the cards would be found littering the floors of the latrines, soaked in beer and piss.

Mark His Words

Sex and politics often seem to conflate in George W. Bush's mind. In 1975, young George, fresh out of Harvard Business School, followed his father to China, where he was keenly testing the receptiveness of the Chinese to infusions of Texas capital. Soon bored by detailed discussions of international finance, Bush began hitting on his translators and other Chinese women. One Yale coed who came into Bush's orbit recalled: "He was always one of the fastest guys on campus in trying to get his hands in your pants." This friskiness didn't set well with the decorous crowd then running China and he was discreetly directed to evacuate the country in order to save his father, the new ambassador to Peking, further embarrassment.

During the 1988 Republican convention, David Fink, a reporter with the Hartford *Courant*, asked Bush what he talked about with his father when they weren't jawing about politics. "Pussy," George W. quipped. Take that mom.

In 1992, W. famously offered his services to his father's moribund re-election campaign. The younger Bush counseled the president to hire private investigators to rummage through the bed trails of Clinton's sex life, hoping to ignite "bimbo eruptions." This advice coming from a man who, according to one of his friends, spent the 1970s "sleeping with every bimbo in West Texas, married or not." George Sr. (who was himself desperately trying to suppress talk of an affair with a State Department employee) demurred, patted Jr. on the head and followed the more tactful advice of Robert Teeter, with fatal results.

George W. vowed not to make the same political miscalculations as his father in his own 1994 run for governor of Texas. With the sepulchral Karl Rove as his political Svengali, Bush set his sights on Ann Richards, the gruff Democrat who ridiculed Bush's sense of privilege, "Little George was born on third base and thinks he hit a triple." It was a campaign marked by unbridled viciousness, backroom slanders and outright lies. Bush didn't attack frontally; he sent surrogates to hurl the mud for him. Naturally, he won in a romp.

Bush's six-year tenure as governor of Texas was unremarkable by almost any standard. He was kept on a short leash by his handlers, Rove and Karen Hughes, and generally turned over policy-making to the yahoos in the Texas legislature. His resume of those days is familiar by now: he slashed taxes for the rich, injected religion into public schools and social welfare programs, signed a law permitting the carrying of concealed weapons in public buildings and churches, privatized public parks, turned Texas into the nation's most toxic state, sent children to adult prisons and supervised the execution of 152 death row inmates. During an interview with Larry King, Bush chortled about sending Karla Faye Tucker to her fatal encounter with death's needle, saying he had no regrets. Later he joked about the execution with his CNN doppleganger Tucker Carlson. Bush mimicked Karla Faye's pleas for mercy, whining in a shrill falsetto: "Oh please don't kill me." Somebody give Bushtail a shot of Jack Daniels before he kills again.

The big change in Bush was his dramatic conversion to a messianic form of Christian fundamentalism. The happy-go-lucky cad of the 60s and 70s had withered away, replaced by a doltish and vindictive votary. His rebirth as a Christian zealot was famously midwifed by Billy Graham, who considered young George "almost like a son." According to Bush during a walk on the beach at Kennebunkport, "Billy planted a mustard seed in my soul." The man has a felicity with metaphor.

The seed sprouted a few months later. In the notorious scene in the bathroom of a Colorado resort, Bush, head pounding from a night of drinking in celebration of his 40th birthday, plunged to his knees before the mirror and pleaded with the Almighty for a heavenly intervention. Lightning struck that morning. Bush, so the family legend goes, kicked the bottle and emerged as a fanatical believer in what he called "the intercessory power of prayer."

A few years later Bush, by then governor of Texas, offered readers of the *Houston Chronicle* a peek into the stern nature of his faith. "Only those who have accepted Jesus as their personal savoir will be permitted entry into heaven," Bush prophesied. Ten years down the road, Bush would do his best to send thousands of heathens to eternal damnation. Of course, Bush, having been granted the moral amnesty of being born-again, rarely attends formal church services.

* * *

Bush wasn't the early favorite of the Texas king makers to retake the presidency for the Republicans. That role fell to the newt-faced senator Phil Gramm, who had amassed a majestic campaign warchest. But no amount of money could soften Gramm's grotesque image and foul tongue. He was the hissing personification of the Republican ultras, an unrepentant whore for industry who seemed to take delight in savaging the poor, blacks and gays. Here's a taste of the Gramm technique: "Has anyone ever noticed that we live in a country where all of the poor people are fat?"

Gramm's dismal showing in 1996 told the Republican powerbrokers that they needed an image makeover, a candidate with Christian sex appeal coating a hard core philosophy. John McCain was too grouchy, carried the whiff of scandal and might prove uncontrollable. Jack Kemp was perceived as soft on blacks and perhaps even was a real libertarian at heart. So they settled on Bush, the smirking governor with the lofty Q-rating among white middle-aged women who'd been devoted watchers of *Dallas* and *Knots Landing*.

As for Bush, he didn't recall being coaxed to run by the RNC power elite. Instead, the green light fell upon him from a celestial source. "I feel like God wants me to run for president," Bush confided to James Robison, the Texas evangelist. "I can't explain it, but I sense my country is going to need me. I know it won't be easy on me or my family, but God wants me to do it."

In a flashy feat of political transvestitism, Bush marketed himself as a "compassionate conservative," a feathery reprise of his father's kinder and gentler Reaganism. It was a ploy to distance himself from the foamy rhetoric of the Republican pit bulls who had nearly self-destructed in their manic pursuit of Clinton. Bush was tight with Tom DeLay, Trent Lott and Phil Gramm, but he didn't want to be tarred with their radioactive baggage while he courted soccer moms. During the 2000 campaign, this grand hoax was rivaled only by Al Gore's outlandish masquerade as an economic populist.

Still Bush, under the lash of Karl Rove, didn't shirk from playing mean, particularly in the bruising inter-squad battle for the Republican nomination. During the crucial South Carolina primary, Bush's campaign goons intimated that his chief rival, John McCain, had fathered an illegitimate child with a black woman. Of course, a more dexterous politician than McCain could have turned this slur to his advantage. After all, Strom Thurmond ruled the Palmetto State for decades and he was widely known to have sired at least one child with his black mistress. The Bush attack dogs also made ungentlemanly whispers about McCain's wife, Cindy, suggesting that she might be a neurotic and a drug addict. Of course, it was McCain himself who was slightly unhinged and he wilted under the fire of the Bush sniper teams, which also included an attack on McCain's war record by the same by claque of mad dog vets who would later fling mud at Max Cleland and John Kerry.

The 2000 campaign itself was unremittingly dull until the final debate, when Gore sealed his fate as he stalked Bush across the stage like he had overdosed on testosterone. As Gore glowered over the governor badgering him with the names of obscure pieces of legislation, Bush merely turned his head to the camera and shrugged his shoulders, as if to say, "What's this guy's problem?" It was the first real moment of the campaign and probably kept Bush close enough so that the Supremes could hand him the presidency.

Bush's 527-vote triumph in Florida is an old and tiresome story by now, but it's worth recalling some of the low points. The stolen election was an inside job, although greatly abetted by Gore's incompetence. The state may very well have been secured before a single vote was cast. That's because Jeb, the Bush who always wanted to be president, ordered Katherine Harris to purge the voter rolls of more than 90,000 registered voters, mostly in

Democratic precincts.

Then, with the recount underway, the Bush junta sprang into action. Using $13.8 million in campaign funds, they recruited an A-list of Republican fixers, tough guys and lawyers. Roger Stone, the former Republican fixer and body builder of Reagan time who fled to Florida following a DC sex scandal, was summoned to orchestrate gangs of rightwing Cubans to harass election officials in Dade and Palm Beach counties. Marc Racicot, later to be elevated by Bush to chair of the RNC, staged similar white-collar riots, all designed to impede the counting of ballots. Jeb and the haughty Harris did their parts as institutional monkeywrenchers.

Meanwhile, the legal strategy was designed by Theodore Olson to fast track the case to the Supreme Court. When Scalia and Thomas refused to recuse themselves from the case despite glaring conflicts of interest (family members worked for the Bush campaign), the electoral theft was legitimized.

The ringmaster of this affair was Bush Sr.'s old hand, James Baker. Baker later boasted to a group of Russian tycoons mustered in London, "I fixed the election in Florida for George Bush." And Gore laid down and took it like a dazed Sonny Liston. He didn't raise a peep about the disenfranchisement of thousands of black voters, as if to say, "If have to be elected by blacks, I don't want the job."

Bush, the Selected One, was anxious to consolidate his power. "If this were a dictatorship, it would be a heck of a lot easier— just so long as I'm the dictator," Bush snickered on December 18, 2000, as the Supreme Court prepared to deliver the presidency to his sweaty hands.

Mark those words.

* * *

The contours of the Bush agenda were established by his transition team. This shadowy group picked the cabinet, outlined the budget, sketched the foreign policy, dreamed up the size of the tax cuts and scouted across the sprawl of the bureaucracy for opportunities for self-dealing contracts.

None had a sharper nose for scenting opportunities to cash in on federal contracts than Dick Cheney, the man who recruited himself as Bush's running mate. Although Cheney flunked out of Yale (he was a working class kid without the academic passes afforded the legacy admittees), he shares several other traits with Bush. Twice Cheney has been arrested for drunk driving. And, although he fervently supported the war, he had no desire to actually go to Vietnam and do battle. Saying he "had other priorities," Cheney sought and received five draft deferments. See Dick run. And so it came to pass: others died so that he might prosper. Don't tell Cheney he doesn't understand the meaning of sacrifice.

As a congressman from Wyoming, Cheney established himself as a hardcore rightwinger, gnashing away at everything from abortion to Head Start. Bush Sr. picked this top-flight chickenhawk as Defense Secretary in 1989. He managed the first Gulf War, amassing through bribery and bullying international support like a CEO on a consolidation binge, and later rationalized the decision not to depose Saddam or support uprisings by Iraqi and Kurdish rebels, predicting that the fall of the Ba'athists would destabilize the entire region. How right you were, Dick.

After Clinton steamrolled Bush, Cheney cashed in, landing a top executive position at Halliburton, the Houston-based oil services and military construction giant. Cheney knew all about Halliburton and they knew Dick. In fact, as Defense Secretary, Cheney had devised the privatization scheme which turned over much of the Pentagon's logistical programs (base construction, food and fuel services, infrastructure, mortuaries) to corporations. He also steered some of the biggest early contracts to Halliburton, including lucrative deals for reconstructing Kuwait's oil fields and logistical support for the doomed venture into Somalia.

At Halliburton, Cheney exploited his government and international contacts to boost Halliburton's government-guaranteed loans from $100 million to $1.5 billion in less than five years. He also created 35 offshore tax-free subsidiaries, a feat of accounting prestidigitation that would soon be aped by Kenny Boy Lay and the corporate highwaymen at Enron. The grateful board of Halliburton soon rewarded Cheney by making him CEO and compensating him to the tune of $25 million a year in salary and lavish stock options. By the time he left Halliburton for the White House, he owned $45 million in the company's stock.

Of course, the question presents itself as to whether Cheney ever really left Halliburton. The company had been bruised a bit in the Clinton era. In 1997, it lost a multi-billion dollar logistics contract with the Army. Yet, soon after Cheney ascended to the Veep's office Halliburton seized the contract back and stood poised to become the prime provisioner for the Pentagon as it embarked on operations in Afghanistan, Iraq, Uzbekistan, Qatar, South Korea, and the Philippines. Within two short years under Cheney, Halliburton cashed in on $1.7 billion in Pentagon contracts. Then, naturally, Halliburton decided to gouge the government, overcharging for everything from gas deliveries to food services.

Then came the big reward: a two-year contract worth $7 billion for rebuilding Iraq's oil infrastructure, bombed to smithereens by the Pentagon. The no bid contract was awarded by the Army Corps of Engineers, who apparently never even considered another company. No surprise here. Halliburton had drafted the Corps' reconstruction plan for Iraq. "They were the company best positioned to execute the oil field work because of their involvement in the planning," explained Lt. Col. Gene Pawlick, a PR flack for the Army.

All the while, Cheney continues to personally benefit from Halliburton's government contracts. He still holds options for 400,000 shares of Halliburton stock and continues to receive $150,000 a year in deferred compensation from his former company.

* * *

Cheney was not a lone emissary from the crude cartel. Of the 41 members of that Bush transition team, 34 came from the oil industry. The mask had slipped off the beast. Not since the days of Warren Harding has big oil enjoyed a firmer stranglehold on the controls of the federal government. Bush's inner circle is dominated by oil men, starting with Bush and Cheney and including 6 cabinet members and 28 top political appointees. Recall that Condoleezza Rice has an oil tanker named after her and that Stephen Griles, the number two man at the Interior Department, was the oil industry's top lobbyist and continued to be paid $285,000 a year by his former firm as he handed out oil leases to his former clients. Griles is the Albert Fall of our time. Fall, the architect of the Teapot Dome scandal, where his crony's oil company was quietly handed the rights to drill in on federal lands in Wyoming, pronounced: "All natural resources should be made as easy of access as possible to the present generation. Man cannot exhaust the resources of nature and never will." More than 80 years later, this reckless nonsense could serve as a motto for the Bush administration. But see how times have changed. Fall went to jail for his self-dealing; Griles got a bonus.

Then came the neo-cons: Paul Wolfowitz, Richard Perle, Lewis "Scooter" Libby, Douglas Feith, Donald Wurmser, Stephen Cambone and John Bolton. This coterie of hawks, many of them veterans of Reagan/Bush I, were deeply marinated in the writings of the darkly iconic Leo Strauss and schooled in the art of political terror by Henry "Scoop" Jackson, the Democratic senator from Boeing. After eight years on the outside, they came in febrile for war from the get-go and charged with an implacable loyalty to Israel, nation of the apartheid wall and the 82 nukes. The neo-cons's devotion to Israel was so profound that several of them hired themselves out as consultants to the Israeli government. At the close of Bush's first term, this same nest of neo-cons finds itself under investigation for leaking top-secret documents to Israel.

To complete the starting lineup, Bush and Cheney also dredged up from the obscurity of far right think tanks some of the most malodorous scoundrels of the Iran/contra era: Eliot Abrams, John Poindexter, Otto Reich and John Negroponte. Soon enough this merry band of brigands were up to their old tricks. Poindexter, from his den at DARPA, devised a big brother program under the name Total Information Awareness, branded with an Illuminati logo, which sought to keep track of the movements and credit card purchases of all Americans. Later Poindexter, convicted of lying to congress in the 1980s, opened up a futures market for terrorist attacks, where traders would be financially rewarded by the Pentagon for accurately predicting suicide bombings. Meanwhile, Abrams, another Iran/contra felon, was put in charge of human rights in the Middle East-a curious brief for the man who backed the butchers of Guatemala and El Salvador. Even Hunter S. Thompson blazing away on blotter acid couldn't dream this stuff up.

More Pricks Than Kicks

Relations inside the Bush cabinet have not always collegial and harmonious. Take Richard Armitage, the longtime diplomatic fixer. Armitage had originally been slated by the Bush transition team for installation as the number two man at the Pentagon. But Armitage despised Donald Rumsfeld's megalomaniacal style and denounced him openly as "a prick." Armitage ended up back at State and Paul Wolfowitz, the crafty neo-con, became Rumsfeld's slavishly devoted deputy.

Rumsfeld had good reason to fear Armitage and some of the other old hands at State. Not because Armitage and Powell weren't itching for war with Iraq. Oh, no. It was a tussle over who would call the shots and how it would be launched: Powell's office wanted a reprise of the 1990 coalition; Rummy wanted war on his own terms. The men and women at Foggy Bottom knew some unsavory tidbits about Rumsfeld's past relations with two pillars in Bush's Axis of Evil: Iraq and North Korea.

In the early 1980s, Rummy was grazing in the corporate pastures as a top executive fixer at G.D. Searle, the drug giant involved in the aspartame scandal. Then Reagan called. The Gipper summoned Rumsfeld to serve as his special emissary for the Middle East, assigned with the delicate mission of delivering back channel communications from the White House to Baghdad. This was the beginning of the so-called Iraq Tilt, the subtle backing of Saddam during the gruesome Iran/Iraq war.

December 20, 1983 found Rumsfeld in Baghdad supping with Saddam and Iraq's foreign minister Tariq Aziz. By all accounts the day long session was amiable and cordial. Rumsfeld chose not to issue a remonstrance about Iraq's lethal use of chemical weapons against Iran. Rumsfeld, known as the Prince of Darkness by some of his staffers, was well acquainted with the slaughter. He was in possession of a State Department memo dated November 1, 1983 by Middle East specialist Jonathan Howe who warned the administration of "almost daily use of CW by Iraq against Iranian forces."

Rumsfeld blew off the reports of atrocities and instead encouraged Saddam to press his war on Iran. By February 1984, a UN investigation publicly confirmed the gassings, but that didn't deter Rumsfeld from meeting with Tariq Aziz again on March 26, 1984, where he again failed to reprimand the Iraqis (now essentially pursuing a proxy war for the US) for the war crimes. Two decades later, Rumsfeld, without cracking a grin, repeatedly invoked Saddam's use of poison gas in the 1980s as a justification for Bush's pre-emptive war.

Cut to 1994. Now Rumsfeld plying his craft back in the corporate milieu, this time for the Swiss engineering giant ABB, which specializes in the construction of nuclear power plants. In the fall of that year, ABB received a $200 million contract to construct two light-water reactors for the Pyongyang government, under a deal sanctioned by the State Department during the Clinton years. Oddly, Rumsfeld was later to cite the reactors as evidence of North Korea's malign intention to pursue the development of nuclear weapons and used the reactors as justification for sinking billions in Bush's Star Wars scheme. When confronted by the fact that the reactors under scrutiny had been sold to North Korea by his very own company, Rumsfeld feigned ignorance, just has he had done when presented with a videotape of him greeting Saddam. But the boys at the State Department knew the score on both counts and Rummy didn't like it.

Indeed, Rumsfeld, the Polonius of the Bush team, so distrusted the ecumenicalists in the State Department that he set up an off-the-shelf operation sequestered firmly under his control called the Office for Special Plans, headed by Douglas Feith. Sound familiar? It should. The OSP is not all that different from the William Casey/Oliver North operation that had its stealthy hands in illegal meddlings from Iran and Afghanistan to Honduras and Nicaragua. But see how far we've matured as a nation in 20 years. Rumsfeld's group was an open secret, shedding even the pretense of covertness.

The OSP operates as kind of cut-and-paste intelligence shop that served up as fact any gothic tale peddled by Ahmed Chalabi or the American Israel Public Affairs Committee (AIPAC). Feith made a pest of himself, meddling in the affairs of the war planners. He was reviled by Gen. Tommy Franks, who called him "the dumbest motherfucker on the face of the Earth."

This didn't deter Feith in the least. He recruited a roster of pliant neo-cons into his office, who generated the phantasmagorical briefs for the war to topple Saddam, which he had hungered for since at least 1994. Feith's OSP office was known by State Department hands as the Fantasy Factory. Among Feith's pack of underlings, two have received special attention, Harold Rhode and Larry Franklin, for their intimate relationship with the state of Israel. Franklin, perhaps the scapegoat for a larger scandal, finds himself the target an FBI investigation into Israeli espionage ring in the Pentagon and National Security Council.

Feith himself is no stranger to such inquiries into leaking classified information to the Israeli government. In 1982, Feith was fired from his position as an analyst on Middle East issues in the Reagan administration's National Security Council on suspicion of leaking material to the an official with the Israeli embassy in Washington. Don't cry for Feith. He simply moved out of the White House and over to the Pentagon as a "special assistant" to Richard Perle, then assistant secretary of Defense for International Security Policy.

When the Republicans were driven from office in 1992, Feith settled into a comfortable niche as a DC lawyer/lobbyist with the firm Feith and Zell, where he represented the interests of many Israeli firms hot to see the demise of Saddam. After Feith joined the Bush 2 administration, his former law partner, Marc Zell, moved the firm to Tel Aviv.

During the war on Iraq, Feith was given the responsibility of planning for the occupation of Iraq and its reconstruction. Obviously, Feith spent little of his attention on the troublesome details of the occupation, swallowing the line that Iraqis would welcome their conquistadors. Instead, Feith devoted himself to the lucrative task of awarding many of the Coalition Provisional Authority's reconstruction contracts. He steered many of the most lucrative deals, often on a no-bid basis, to clients associated with his former law firm, including Diligence, New Bridge Strategies and the Iraqi International Law Group, headed by Salem Chalabi-the nephew of Ahmed Chalabi. No sooner had Salem Chalabi, whose Law Group billed itself as "your professional gateway to the new Iraq," been appointed chief prosecutor in war crime trial of Saddam Hussein than he found himself indicted by an Iraqi prosecutor for involvement in a strange political murder plot. Now Salem Chalabi is on the lam in London.

Feith is one of those Washington creatures who seems to live his political life on the ropes, always saved by the paranoid solidarity of the neo-con claque, which suspects, rightly, that if one of their number topples he may take the rest down with him. Of course, even if Feith is forced to walk the plank at the Pentagon, he will almost certainly make a soft landing in the private sector, embraced by the firms he abetted while in office.

Sometimes even the stupidest motherfucker on the face of the earth can make out like a bandit.

* * *

Thanks to Paul O'Neill, Bush's former treasury secretary, we now know what we'd suspected all along: that the Iraq war was plotted long before al-Qaeda struck New York and Washington. Bush himself is depicted as entering office seething with vindictive rage like a character in a Jacobean revenge play. After all, he believed that Saddam had tried to kill his daddy in a bungled bomb plot during Bush Sr.'s triumphal entry into Kuwait City in 1993. Here we have one of the colorful features of the new dynastic politics of America: familial retribution as foreign policy.

O'Neill's version is backed up by Richard Clarke, the former NSC terrorism staffer. Clarke charges that Iraq was an idée fixe with the Bush team since their entry into Washington. In his book *Against All Enemies*, Clarke describes a meeting with the president a few days after the 9/11 attacks when it was clear to nearly everyone that they had been orchestrated by Bin Laden. Bush needled Clarke about finding a link to Saddam. Clarke said there was none. But his answer seemed to bounce off Bush's brain like a handball off the back wall.

A few months later the invasion on Iraq seemed set in stone. "Fuck Saddam," Bush fumed at a meeting of the National Security Council in March of 2002. "We're taking him out." Call it a case of pre-meditated pre-emption.

The game plan for deposing Saddam, seizing his oil fields and installing a puppet regime headed by a compliant thug such as Ahmed Chalabi or, as it turned out, the CIA favorite Ahmed Allawi, was drafted and tweaked by the National Security Council within weeks of taking office. Cheney's shadowy energy task force even produced maps allocating Iraqi reserves to different oil companies. Of course, they didn't offer an exit strategy. Perhaps, they didn't plan on leaving?

On the remote chance that impeachment charges are ever leveled against this coven of pre-emptive warriors, Bush may have a minor case for plausible deniability here. According to O'Neill, the president drifts off during the excruciating tedium of these sessions. Bush only perks up during cabinet meetings when Condi Rice strolls into the room, whereupon he cleaves to each sanguinary phrase, nodding excitedly like his very own bobblehead doll.

Not that Bush seems to care all that much about the veracity of his briefings, but Rice's information is not always noted for its reliability. For example, Rice, who got her start in politics working on the 1988 presidential campaign of Gary Hart, persisted for months in pushing the preposterous notion that Iran was working with Pakistan to inflame anti-American sentiments across Southwest Asia. Of course, the rulers of Iran are Shiites and the elites of Pakistan are Sunni Muslim and, thus, as bitter rivals as Iran and Iraq—that is, until, the Bush administration succeeded in congealing their desperation and rage.

Jesus Told Him Where to Bomb

Get George Bush in front of a bunch of preachers and his tongue tends to loosen up a bit and occasionally some luminous black pearls spill out. Shortly after the Supremes invested him with the presidency, Bush confided to the Reverend Jim Wallis, head of the Call of Renewal coven of churches, the following: "I don't understand how poor people think."

This presidential gem, worthy of Antoinette herself, neatly mirrors a statement made during the darkest trench of the recession by Bush's director of Housing and Urban Development, Alphonso Jackson, who deflected criticism of the Bush economic disaster by pronouncing that "being poor is a state of mind, not a condition."

Jackson's coarse declaration reflects a kind of economic phenomenology that might even give Milton Friedman the willies. Naturally, Bush doesn't know the difference between phenomenology and proctology, but he keenly intuits its essential meaning: The suffering of the poor is entirely self-inflicted. They simply lack faith. And the circle of blow-dried Cotton Mathers the president surrounds himself with sanction his cold sense of compassion. Blaming the victim is not only a political device; it's infused with ecclesiastical authority. The downtrodden must be blamed for their own good.

Bush presided over the loss of more than 2 million jobs, the cruelest blow to working people since the Great Depression. Not his fault. Homeless and poverty rates have soared as a result and thanks to Clinton when this recession hit the social safety net of welfare and food stamps had already been sheared away. Not Bush's responsibility. The mounting piles of corpses in Afghanistan and Iraq. Others are to blame.

Here you have the prime virtue of being a born-again politician: automatic absolution from responsibility for inflicting even more deprivations on the weakest in society. (For more on Bush and the fundamentalists I highly recommend David Domke's excellent new book, *God Willing: Political Fundamentalism in the White House, the 'War on Terror' and the Echoing Press*.)

All of this feeds Bush's stunted capacity for human empathy. His joking about executions. His reluctance to comfort the families of the slain in Iraq and Afghanistan. His imperviousness to the plight of the poor. How else can you explain his bizarre remarks at a White House Christmas party in 2001 made in front of Billy Graham and other guardians of the faith. "All in all, 2001 has been a fabulous year for Laura and me," Bush gushed, even though the ruins of the Twin Towers were still warm to the touch and cruise missiles were cratering hovels in Kandahar.

In the spring of 2001, Bush invited a flock of religious leaders to the White House for tea, followed by the obligatory prayer session. The president soon strayed from his prepared script. "I had a drinking problem," he confessed during the gathering. "Right now, I should be in a bar. Not the Oval Office." There's no record of any objection being lodged.

Of course, perhaps the pastors of doom and damnation sensed that the cure had not entirely taken hold. There's plenty of anecdotal evidence that Bush continues to nip at the bottle every once in a while—and it's almost certainly good for the country and the world that he does imbibe. An Austin musician told us of a night in the mid-1990s, a decade after Bush went on the wagon, when he hustled into the bathroom of a bar between sets only to find the Governor face down on the less than spic-and-span floor, mumbling inanities. It was an episode of foreshadowing worthy of O. Henry, for years later Bush would be similarly felled on the floor of the Oval Office by a renegade pretzel.

Some presidents need a blowjob to unwind; others just crave some blow. Save an Iraqi child; get George high.

* * *

Some leaders of state have a hotline to other bigwigs. Like an Old Testament king, George Bush gets operational faxes straight from the Supreme Deity. "God told me to strike at al Qaeda and I struck them, and then he instructed me to strike at Saddam, which I did, and now I am determined to solve the problem in the Middle East," he told Abu Abbas, the former Palestinian Prime Minister. "If you can help me, I will act, and if not, the elections will come and I will have to focus on them."

He is surrounded by Christian soldiers, the real coalition of the willing. One of them, Gen. Jerry Boykin, proclaimed that God put Bush in office — apparently Jim Baker was merely an unwitting instrument of the Supreme Deity. Boykin also fumed that God had told him that followers of Islam where heathens and it was his duty to smite them. This is the same brand of bracing biblical exegesis that marked the Fifth Monarchists of puritan

England, who believed they could hasten the Apocalypse by firing off their blunderbusses in unison inside the Houses of Parliament. Praise the lord and program the cruise missiles.

Bush's wash-and-wear fundamentalism has revved up liberals into a frenzied panic. But aside from Boykin and Ashcroft, Bush hasn't surrounded himself with that many more religious fanatics than Reagan or even Carter embedded into their ranks. After all, who is Bush's guide to God? None other than, good old Billy Graham, the sky pilot for nearly every president since LBJ, who has absolved official villainy for more than 40 years. Is there a more stable fixture of the federal government than Graham? Alan Greenspan is a mere piker compared to Billy G.

When Bush talks religion, it's a surefire sign that's he's in trouble. His public utterances of piety serve as a distress call to the stalwarts, the base that never wavers. Hence the fervid imprecations against gay marriage issued in Bush's darkest hour.

Bush's stop-and-go pursuit of a religious agenda has been perfunctory at best, backfiring deliriously more often than not. Indeed, John DiIulio, the arch zealot in the Bush inner circle, quit in a huff and denounced the administration as sellouts and frauds, more interested in MOAB bombs and tax cuts than state-coerced conversions to Christ.

"There is no precedent in any modern White House for what is going on in this one: a complete lack of a policy apparatus," DiIulio told Ron Suskind, writing for *Esquire*. "What you've got is everything—and I mean everything—being run by the political arm. It's the reign of the Mayberry Machiavellis."

One of those Mayberry Machiavellians was John Ashcroft, the Savonarola of the Potomac. Ashcroft, the singing senator who lost his reelection to a dead man, is an unapologetic bigot, who launches weekly sorties against the Bill of Rights. (Apparently, no one informed Ashcroft, who daily anoints his forehead with Crisco oil, that his raids on the Constitution were the equivalent of a saturation bombing strike on a Potemkin village— Madison's carta of liberty having been hollowed out by more fiendish minds, long, long ago.) But the censorious Missourian, who sought and received three draft deferments during the Vietnam war, rumbles on, rummaging through the private corners of our lives, like one of Moliere's pious buffoons, draping the breasts of Lady Justice one day and condemning homosexuality as "a sin" the next. In *The Bush Betrayal*, the libertarian writer James Bovard's pitiless dismantling of the Bush era, Bovard quips that the Persecutor General wanted to "repeal 1776."

Whether or not anyone briefed the president to this fact remains unclear, but Ashcroft became an oozing liability to the Bush crowd, ridiculed even by Republican ultras such as Bob Barr and Dick Armey and repudiated by federal judges in nearly every circuit. Ashcroft overreached so far that he made Ed Meese seem like Ramsey Clark.

There's nothing spiritual about Ashcroft's jihad and that's why, ultimately, his vindictive crusade floundered on its own rectitude and rigidity; he offered only persecution and purges, no transcendence. Frail Billy Graham could teach the Reverend Prosecutor a thing or two about how to con a congregation into compliance.

That's not to say that the Patriot Act (and its odious offspring) doesn't qualify as one of the spookiest legislative incursions on civil liberties since the McCarran Act. But Ashcroft can't be saddled with all the blame for that inquisitorial bill. After all, he didn't write it. He merely plucked it fully-formed from one of Janet Reno's shelves, dusted it off and dumped it on a complicit Congress, which passed it nearly unanimously. Only Russ Feingold, the Wisconsin progressive, and Ron Paul, the Texas libertarian, spoke out as prophetic voices of dissent, warning that we were slipping into a culture of official suspicion and interrogation. And so it came to pass: warrantless searches and wiretaps, governments snoops in libraries, infiltration of dissident groups, immigrants rounded up and sent to detention camps without legal redress, prosecution of lawyers who work too sedulously in the defense their clients, and on and on. Paranoia as federal policy.

(The Patriot Act proved sturdy enough to survive Ashcroft's resignation in late 2004. He turned over his seat as chief prosecutor to Alberto Gonzales, the long-time Bush confidant who, as White House counsel, drafted legal memos supporting the use of torture against detainees at Gitmo, Bagram and Abu Ghraib prisons.)

The maintenance of this creepy state of affairs depends on the mainlining of anxiety, inculcating an ever-tender sense of trauma in the psyche of the populace. Thus, the color-coded terror alerts, issued with the precision of a metronome. But here Bush faces his most puzzling problem: keeping the whole thing knotted up tight. Unless he, by some miraculous heresy, legalizes pot, there's no way this condition of perpetual paranoia can be sustained. The republic is too diverse, too innately averse to prosecutorial probings (memo to K. Starr), too unwieldy and restless to be kept sedate under the looking glass for long before minor rebellions begin to erupt, sending out little fuck-yous to the system.

Bush began to lose ground in the winter of 2004: from Janet Jackson flashing her right tit at a scandalized Michael Powell to US soldiers refusing to serve in Iraq to John Dean calling for the impeachment of the president to the exposure of the Sadean circus at Abu Ghraib to the punch-drunk economy, seemingly face-down for the count. It had begun to unravel. By early summer, the once unsinkable Bush was listing, desperate for any life-ring in the sucking maelstrom.

Of course, that's where the Democrats come in.

Bush's Mask of Anarchy

And many more Destructions played
In this ghastly masquerade,
All disguised, even to the eyes,
Like Bishops, lawyers, peers, or spies.
. . .
And Anarchy, the Skeleton,
Bowed and grinned to every one,
As well as if his education
Had cost ten millions to the nation.

Percy Bysshe Shelley, *The Mask of Anarchy*

By the smirk, ye shall know him. It is Bush's identifying mark. The cruel sneer fissures across his face at the oddest moments, like an execution or a spike in the deficit or the news of a light-stick being rammed up the anus of an Iraqi prisoner. It hints at its own sense of inviolateness, like the illicit grin of some 70s porn star—which may not be so far off target given the disclosures by Kitty Kelley about Bush's peregrinations in her delicious book *The Family*.

Flash to Bush's most famous moment, the instant when he supposedly redeemed his tottering presidency. There at ground zero, megaphone in hand, using firefighters as props, Bush squeaks out his war cry. It won't be a war of justice, but revenge, cast as a crusade against evil. Then, hands palsied with anxiety, he closes with his signature sneer and gives the game away.

The mask drops, revealing in a flash, like a subliminal cut, the dark sparkle of the real Bush. You get the sense that he detests his own supporters, those who refuse to see through the act. But perhaps that's giving Bush too much credit. He reminds me of one of the early popes or one of the more degenerate emperors, such as Domitian: cruel, imperious, humorless, and psychologically brittle.

Bush and his team turned 9/11 into a kind prime-time political necrophilia, an obscene exploitation of the dead. For example, Flight 93 was transformed into Bush's Masada, where the passengers committed group suicide by bringing the plane down into the remote Pennsylvania field in order to save the White House. Of course, this was a lie.

Bush lied about his actions in the aftermath of the 9/11 attacks. He lied about why the US was attacked. He lied about what his own government knew in advance about impending plans by al-Qaeda to attack targets in the US. He lied about how much the wars would cost. About weapons of mass destruction. About the relationship between Saddam and Bin Laden. About the progress of the war. These daily manipulations of the truth aren't impromptu faux pas. Bush is kept on a tighter leash by his staff than any president in US history. He's not permitted extemporaneous comments. Bush's prevarications roll right off the teleprompter.

In the memorial service at the National Cathedral, Bush announced his mission: "Rid the world of evil." Part of that evil would, naturally, be the burdensome tax rates on the super-rich.

Bush was hot for war without congressional debate. "I'd rather have them [American troops] sacrificing on behalf of our nation than, you know, endless hours of congressional testimony." And they were primed to give him any thing he wanted. Any thing at all. No one rose to stop him. No one would even question him at the precise moment he most needed to be restrained.

The remote-control war on Afghanistan is a shameful chapter in American history. It rode unbridled on the fervor of a kind of national bloodletting against one of the most destitute nation's on earth, which had only the most tangential responsibility for the events of 9/11. More than 3,400 civilians perished, most of whom had never heard of Osama Bin Laden.

The Pentagon drilled Kandahar and other Taliban strongholds with cruise missiles and pulverized convoys of pack mules with unmanned Predator planes armed with Hellfire guns. The ground war was turned over to the Northern Alliance, a CIA-financed band of thugs with a bloodier reputation than the Taliban.

Why do they hate us? Bush proffered the two word cue-card answer: Our freedom. But how could this be? Only a few years ago the Mujahideen, the Taliban and the Chechen separatists were hailed by neo-cons and neo-libs alike as "freedom fighters."

Yes, they knew them very well indeed. They had not only traded with the enemy. They had created them. Bin Laden and Mullah Omar were armed, funded and sheltered by the CIA in its insane proxy war in Afghanistan against the Soviet Union. A $3 billion war that brought to power the most tyrannical and fundamentalist's sect this side of Falwell's Liberty Baptist College. The Taliban regime was fired by an unquenchable hatred of the West, a political pathology it acted out through the violent suppression of the nation's own women, homosexuals and academics. Then came the first Gulf War, the US bases on Saudi soil, the misguided adventure into Somalia, the blind support of the bloody Israeli suppression of the second Intifada. Al-Qaeda, financed by Saudi millions and sequestered by the Taliban, turned its attention to the great Satan, which was indeed acting like a malevolent titan across the globe. The events of 9/11 have blowback written all over them.

In the end, though, the Taliban weren't toppled. They simply dispersed back into the Pashtun tribal areas from which they arose, where they knew the US and its mercenary army would never come to get them. As recounted in Seymour Hersh's *Chain of Command*, the few ground engagements where US troops faced off with the Taliban proved embarrassing for the Pentagon. And today the Taliban have reasserted their control over most of Afghanistan. The only city that remains under the uneasy grip of Hamid Karzai and his CIA masters is Kabul, the old British capital which has never been a Taliban stronghold.

So much for the opening act. As Condoleezza Rice put it, Bush, the conquistador in a jogging suit, soon got bored with "swatting flies."

(Torturing flies was, of course, a favorite past time of Domitian. According to Suetonius, "At the beginning of his reign, Domitian used to spend hours in seclusion every day, doing nothing but catching flies and stabbing them with a keenly sharpened stylus. Consequently, when someone once asked if anyone was in there with the Emperor, Vibius Crispus made the witty reply, 'Not even a fly." Domitian, that wanton boy emperor, was also the inspiration for the famous line in Lear, "as flies are to wanton boys, are we to the gods: they kill us for their sport."

Bush wanted to put away such childish things and squash bigger game. Iraq, naturally.

Coda: The House Rules

Even Laura couldn't stop him. By most inside accounts, the first lady opposed the war on Iraq. She told Bob Woodward on the eve of the war that she found the prospect of the invasion horrifying. Later she whispered to others of being repulsed by the killing of Iraqi children and American soldiers. Generally, Bush cleaves to Laura like a security blanket. Since 1988, he hasn't spent more than two consecutive nights away from her. Still, he denied her on Iraq, just as he has done on abortion, which Laura demurely supports.

His father also couldn't deter him. Poppy Bush opposed the invasion of Iraq, reportedly fretting that Junior was wrecking the global coalition that he'd built. The old man thought that the toppling of Saddam would destabilize the Middle East and the occupation would be a bloody quagmire that would end with many Americans dead and a fundamentalist regime in control of much of Iraq. He sent his warnings through emissaries, such as his old National Security Advisor Brent Scowcroft. Scowcroft wrote an op-ed in the *Wall Street Journal* opposing the war. The text of the piece had been floated by Bush, Sr., who gave it the thumbs up. It went to press on August 15, 2002 under the title "Don't Attack Saddam." Plank by plank, Scowcroft ripped apart the Bush brief for war, as if it were a dilapidated barn. He said that the sanctions and UN inspections were working. Saddam was essentially contained and didn't pose a threat to the US, Israel or other protectorates in the Middle East.

Scowcroft also blew up the notion that Saddam had cosseted Al Qaeda. "There is scant evidence to tie Saddam to terrorist organizations, and even less to the September 11 attacks. Indeed, Saddam's goals have little in common with the terrorists who threaten us, and there is little incentive for him to make common cause with them...There is virtual consensus in the world against an attack on Iraq at this time. So long as that sentiment persists, it would require the US to pursue a virtual go-it-alone strategy against Iraq, making military operations more difficult and more expensive." The occupation and reconstitution of Iraq, Scowcroft warned with vivid prescience, could be bloody, protracted and might ultimately result in a fundamentalist regime more hostile to US interests than Iraq was under Saddam.

The article was warmly received by Colin Powell and Richard Armitage at the State Department, who wanted some breathing room from their rivals in the Pentagon. Armitage in particular seemed to be looking for a way to stick it to Cheney and Rumsfeld. He advised Powell to use the Scowcroft column to tell Rumsfeld to "Fuck off." Typically, Powell, always reflexively subservient, declined to press the advantage opened by his former colleague.

Meanwhile Scowcroft's broadside enraged Cheney and Rumsfeld. Being experienced hands at this game, they didn't attack their old associate frontally. Instead, they sent Condoleezza Rice out to lambaste Scowcroft. She accused the apex insider of betraying the home team and demanded that he muzzle his objections to the war. Shamefully, Scowcroft backed down, sulking mutely in his holding pen at the Scowcroft Group, his international lobbying firm headquartered in DC, content to be Cassandra for a day.

The prickly George W. was peeved at his father for trying to pull the rug out from under his planned conquest of Baghdad. He sniped that he wasn't about to recapitulate the mistakes of his father in regard to Saddam or the tax code. He privately ridiculed his father's lack of bravado in failing to take out Saddam in 1991, which the president characterized as a lack of nerve typical of those inclined toward diplomacy. Then in an interview with Bob Woodward, Bush, Jr. twisted the knife one last, fatal time. Bush confessed that he never consulted his father on the Iraq war. "You know, he is the wrong father to appeal to for strength," Bush said. "There is a higher father that I appeal to." Notice the implication here: his own father was weak. W.'s war on Saddam was in many ways not to redeem his father or avenge him, but a way to outdo him. Bush downshifts from choir boy to frat boy in a nanosecond. On the eve of the war, he gloated to Italian prime minister Sylvio Berlusconi, "Just, watch us, we're going to kick Saddam's ass."

As Hersh discloses in *Chain of Command,* the decision to invade Iraq, high on the agenda of the neo-cons in Cheney's office and the Pentagon since the election, had been given the greenlight almost immediately after the planes hit the World Trade Center and the Pentagon. At 2:40 in the afternoon on September 11, Rumsfeld convened a meeting of his top staffers. According to notes taken by an aide, Rumsfeld declared that he wanted to "hit" Iraq, even though he well knew that Iraq was not behind the attack. "Go massive," ordered Rumsfeld. "Sweep it all up. Things related and not."

For Rumsfeld and his gang, 9/11 was an opportunity more than a hardship. It augured a war without end, a war without rules, a war without fiscal constraints, a war where anything was permitted and few questions asked. Almost immediately the Secretary of Defense conjured up his own personal hit squad, Joint Task Force-121, which he endearingly refers to as his "manhunters." Though we wouldn't hear about it for months, this operation launched the kidnappings, wholesale round-ups, assassinations, and incidents of torture that are only now coming partially to light.

Of course, it can't all be pinned on Rumsfeld and his band of bureaucratic thugs. It goes right to the top. On February 7, 2002, Bush signed an executive order exempting captured members of al-Qaeda and the Taliban from the protections of the Geneva Conventions. With that stroke of the pen, Bush affixed his imprimatur to the prosecution of his wars unbound by the constraints of international law. That secret imperial decree set into motion the downward spiral of sadism-as-government-policy which led directly to the torture chambers of Camp Cropper and Abu Ghraib and obliterated the last molecule of moral authority from Bush's global war. Of course, such concerns are mere trifles to these cruise missile crusaders.

* * *

From the beginning, the problem was concocting a rationale for the Iraq war, as the hunt for al-Qaeda in Afghanistan turned into a futile game of bomb and chase and anthrax letters and terror alerts kept the American public pinioned on tenterhooks. Rumsfeld ordered his number 3, the arch-neocon Douglas Feith, to establish the Office of Special Plans to develop the case for war against Iraq, a case built on raw information supplied mainly by Iraqi defectors under the control of Ahmed Chalabi. Another crucial source was Israeli intelligence, which was pushing hard for the ouster of Saddam. A similar war council was set up in Cheney's office, under the control of his chief of staff Scooter Libby.

For its part, the CIA realized that its rivals in the Pentagon and the White House were attempting to wrest control of the brief for war. Cheney and Rumsfeld had long loathed George Tenet for his timidity and distrusted many CIA analysts as being sympathetic to the Powell / Armitage axis of diplomacy at the State Department. Cheney in particular fumed that the CIA and the State Department were badmouthing his pal Chalabi and had conspired to freeze $92 million payments to the Iraqi National Congress. "Why are they denying Chalabi money, when he's providing unique intelligence on Iraq Weapons of Mass Destruction?" The spigot was soon turned back on.

And to stay in the game, the CIA began to play along. Over the course of the next year, the CIA briefings for Bush became more and more bellicose. But they contained all the empirical rigor of silly-putty. Agency analysts knew that Iraq's military was in a decrepit condition; its nuclear, chemical and biological weapons programs were primitive at best; and its links to al-Qaeda non-existent. Yet, as James Bamford reported, CIA analysts were instructed to bend their reports to bolster Bush's martial ambitions. "If Bush wants to go to war, it's your job to give him a reason to do so," a top CIA manager told his staff. It wasn't long before George Tenet himself was calling the case for war "a slam dunk."

This wasn't exactly a covert operation. In fact, Paul Wolfowitz let the cat out of the bag before the bombs started falling on Baghdad. "For bureaucratic reasons, we settled on one issue, weapons of mass destruction because it was one reason everyone could agree on," Wolfowitz gloated.

Why WMDs? For starters, they knew they could hook the Democrats into biting on that issue. After all, back in 1992 Al Gore himself had led the charge against Bush I for failing to topple Saddam in 1991, invoking the very same threat. "Saddam Hussein's nature has been clear to us for some time," Gore wrote in a *New York Times* essay. "He is seeking to acquire ballistic missiles and nuclear weapons; it is only a matter of time...Saddam is not an acceptable part of the landscape. His Baathist regime must be dismantled as well...We should have bent every policy—and we should do it now—to overthrow that regime and make sure that Saddam is removed from power."

Wolfowitz understood the political lay of the land. The WMD threat paralyzed the Democrats into giving Bush carte blanche for war. Wolfowitz also knew he could count on the press playing along, fanning anxiety on the homefront about Saddam's murderous intentions. Shortly after 9/11, Rumsfeld and his gang set up a special propaganda office in the Pentagon, which admitted that it intended to plant false stories in the foreign press. Evidently, they didn't have to worry about a similar operation for the US press, which seemed eager to cultivate its own fantastical scenarios.

The Brahmins at the *New York Times* gave reporter Jayson Blair a merciless public flogging for his harmless flights-of-fancy. The destruction of Blair was overtly racist, suggesting that the scandal illustrated the perils of a zealous pursuit of affirmative action. Contrast this with the *Time's* agonizing comedown on its mound of stories on Iraq's non-existent weapons of mass destruction that daintily elided all mention of the name Judith Miller. Yet, Miller's cynical and malign front-page fictions, cribbed from her intimate contacts with the crook Ahmed Chalabi and his frontman Richard Perle, functioned as official fatwas for Bush's jihad against Saddam. Thousands perished due in part to Miller's fantasies, but she writes on, immune to the carnage her lies sanitized.

The thinly sourced stories were patently bogus to the attuned eye, but that didn't stop the flock of other war-maddened reporters, such as the equally gullible Jeffrey Goldberg at The *New Yorker*, from peddling their alarmist fantasies. Take Dan Rather, lately stung by airing apparently forged documents regarding Bush's ghostly tenure in the Texas Air National Guard. These days the Rove machine targets Rather as the poster boy for liberal bias in the media. Yet not so long ago Rather, part owner along with Donald Rumsfeld of a sprawling high desert ranch in New Mexico, confessed that he was willing to give the Bush administration the benefit of the doubt when it came to war and measures like the Patriot Act.

"I want to fulfill my role as a decent human member of the community and a decent and patriot American," Rather told Howard Kurtz of The *Washington Post*. "And, therefore, I am willing to give the government, the president and the military the benefit of any doubt here at the beginning. I will give them the benefit of the doubt, whenever possible, in this kind of crisis, emergency situation."

Hold on, Mr. Rather. That's not a slippery slope; it's the sheer face of Half Dome.

So, with no resistance from the press or the so-called opposition party, Bush got his war.

Despite the fear mongering and threat inflation, Saddam's slave army of conscripts didn't fight back. Battered by a decade of sanctions and two week's worth of saturation bombing (including illegal cluster bombs), they didn't have the means, the will or the desire. Not until later, when the occupation, where the military essentially served as armed guards for what the neo-cons hoped would be the corporate plunder of Iraq, turned vile and bloody.

Anxious for a victory celebration, Bush, the cross-dresser-in-chief, put on his flight suit and was ferried onto the deck of the USS Abraham Lincoln, where, braying like Caligula on the shores of Britain, he pronounced the war over and hailed himself as victor. Up to that day, when Bush told the world that major combat operations had concluded, 141 American soldiers had died in Iraq. Then the real killing began.

Two or three a day. One day after another. Week after week. Month by month. Bring 'em on, he said, hiding out in his ranch. And so they did. A current of blood swirled through the summer and autumn, Americans, Brits, and Italians. And Iraqis. By the thousands.

There wasn't a good photo-op to be found. Normally, war presidents find time to console the wounded and grieve with the families of the slain. But Bush didn't want any bloodstains on his flight suit, fearing political forensics teams would use the evidence against him in the 2004 election.

The longer the occupation went on, the worse it got. In July, Saddam's sons Uday and Qusay, the sadists of the Tigris, were killed in a villa in Mosul. Their corpses were displayed before the world press in a wind-buffeted tent like slabs of meat in a butcher shop. No one in Iraq cared about their fate. Until that barbarous moment. Then came the uprisings in Fallujah and Najaf, the rise of al-Sadr, and the exposure of the Sadean circus going on after dark at Abu Ghraib. By June of 2004, it was obvious to nearly everyone who was paying attention the US had lost Iraq.

Bush acted oblivious to the carnage. He sequestered himself from the press, refused to read the papers, got his news ladled to him in palatable bite-sized bits by Condi Rice. When he made the occasional public appearance, he delivered fidgety non-sequiturs, as divorced from reality as the vapid mutterings of Liza Minelli.

So what was it all about? It was about oil, of course. Oil and fealty to Israel. And blood vengeance. And politics. And multi-billion dollar no bid contracts for political cronies. And empire building. And even cowboy chutzpah. Most of all, it was about collusion. That's how republics are undermined and replaced by empires. Go read Tacitus or Twain.

Bush's path to war was cleared by the Democrats, who were passive at best and deeply complicit at worst. Take House Minority Leader Dick Gephardt and Senator Joe Lieberman, who rushed to the White House to stand side-by-side with Bush in a Rose Garden war rally, where they pledged their support for the invasion of Iraq.

John Kerry, a man who gives gravitas a bad name, went along with the war and refused to retract his support even after it became obvious that the grounds for the invasion were bogus at best and fabricated. (Kerry has been wrongly diagnosed as a chronic flip-flopper. He's simply a flipper. The senator and war criminal does a lot of gymnastical contortions of his position, but he keeps landing in the same place time after time.) So did his faithful sidekick John Edwards. And the rest of the Democratic leadership.

Look across the political taiga of the Democratic Party; it is a landscape denuded of any fresh sprigs of resistance. Even the august Russ Feingold's regular objections seem like perfunctory exercises, mere footnotes for the record. Feingold is the bland moral accountant of the senate. Dry and austere. He is also ignored, by the press and the bosses of his own party, partly because he is so bland. But mostly because he is usually right.

But most don't even express regrets. Take Senate Minority Leader Tom Daschle. Nearly a year after the war was launched, after every pretext had dissolved away and the US military found itself mired in a bloody and hopeless occupation, Daschle pronounced himself satisfied with the progress of the war. On February 19, 2004, Daschle told the South Dakota Chamber of Commerce: "I give the effort overall real credit. It is a good thing Saddam Hussein is no longer in power. It is a good thing we are democratizing the country." He also assured the business leaders of the Great Plains that he was not the least upset the over the bogus pre-war intelligence on weapons of mass destruction. As the summer of 2004 turned to autumn, Daschle, locked in a tight reelection race with Jim Thune, launched TV ads touting his support of the war, highlighted by a photograph of the senator being hugged by Bush. There you have it. Harmony in government. It boils down to a shared faith in the imperial project, a raw certitude in the righteousness of their collective crusade.

The cardinal rule of a grifter's game is to control both sides of the action. Under those rules of engagement, the house (read: empire) always wins.

October, 2004

Eight

How Bush Got (and Lost) His Wings

The early winter of 1968 was a season of acute anxiety for the young George W. Bush. As his academic career at Yale sputtered to an inglorious denouement, the war in Vietnam was hurtling forward at full-bore with the onset of the Tet Offensive. In those perilous months, there were 350,000 US troops in Vietnam, dying at a rate of more than 350 a week. From Bush's perch in New Haven, hamlet of his birth, the draft loomed, casting a chill shadow over his future.

Bush faced limited options. Unlike his warden-to-be, Dick Cheney, Bush wasn't prepared to anchor himself down in wedlock, which would entitle him to a marriage deferment. There were too many oats yet to be sown. How many oats in how many fields? Tough to say precisely, but in the ripe phrase of one of Bush's drinking buddies from the 1970s "he bedded nearly every bimbo in West Texas, married or not."

His grades at Yale, already inflated beyond all merit courtesy of his legacy admission, were so paltry that the escape hatch of graduate school was out of the question. Only one sure sanctuary remained: the National Guard.

In January of 1968, Bush sent inquiries to the National Guard. It seems Bush had had an epiphany: he wanted to be a pilot, just like his dad. Well, not exactly like Pappy, who was shot down flying a fighter in World War II. Yes, Lil' Bush wanted to fly fighter jets, but not in dicey combat situations. That, naturally, would defeat the entire purpose of joining the Guard.

In 1989, Bush explained the coarse calculus behind his decision to a reporter from the Lubbock *Avalanche-Journal*, "I'm saying to myself, 'What do I want to do?' I think, I don't want to be an infantry guy as a pilot in Vietnam. What I do decide to want to do [sic] is learn to fly."

The National Guard commanders responded warmly to Bush's initial probings, but noted, somewhat ominously for the fratboy flier, that before his application could be accepted he had to submit to a battery of physical and mental tests. Damn, the remedial student must have shivered, more exams and no helpful tutors from the egghead division of Skull and Bones to guide him through the intellectual shoals!

At the time Bush applied to the National Guard, there were 100,000 other young men in line before him, stalled on a crowded waiting list hoping their number would be called before they were sucked up by the draft and dropped onto the killing fields of the Mekong Delta. In Texas alone, there were 500 applicants frantically vying for only four open slots for fighter pilot-training in the Air National Guard.

At first blush, Bush didn't seem to have much of a shot at landing one of those choice positions. First, he flunked his medical test. Then he flunked his dental exam. And finally, as Ian Williams reveals in *Deserter*, his merciless indictment of Bush's disappearing act in the National Guard, he scores a rock-bottom 25 percent on his pilot aptitude examination. That's one out of four correct answers, a ratio that is not even a credible mark in cluster-bombing class. To put this achievement in perspective, the average score of applicants taking the pilot aptitude test was 77 percent, a whopping fifty-two percent higher than the proud product of the Yale ancestral admissions program. More than 95 percent of the testers scored higher than Bush, the Ivy Leaguer.

Aptitude for piloting a fighter jet notwithstanding, on May 27, 1969, just twelve days before the expiration of his student deferment, Bush the Younger was accepted into the Texas Air National Guard. On his application form under the heading "Background Qualifications," Bush declares in a refreshing outburst of honesty "None."

Today the pipsqueak commander-in-chief has exploited the Guard and Army Reserve as a form of covert conscription to beef up troop numbers in Iraq and Afghanistan. But in those days National Guard squadrons were generally not being sent off to the frontlines in Vietnam. But just to be sure, Bush checked the box on his enlistment form saying he was unwilling to do time overseas. That box was a comfy failsafe that is no longer available to young people seduced into signing up as weekend warriors in Bush's National Guard.

Flush with excitement at his triumphal entry into the Air National Guard, Bush averred to one-and-all that he had caught the flight bug. He duly submitted to the Guard brass a "Statement of Intent," pledging that he had "applied for pilot training with the goal of making flying a lifetime pursuit and I believe that I can best accomplish this to my own satisfaction as a member of the Air National Guard."

This seems like boilerplate stuff. But it is a crucial document in at least one respect. Getting the dunderheaded Bush air-ready was going to take a lot of training and the Guard wanted to get a guarantee that it would get a minimal return on its investment—if not a special line-item in the appropriations bill, at least commitment from Bush that he would stick around as a pilot for the duration of his commitment, if not beyond. Ian Williams estimates that the Guard spent more than a million dollars training Bush how to fly. Bush was warned that any prolonged absence from the Guard would result in him being ordered to "active duty" for a period of two years.

What the commanders of the Guard may not have known at the time was that in Bush's mind it was either the Guard or Canada. In 1994, the gun-shy Bush, who tortured animals as teen-ager, fessed up to the *Houston Chronicle* that being sent to Vietnam was simply not an option for him: "I was not prepared to shoot my eardrum out with a shotgun in order to get a deferment. Nor was I willing to go to Canada. So I choose to better myself by learning how to fly airplanes...I don't want to play like I was somebody out there marching when I wasn't. It was either Canada or the service. Somebody said the Guard was looking for pilots. All I know is, there weren't that many people trying to be pilots."

As we now know, there were more than 500 people looking to be pilots in Texas alone, nearly all of them more qualified for the slots than Bush.

So how did this miraculous induction come about? Bush has long denied he got any favored treatment, which would seem unmanly. But there's now little doubt that the draft evader benefited from at least three pairs of helping hands: Sid Adger, a Texas oilman and Bush family crony, Ben Barnes, then Speaker of the House in Texas, and Gen. James Rose, former commander of the Texas Air National Guard.

The truth began to trickle out in 1999, when Barnes, then a top lobbyist and political fixer in Austin, became a witness in a lawsuit by Laurence Littwin. Littwin was suing the State of Texas for firing him as lottery directory, which he claimed was politically motivated. The Littwin lawsuit is a complex and confusing affair that provides a glimpse at the baseline of corruption pullulating through the Texas political system.

In sum, Littwin claimed that he was forced to hire a company called GTech to run the Texas lottery in order to suppress the real story of how Bush won entry into the Guard—namely that Ben Barnes had pulled strings with Gen. Rose. In the 1990s, Barnes worked a lobbyist for GTech. Indeed, GTech had paid Barnes $23 million for his expert services.

In his deposition, Barnes denied blackmailing Littwin into giving GTech the lucrative contract. But he confessed, with the haughty sense of accomplishment that only an apex politico can impart, that he had indeed opened the backdoor for Bush into the Air National Guard. Barnes said that he responded to a distress beacon from Bush intimate Sid Adger, a now dead Texas oil tycoon, and prevailed on Gen. Rose to adopt the young Bush as a member of the Guard's flying elite, which then included the war aversive sons of Gov. John Connelly and Sen. Lloyd Bentsen. It helped that Barnes's chief of staff, Nick Kralj, also served as a top aide-de-camp to the general. Mission accomplished.

But the handouts didn't stop there. Bush didn't want to remain a lowly private or corporal in those drab uniforms. He saw himself as officer material. Yet, he had no desire to subject himself to the mental and physical rigors of Officer Candidate School. In his mind, he was a birthright officer. And so it came to be. After a mere six weeks of training, Bush was promoted to the rank 2nd Lieutenant. He didn't even have his pilot's license.

In the wake of this astounding achievement, Bush felt it was time for a breather. He abandoned his training with the Guard for two months, hightailing it to the beaches and bars of Florida, where he claimed to have occasionally lent the services of his agile political mind to the senatorial campaign of rightwing, neo-segregationist congressman Ed Gurney, a favorite of Richard Nixon. Gurney won, but his victory was short lived. Gurney was later indicted by a federal grand jury on charges of political corruption, bribery and perjury. He walked away a free man courtesy of a hung jury.

* * *

After the election, Bush headed for Moody Air Base in Georgia to complete his pilot training with the 359th Student Squadron. Around Thanksgiving, Bush was once again whisked away from the monotony of life as a fighter-pilot-in-training, this time courtesy of Richard Nixon. The president sent a plane to Moody Air Base to pick up the young Bush so that the newly brevetted lieutenant could escort Nixon's fabulously neurotic (and what child of Nixon's wouldn't at least be neurotic?) daughter Tricia out on a date. Sparks didn't fly. The young officer made clumsy advances, which Tricia deflected. She later described Bush as "testy."

And so the days and weeks of Bush's service to the country, as the commander-in-chief likes to put it, during the war in Vietnam rolled on. His instructors at the Moody Air Base assigned Bush the task of learning how to fly the F-102, an obsolete fighter soon destined for the scrap heap.

Finally, on June 23, 1971 Bush graduated from combat flight training school. Now he was ready to defend the airspace of Texas from hostile incursions from Mexico, Belize or the Virgin Islands.

Except that George the Younger apparently had formed other plans. Without informing the Guard commanders who had saved him from going to Vietnam, Bush quietly applied for admission to study law at the University of Texas. For one of the few times in his life, Bush didn't get immediate gratification.

The flying fratboy's application to the University of Texas law school was ungraciously declined, despite the pleas of his father, then pitted in a fierce senatorial election battle with Lloyd Bentsen that he would end up losing. Whatever its faults, apparently the University of Texas isn't prone to handing out legacy admissions to New Haven-born whelps of the political elite. Even in Texas, you have to draw the line somewhere.

Sulking at this unfamiliar rebuke, Bush slunk off to Ellington Air Base near Houston to join the 111th Fighter Squadron. By most accounts, his drinking, already problematic, began to intensify. By other accounts, it was during this time in Ellington that Bush began to refamiliarize himself with his narcotic of choice at Yale … cocaine.

Now we come to the crucial lost years of 1971 and 1973. Shortly after Bush arrived at Ellington, his political ambitions begin to percolate to the surface. He tells the *Houston Post* that he is considering a run for the Texas state senate. His testing of the waters doesn't excite much interest and nothing comes of it.

So he continues flying, mainly on weekends, over the course of the next year. And he continues getting inebriated. On a trip back to Washington, DC at Christmastime, Bush treats his younger brother to a night cruising the bars of Georgetown. In the early hours of the morning, a shit-faced Bush crashes his car into a row of garbage cans in front of the family house. Roused from his slumbers by the racket outside, his father confronts him in the driveway about driving around drunk. Bush the Younger threatens to pummel his father with his fists, but Marvin, also drunk, intervenes and Bush is sent packing back to Texas.

In April of 1972, two seminal events coincide. The Air Force mandates drug testing for all pilots during medical exams and Bush takes what will turn out to be his last flight as a pilot for the Air National Guard.

Less than a month later, Bush flees his Texas Guard base for Alabama, where he signs up to work on the congressional campaign of Winton "Red" Blount, a friend of Bush's father and Nixon's postmaster general. He didn't inform his superiors at Ellington that he had left Texas until two weeks later, when he requested a transfer to the 9921st Air Reserve Squadron, a postal unit with no fighter jets. Initially, the transfer is granted.

No one recalls seeing Bush report for duty and there is no documentary record supporting his service there, which, in any event, was to consist only of reading flight manuals. On July 6, Bush is scheduled to take his required flight physical, which will for the first time include a drug test. He fails to show up. Failure to take a flight physical is grounds for immediate suspension of his pilot's license.

These days Bush claims that he simply blew off the physical because the Guard was phasing out the F-102 and he didn't expect to be piloting any more flights. This excuse is circumspect for two reasons. First, although the F-102 was on its way out, the jet had not yet been mothballed and Bush still had the opportunity to learn to fly the new generation of fighter jets. Indeed, there was a fleet of them just down the highway at Dannelly Air Base in Alabama. Moreover, the flight physical was a mandatory requirement of service. This was not a matter of getting a permission slip to play intramural polo at Yale. For most Guardsmen, failure to abide by such orders resulted severe consequences, like being compelled to spend two-years in active duty, perhaps in Vietnam.

On July 31, Bush's transfer to the Montgomery postal unit was overturned by the DC office, which deemed him "ineligible for reassignment to the Air Reserve Squadron. He is ordered to return to Ellington. But Bush doesn't pay any attention. Instead, he retreated to Miami with his father for the 1972 Republican National Convention, the last hurrah of Nixon.

Two weeks later Bush returns to Alabama, where he files a new transfer request, this time to the 187th TAC Recon Group in Mobile. The transfer is approved on September 5, 1972. The following day the Air Force officially revokes his flight privileges for "failure to accomplish annual medical examination."

Bush wasn't alone in losing his wings. The other pilot suspended alongside Bush was none other than his close friend, James M. Bath. Yes, *that* James Bath, who would in just a few short years become the financial factotum for the Bin Laden family in Texas. In the 1980s, it was Bath, backed by the Bin Laden fortune, who bailed Bush out of the financial ruin he had made of Arbusto Drilling and Harken Energy. Old friends down there are not forgotten.

The de-winged pilot was ordered to report for duty to Lt. Col. William Turnipseed, commander of the 187th Recon Group. The Colonel says he never met Bush and there is no record that junior ever showed up at the base. "Had he reported in, I would have had some recall, and I do not," said Col. Turnipseed. "I had been in Texas, done my flight training there. If we had had a first lieutenant from Texas, I would have remembered."

On September 29, Bush was sent a letter commanding him to appear before the Flying Evaluation Board to explain why he had refused to take the medical exam. Bush never responded. At this point, Bush was not only AWOL, but in breach of two direct orders.

Blount lost the election, but remained tight with the Bush clan. His company, Blount International, continues to benefit from its close association with the Bushes and their wars. In 1991, Blount International got a multimillion-dollar contract to help reconstruct bombed out Kuwait City. Later, it won one of the largest private contracts ever awarded by the Saudi Royal family. Now, Blount's firm is working as a subcontractor for Halliburton in Iraq.

In the fall of 1972, things began to look grim for the fatuous flyboy from New Haven. The National Guard was on his tail, demanding an explanation for why he had jilted them after they had saved him from Vietnam and had invested a million dollars in teaching him how to fly fighters.

It was in this window of months that Bush apparently got a Houston woman pregnant and gallantly paid for her to have an abortion. It was also in this period that Bush, according to his biographer J.H. Hatfield, was arrested for possession of cocaine. Instead of landing in prison, the judge presiding over the case bent to the pleadings of Bush's father, then US ambassador to the UN, and ordered the young derelict to perform a year's worth of community service at PULL, a center for black youths in urban Houston.

Williams' book *Deserter* lends credence to Hatfield's account and raises new questions. According to Bush's autobiography (ghostwritten by his political au pair, Karen Hughes), *A Charge to Keep*, he met former

Houston Oiler tight end John White in December of 1972. White, Bush claims, asked him to come work full-time at his Houston youth center, called Project-PULL. Bush, who until this charmed moment had never exhibited the slightest charitable instinct, agreed. He started work at PULL in January of 1973.

Now keep in mind that Bush supposedly already had a job, working for the National Guard. Yet over the next six months there's not one confirmed Bush sighting by his Guard commanders. In the ornithology of the Air National Guard, Bush is the rarest and stealthiest of birds, passing through Guard air space like a ghostly passenger pigeon. Indeed, when his superiors tried to fill out an annual evaluation of Bush's service they are unable to complete the form, writing on May 2, 1973: "Lt. Bush has not been observed at this unit during the period of the report."

A month later, National Guard HQ in Washington sent Texas Guard commanders an official query about Bush. The DC brass instructed the Texas crew to prepare a Form 77a on Bush "so this officer can be rated in the position he held." The Texas Guard, then run by Bush family cronies who now saw themselves implicated in the transgressions of the absconder fratboy, balks at the order. Indeed, they delay filing a response until November 12, 1973, by which time Bush has been honorably discharged from the Guard. Even then the response from the Texas HQ is coy, though ripe with nefarious possibilities: "Not rated for the period 1 May 1972 through 30 April 73. Report for this period unavailable for administrative reasons."

So the bureaucratic vise began to tighten on young George. Then mysteriously Bush is recorded as having performed 36 days of duty between May and July of 1973. Bush doesn't recall precisely what he did. There are no pay records to confirm his service. No one in the Guard witnessed him on the base. Indeed, Bush couldn't have done the Guard service because by his own admission he was working full-time for John White at PULL—if he'd gone AWOL from that job he might have very well landed in jail. It now seems likely that the entry of those 36 days of service was made by someone in the Texas office not only to protect Bush, but also to shield his retinue of enablers in the high command of the Texas Air National Guard.

In September Bush completed his tour of duty at PULL, applied to grad school, and despite being AWOL from the National Guard from May of 1972 through October of 1973, is granted an honorable discharge.

That fall Bush evacuated to Cambridge, making a soft landing at

Harvard Business School, another reliable safehouse for the brattish scions of the ruling class. Fellow students at Harvard remember Bush prancing into lecture halls wearing his uniform. Even then, he had a taste for military cross-dressing, though no one in the Massachusetts National Guard ever recalls the tyro-in-a-jumpsuit showing up for duty at the base, although he did drop by once to have his choppers cleaned gratis by the Guard's dentist.

Whenever Bush plays dress-up, as he does at nearly every photo-op on a military site from the USS Lincoln to Ft. Bragg, he comes off as the missing member of the Village People, which probably explains his enduring appeal to the latent types manning the controls of the Christian right these days.

In the mid-1990s, as Bush began to plot his run for the White House, the governor and his handlers (Dan Bartlett, Karen Hughes and Karl Rove) realized that Bush's missing years in the Guard might prove problematic. After all, during the 1992 presidential campaign, Bush's father assaulted Clinton for his deft manipulation of Col. William Holmes, the commander of Arkansas's ROTC, to sidestep the draft.

Bush's dilemma was more complicated and more unseemly than Clinton's. In order to escape service in Vietnam, he had exploited his family's political connections to secure a choice spot in the Texas Air National Guard, despite failing his pilot aptitude test. Though a blatant act of patronage, Bush was promoted to officer status before he earned his pilot's license and without going to officer training school. He refused to take his mandatory flight physical and also refused to show up for a mandatory evaluation. He went AWOL for a year and a half and then requested and received an early discharge. All this after promising to "serve as long as possible" and to devote himself to a lifetime of flying...flying planes, that is.

In the offices of the Texas Air Guard there were records documenting Bush's dubious career and exposing the holes in his extravagant version of his military service to the country. The most potentially damning of those documents (Bush's pay records) are now missing. Where did they go?

One intriguing explanation comes from Lt. Col. Bill Burkett, a top aide to Maj. Gen. Daniel James, III, then commander of the Texas Air National Guard. In 1997, Burkett claims he was just outside the open door of Maj. Gen. James's office when the general received a conference call from Joe Allbaugh, Bush's chief of staff, and Dan Bartlett, Bush's communications director. The conversation played out over James's speakerphone, where

Burkett claims he overheard Bush's men order James to cleanse Bush's military files. Burkett said he recalled Allbaugh's saying: "We certainly don't want anything that is embarrassing in there."

A few days later, Burkett says that he saw Brig. Gen. John Scribner dispose of Bush's pay and performance records in a 15-gallon metal waste can inside the Texas Air National Guard Museum. "The files had been gone through over the years," Scribner quipped to Burkett, pointing to the garbage can. "Not as much in here as I thought." Apparently, this was a mop-up operation to make sure that nothing had been missed in previous search-and-destroy raids on Bush's files.

Burkett went public with his recollections in the spring of 2004 during the mini-tempest in the corporate press over Bush's military record sparked by Michael Moore's assertion that the president was a "deserter." The president's praetorian guard went into action, smearing Burkett as a disgruntled malcontent with an ax to grind against Maj. Gen. James, who Bush had elevated to the head of the Air National Guard for the entire country. Although the Burkett story quickly faded, phone records and other documents back up the circumstances of his claims. And Burkett himself hasn't backed down despite the assaults on his character from Bush's political mercenaries. "If President Bush is going to be the first president in over one hundred years that puts himself in a uniform and uses taxpayer's money for a photo opportunity to land on a flight deck and say hooray," Burkett told reporters. "He's put it on the table and we deserve to know." But the press bus had long since pulled away, never to return to the scene of the crime.

Given this vaporous record of service during Vietnam, it takes a perverse kind of hubris for Bush to assail the military careers of a POW (John McCain), a bona fide killing machine (John Kerry) and a triple amputee (Max Cleland). It's the trademark of a pampered bully.

* * *

The moment George Bush refused to go spill blood in Vietnam may have been the moral highpoint of his life. But he has long since buried that singular act of conscience beneath a stench-heap of projection and hypocrisy. He remains a brat and a coward at the core, dodging rules he forces others to abide by with unforgiving strictness. Festooned in a flight jacket he never deserved, Bush has ordered National Guard troops into a bloody desert war he and his cronies launched under fabricated pretexts. Then in order to hand out tax cuts to the super-rich and billion-dollar contracts to favored arms makers, Bush scrimped on the funding of his precious war itself: too few troops, under-armed, over-worked, operating with no occupation plan and no exit strategy.

In their quest to transfer every possible federal dollar to their fatcat base, the Bush regime even went so far as to try to slash combat pay and separation allowances and increase co-payments for the treatment of those maimed in battle. Although he opted out of the Guard early, Bush has now implemented (perhaps illegally) "stop-losses" orders, a kind gang-pressing by Oval Office fiat that keeps National Guard and Reserve troops in Iraq far beyond their contracted tour of duty. They are war slaves.

Explain his actions? Not then, not now. Just as he stiffed the Flight Evaluation Board in 1972, so he now refuses to offer an explanation for his illegal war that has killed and maimed tens of thousands. "I'm the commander—see, I don't need to explain," Bush boasted to Bob Woodward. "I do not need to explain why I say things. That's the interesting thing about being the president. Maybe somebody needs to explain to me why they say something, but I don't feel I owe anybody an explanation." That's the distilled essence of Bush from his very own mouth: a bellicose and imperious asshole who has never once been held to account for the mayhem he leaves in his wake.

So once again Bush has succeeded in doing the impossible: He has sullied the once heroic term "draft evader."

September, 2004

Nine

They Call Him Star Child

Rummy's Rise to Power

The best thing that you can say about Donald Rumsfeld is that Henry Kissinger hates him. The antagonism dates back to the Ford presidency when Rumsfeld undermined Henry K's freelance diplomacy and quietly tried to destroy Kissinger's détente project.

Rumsfeld ("Rummy to his friends"—though he confessed to Nixon in 1971 that he never drank with reporters or Secret Service agents) isn't all that close to George Bush Sr., either. Remember Rumsfeld launched a presidential bid against Bush in 1988. Unable to raise much cash, Rumsfeld backed out and promptly endorsed Bush's arch-rival Bob Dole.

And back in the Ford days, when Rumsfeld was charged with picking a CIA director to replace William Colby, Rumsfeld developed a list of 10 names for the post, including Robert Bork, C. Douglas Dillon, Stanley Resor and Lee Iacocca. Bush, who was being pushed by Republican powerbrokers, wasn't on it. In fact, in memo to Ford, Rumsfeld argued that Bush was ill-equipped for the job and was probably using it a means to rehabilitate his career and start a run at the presidency. Rumsfeld's memo warned that Bush's "RNC role lends an undesirable political cast." Ford agreed and offered the post to superlawyer, Edwin Bennett Williams, who rejected it and the slot finally fell to Bush, who had been backed only by Dick Cheney.

For better or worse, the choice of Rumsfeld to run the Pentagon proves that Dick Cheney is in full control of the White House. Bush apparently had his heart set on Dan Coates, the rather laid back former senator from Indiana. But Cheney intervened, saying that Coates was no match for Colin Powell. Perhaps not. But Bush's initial instinct may have been right. Coates is something of a free-thinker and had a tendency to buck his own party, a valuable trait in a party run by the likes of Tom DeLay and Trent Lott.

Cheney's call for a system of checks and balances between the Pentagon and Foggy Bottom suggests that Powell and Rumsfeld might not be in harmony on some issues. Unlikely. Powell, like Cheney, is a Rusmfeld protégé. Powell worked as a lowling under Rumsfeld in the mid-70s when he first came to Washington as a Lieutenant Colonel on the move. Then during the Carter administration Powell really made his mark in the Pentagon under Frank Carlucci, another Rumsfeld associate.

Rumsfeld has a reputation as a moderate on social issues. This dates back to the 60s, when he was a young congressman from Illinois, in the mold of more liberal northern Repubs such as Richard Schwieker and Nelson Rockefeller, and seemed to constantly at odds with the party leadership. He was denied a spot in the party leadership in 1968 and fled into the Nixon administration—a refuge for liberal Republicans. Rumsfeld headed up the Office of Economic Opportunity, where they concocted such Nixon measures as price controls and cost of living adjustments. Rumsfeld used his office as a training ground for a new generation of Republican (and Democratic) politicians. He hired Dick Cheney, Bill Bradley, and Christy Todd Whitman.

Rumsfeld was one of Nixon's favorite cabinet members and the two apparently spent many evenings in the Oval Office drinking Scotch and plotting the future of Rumsfeld's political career. Some of these conversations were captured by Nixon's tape recorders. Rummy and Nixon kicked around a number of positions in the executive office that might catapult his career: head of HUD, secretary of transportation, head of the newly created EPA. Rumsfeld noted all those were fine, but that he needed to pad his resume with foreign policy credentials. Nixon warned him against working under Kissinger and Rumsfeld nodded that he had no desire for that arrangement. He suggested ambassador to NATO, although he didn't want to look like "he was being dumped."

Nixon said he didn't think "it would look that way now." But the president questioned whether it would be the best spot for his political career. "I don't know what the hell it would do for you in Illinois. Maybe it's not the thing in Illinois."

Rumsfeld said he was willing to take the chance because "it would certainly fill a gap in my background." The two go on to berate the Democrats for being warmongers. "When we get down to it, the war will be over one way or another, next year at this time," Nixon says. "They [the Democrats] got us in, we got us out."

"Exactly, that's right," Rumsfeld says. "Republicans got us out of Democrat wars four times in this century."

"Four times in this century," Nixon says. "They got us into World War I, they got us into World War II...They got us into Korea, Eisenhower got us out. They got us into Vietnam, Nixon got us out."

"The Democratic mentality," Rumsfeld says, "is to smother, to intervene, to try to manage things...The Nixon doctrine, and its domestic program, have a different philosophical base. It's to create, develop capabilities on other things."

In 1971, Rumsfeld, then counselor to the president, chatted it up again with Nixon in the Oval Office. Nixon was in a snit about Spiro Agnew's disastrous trip to Africa, where the vice-president got drunk with the press corps and pronounced his opinion that black Africans were smarter than black Americans.

"It doesn't help," Nixon fumed. "It hurts with the blacks. And it doesn't help with the rednecks because the rednecks don't think any Negroes are any good."

"Yes," agreed Rumsfeld.

As for the notion that "black Americans aren't as good as black Africans," Nixon said, "most of them are basically just out of the trees.... Now, my point is, if we say that, they [opponents] say, 'Well, by God.' Well, ah, even the southerners say, 'Well, our niggers is [unintelligible].' Hell, that's the way they talk!" said Nixon, putting on a southern accent.

"That's right," Rumsfeld said.

"I can hear 'em," Nixon said.

"I know," Rumsfeld replied.

"It's like when our black athletes, I mean in the Olympics, are running against the other black athletes, the southerner may not like the black but he's for that black athlete," Nixon said.

"That's right," Rumsfeld said.

"Right?" Nixon asked.

"That's for sure," Rumsfeld said.

Fortunately for Rumsfeld, he escaped the politically toxic fallout from Watergate when Nixon appointed him ambassador to NATO in 1972. In Brussels, he pushed for a stepped up US presence in Germany and for a new generation of mobile tactical nuclear weapons.

On defense issues Rumsfeld can't qualify as a moderate even by today's warped standards. He's always been a hawk. In 1975 Ford appointed Rumsfeld to replace James Schlesinger as secretary of defense. At 43, he was the youngest to hold the post. Now at 68, he (tying George Marshall) will be the oldest. Rumsfeld apparently didn't spend much time overseeing day-to-day matters at the Pentagon. Instead, according to an internal history of his tenure prepared by the Defense Department, he tried to politicize the office, hobnobbing with members of congress, playing to the press and "more than any of his predecessors, he served as a roving ambassador for the Defense Department."

Rumsfeld bemoaned the decline in defense spending that followed the Vietnam War, much of it under Ford's administration. He predicted (wrongly, of course) that it would generate "a fundamental instability in the world." As defense secretary, he lobbied hard for the very programs that would be the heart of the Reagan defense spending spree five years later: the B-1 bomber, a fleet of new submarines and nuclear powered ships, the Trident missile and the MX intercontinental ballistic missile. By all accounts, Rumsfeld despised SALT II because in his view, it didn't leave the US with superiority and tried to undermine it at every turn both inside and outside the administration.

At the Pentagon, Rumsfeld became known for his public relations stunts. As part of his campaign to sell the B-1 bomber, Rumsfeld, a former fighter pilot, got behind the controls and piloted one of the planes up the California coast while being filmed by a TV crew. "He thought he could jump from secretary of defense to the presidency," a longtime Pentagon analyst told me. "But even with the theatrics, Rummy was just too dull to excite anyone but the defense contractors."

Rumsfeld's ponderousness has given him the reputation of a Sphinx, a brooding and secretive policy whiz. Rumsfeld seems to hold this opinion of himself and he published a book of belabored and corny aphorisms on how to manage presidents, called *Rumsfeld's Rules*—imagine *The Prince* written by a mind as boring as Jim Lehrer's. An example: "Avoid public spats. When a department argues with government agencies in the press, it reduces the presidents options."

But some think it's all a pose, an act to disguise his shallowness. Here's how Nixon crony Pierre Rinfret described Rumsfeld: "What he contributed to the United States all the years he played in politics is beyond me. He is the perfect example of the absolutely perfect cover with very little inside. Or at least that is the way I knew him over the years. What substance he had is anybody's guess…But in all those years I never felt there was much there, and he held some of the highest positions of the land. That tells you a great deal about why and how the government is so fouled up. It doesn't attract the best and brightest, but mainly those who think they are and frequently aren't."

During the 1980s, Rumsfeld made his millions in the private sector, heading up two big corporations: pharmaceutical giant GD Searle and technology firm General Instruments. It was the era of downsizing and Rumsfeld was one of the most ruthless, slashing the workforces in both companies more than 30 percent. Searle's stock soared more than 500 percent and Rumsfeld earned *Fortune* magazine's kudos as one of America's "toughest bosses."

Rumsfeld rarely played the role of talking head. He's part of that dwindling group of politicos which still considers congressional testimony and presidential commissions to be a sign of political cachet. And over the past decade he's been on a lot of them. He was part of a group that actively opposed the Comprehension Nuclear Test Ban Treaty. And he testified vehemently before congress against the Chemical Weapons Convention, opposing the ban because it would be bad for American businesses. "Most of us in business are engaged with joint ventures and partnerships with companies across the globe and we share proprietary information in the same facility," Rumsfeld testified. "And were these inspections to be imposed, it's entirely possible that not only your own proprietary information would be compromised, but so would the proprietary information of joint venture partners. I don't believe that the thousands of companies across this country know about this treaty in any detail, believe that the treaty would apply to them, understand that they could be subjected to inspections, or appreciate the unfunded mandates that would be imposed on them in the event this were to pass."

He zeroed in on the Anti-Ballistic Missile Treaty with similar vigor, calling it outmoded and destabilizing. In 1998, Rumsfeld was tapped to head a commission to evaluate the evolving missile threat to the United States and the need to accelerate funding for a ballistic missile defense system. Predictably, Rumsfeld's report on Star Wars reiterated the "rogue" nation rationale put forth by Gore, Madeleine Albright and other Clinton administration hawks. It was largely hailed in the press as bi-partisan proof of "the emergence of a new window of vulnerability."

But Rumsfeld could scarcely be considered a dispassionate or neutral investigator on the matter. His disciple Frank Gaffney, a leading agitator for Star Wars, heads the Center for Security Policy, a group that lists Rumsfeld as one of its top contributors. Rumsfeld is also a member of Empower America, a group which ran a public relations and advertising campaign in favor of increased spending on Star Wars during the 1998 elections.

"Rummy's gone a little fruity over the past few years," a senate staffer on the Foreign Relations committee told me. "Some have taken to calling him the Star Child, after the demonic figure at the end of Kubrick's film 2001. First, he comes out full-bore for a new $60 billion edition of Star Wars, pointing the finger at the supposed missile threat from North Korea and Iran—two countries that can barely keep their traffic lights working. Now he's back obsessing on killer satellites, space lasers and using nukes against runaway asteroids. The question around here is: has he cleared all this spending with Greenspan?"

January, 2001

Ten

Rumsfeld's Enforcer

The Secret World of Stephen Cambone

The chill fellow in the business suit sitting between two uniformed generals at the witness table during the senate hearings on the Taguba Report about abuse of Iraqi prisoners of war was Dr. Stephen Cambone, the undersecretary of defense for intelligence, known throughout the Pentagon as Donald Rumsfeld's "chief henchman". In his testimony before the committee, Cambone was unapologetic and almost as dismissive as the ridiculous Sen. James Inhofe about the global disgust which erupted over the abuse and murder of Iraqi prisoners of war. Cambone, an apex neo-con and veteran of the Project for the New American Century, evinced disdain not only for the senatorial inquiry but also at a squeamish Lieutenant General Antonio Taguba, who sat next him, looking as if he suspected that he might well be the next one leashed to Cambone's bureaucratic pillory.

A Republican staffer on the Senate foreign relations Committee told me that the little-known Cambone, who like so many others on the Bush war team skillfully avoided military service, has quietly become one of the most powerful men in the Pentagon, rivaling even Paul Wolfowitz. "Cambone is a truly dangerous player", the staffer said. "He is Rumsfeld's guard dog, implacably loyal. While Wolfowitz positions himself to step into the top spot should Rumsfeld get axed, Cambone has dug in and gone to war against the insurgents in the Pentagon. Cambone's fingerprints are all over the occupation and the interrogation scandal. For him, there's no turning back."

Cambone has stealthily positioned himself as the most powerful intelligence operator in the Bush administration. On May 8, 2003, Rumsfeld named him Undersecretary of Defense for Intelligence, a new position which Deputy Secretary of Defense Paul Wolfowitz described thus: "The new office is in charge of all intelligence and intelligence-related oversight and policy guidance functions". In practice, this means that Cambone controls the Defense Intelligence Agency, the National Imagery and Mapping Agency, the National Reconnaissance Organization, the National Security Agency, the Defense Security Service and Pentagon's Counter-Intelligence

Field Activity. Cambone meets with the heads of these agencies, as well as top officials at the CIA and National Security Council twice a week to give them their marching orders.

One senate staffer tells us he has more operational sway than George Tenet or Condi Rice. His rise to power has been quiet, almost unnoticed until the Abu Ghraib scandal forced him briefly into the spotlight. Indeed, prior to the events of May, Cambone completely evaded detection by Bob Woodward, who in two thick volumes on Bush's wars failed to mention the name Cambone once. Of course, this may reveal more about Woodward's reportorial method than Cambone's skill at bureaucratic camouflage.

Yes, Cambone has neo-con credentials. He got his masters and doctorate at Claremont College in southern California, an elite Straussian enclave. He went on to draft sections of the Project for a New American Century's 2001 Report, *Rebuilding America's Defenses*, a document notable for urging that the US develop ethnic and race-based weapons. But more crucial for the speedy trajectory of his career is Cambone's resume as a devout Rumsfeldian. In 1998, Rumsfeld selected Cambone to serve as staff director of the Rumsfeld Commission on Ballistic Missile Defense, the Congressionally-appointed panel which justified implementation of the Strategic Defense Initiative on the grounds that the US was vulnerable to strikes from missiles freighting nuclear, chemical and biological weapons launched by rogue nations, such as North Korea, Iran and Iraq.

Cambone was no newcomer to the Star Wars scheme. From 1982 through 1986, he toiled at Los Alamos developing policy papers about the need for space-based weapons. In 1990, George Bush, Sr. picked Cambone to head up the Strategic Defense Initiative Office at the Pentagon. After Bush lost, Cambone migrated to the Center for Strategic and International Studies, a DC holding pen for hawks, where he continued to hammer away in essays and speeches about the windows of vulnerability in the skies over America.

Rumsfeld first brought Cambone into his inner circle not as an overlord for intelligence, but as the chief Pentagon strategist for pushing SDI through Congress. Recall that in the early days of the Bush administration, Star Wars and the obliteration of the Anti-Ballistic Missile Treaty were the twin obsessions of the Rumsfeld gang at the Pentagon.

After 9/11 Rumsfeld moved Cambone over to work on war planning and intelligence as Deputy Secretary of Defense for Policy, where he labored under the neo-con luminary Douglas Feith. There's reason to believe that Cambone's real mission was to keep tabs on Feith, a notorious hothead and Cheney loyalist whom Rumsfeld distrusts. Rumsfeld wasn't the only one who loathed Feith. Gen. Tommy Franks, who commanded the Afghan and Iraq wars, told Woodward that Feith was "the stupidest motherfucker on the face of the Earth".

Cambone and Feith reportedly soon developed an equally acrimonious relationship. But as Feith's star fell, Cambone's rose. In July 2002, Rumsfeld moved Cambone to the Office of Analysis and Evaluation, where his mission was to implement Rumsfeld's plan to reorganize the military and trim some of its most highly-prized weapons systems. "Cambone loomed as a huge threat to the generals", a senate staffer told me. "The message was pretty simple. Go along with our war plans or risk losing your big-ticket items and perhaps your command. Cambone was the enforcer". At the Pentagon, the most feared weapon isn't a dirty nuke, but a line item in the budget.

In April of 2003, Rumsfeld placed Cambone in charge of counter-terrorism teams operating under the code-name "Grey Fox". This covert operation is a kind of sabotage and assassination squad run out of the civil wing of the Pentagon. Rumsfeld had grown frustrated with the military's reluctance to assassinate suspected al-Qaeda and Iraqi resistance leaders, an understandable reluctance in light of US executive orders restricting the use of assassinations. So Rumsfeld seized control of the hit teams from the generals and assigned it to Cambone, a civilian appointee with no military experience. The Gray Fox project, so one *Washington Post* report concluded, is geared to perform "deep penetration" missions in Iraq, Afghanistan, Pakistan, Iran, Syria and North Korea, setting up listening posts, conducting acts of sabotage and assassination. When questioned about Gray Fox, Cambone snapped, "We won't talk about those things".

However, military officers did talk about Gray Fox. "The people in these units are available 24 hours a day, seven days a week, anywhere around the world. They are very highly trained, with specialized skills for dealing with close-quarters combat and unique situations posed by weapons of mass destruction", a military officer told *Army Times*. "If we find a high-value target somewhere, anywhere in the world, and if we have the forces to get there and get to them, we should get there and get to them", the official said. "Right now, there are 18 food chains, 20 levels of paperwork and 22 hoops we have to jump through before we can take action. Our enemy moves faster than that".

Aside from guarding Rumsfeld from assaults from within the Pentagon, Cambone's main role seems to be cutting through red tape and bothersome codes of conduct, such as the Geneva Conventions, to institute legally questionable policies. Take the treatment of Iraqi prisoners. The orders to soften up Iraqi prisoners for intelligence interrogators (both military and private contractors) came directly from Cambone's office.

In August 2003, as the occupation of Iraq began to turn bloody, Cambone ordered Brigadier General Geoffrey Miller, former commander of the detention facility at Guantanamo, to go to Iraq along with a team of experienced military interrogators, who had honed their inquisitorial skills with the torture of al-Qaeda and Taliban detainees captured in Afghanistan. His instructions were to "Gitmoize" the interrogations at Abu Ghraib and other prisons, including the notorious Camp Cropper on the outskirts of the Baghdad Airport, where the Delta Force conducted abusive interrogations of top level members of Saddam's regime.

Cambone's top deputy inside the military is none other than Lt. General Jerry Boykin, the Christian warrior, whom Cambone and Rumsfeld elevated to the position to the position of intelligence czar for the US Army last fall. Boykin rose to this lofty eminence after he went on a revival tour of evangelical churches in Oregon, where he disclosed the top secret intelligence that the US "had been attacked because we are a Christian nation". Boykin also leaked the news that Bush's war on terrorism was actually "a war against Satan".

Boykin calmed the congregations by saying there was little reason to fear because the Christian god is mightier than Allah. "I know that my god is bigger than his", Boykin preached. "I know that my god is a real God and his an idol". The general also revealed to the faithful that the supreme deity of the Christians had hand-picked Bush to be president during these fraught times. It was obvious, the general reasoned, that Bush didn't win the election. He became president through a kind of preemptive strike by the Almighty.

When word of Boykin's sermons landed on the front page of the *Los Angeles Times* in October of 2003, there was outrage in the American Islamic community that this two-star zealot was now directing US military intelligence operations in the Middle East. There were calls for his ouster and the Inspector General of the Army launched an investigation of Boykin.

But Rumsfeld and Cambone shrugged off the probe and stood by Boykin.

It now turns out that Boykin, the Islamophobe, played a central role in the torture scandal now gripping the Bush administration. In the summer of 2003, Boykin briefed Cambone on a list of no-holds-barred interrogation methods that he thought should be used to extract more information from Iraqi detainees.

These torture techniques included humiliation, sleep deprivation, restraint, water torture, religious taunting, light deprivation, and other techniques of torture that have since come to light. A few weeks after this crucial meeting in June, Cambone sent General Miller to Iraq with instructions to oversee the implementation of the Boykin interrogation plan in order to "rapidly exploit internees for actionable intelligence". According to Lt. General Antonio Taguba, who investigated the abuses at Abu Ghraib, Miller then instructed the Military Police to become "actively engaged in setting the conditions for successful exploitation of internees". The grim trio of Cambone, Boykin and Miller also conspired to put the control of the detention facilities in Iraq under the tactical control of military intelligence. At Abu Ghraib, the job fell to Col. Thomas M. Pappas, commander of the 205th Military Intelligence Brigade, a move that Lt. General Taguba called contrary to established military doctrine.

It now seems likely that Cambone was the U.S. official who invited Israeli advice (and perhaps interrogators) on how to extract information from Iraqi detainees. Before the Abu Ghraib scandal broke, Cambone freely admitted to the *Washington Times* that he was taking advice from the Israelis and sharing intelligence with them on the mechanics of occupation and interrogation. "Those who have to deal with like problems tend to share information as best they can".

These days advancement through the ranks of the Pentagon often goes hand-in-hand with opportunities to deliver sweetheart deals to corporate allies. Here too Cambone has not disappointed his backers. From 1986 to 1990, Cambone worked as a top lobbyist for SRS, a murky software company with deep roots in the Pentagon and CIA. Although Cambone left SRS for government work, he didn't forget his old employers. With Cambone's approval, the Pentagon awarded SRS a $6 million contract to provide management support for the Missile Defense Agency, the wing of the Defense Department charged with managing the SDI program and the development of space-base weapons.

In addition, SRS benefited from Cambone's transfer to the spying wing of the Pentagon. An SRS subsidiary called Torch Concepts was hired by the Pentagon to conduct a data mining foray into passenger records of JetBlue airlines. Bart Edsall, SRS's vice-president, described the work Torch did this way: "the company got a contract from the Pentagon to work with the Army to ferret information out of data streams [in an effort to detect] abnormal behavior of secretive people". Sound familiar? It should. The scheme was essentially a privatized version of the kind of work that John Poindexter wanted to conduct with his discredited Total Information Awareness operation. No surprise that the contracts for this outsourced form of snooping should fall to SRS. It is already the primary private contractor working with the Information Awareness Office of DARPA, the agency which Poindexter ruled and which continues the nefarious work of prying into the private lives, including travel, health and financial records, of American citizens.

As Rumsfeld's hatchetman, Cambone has become so hated and feared inside the Pentagon that one general told the *Army Times*: "If I had one round left in my revolver, I'd take out Stephen Cambone". This raises the concept of fragging to an entirely new level.

May, 2004

Eleven

The Mark of McCain

"The Senator Most Likely to Start a Nuclear War"

It's November 19, 2004, a mere two weeks after the election that returned George W. Bush to power, and Senator John McCain has traipsed off to New Hampshire to give a speech calling for 50,000 more troops to be sent into the quagmire of Iraq, press flesh and raise money for an expected run at the presidency in 2008. John Sununu, former New Hampshire governor and Bush family consigliere, wryly quipped about McCain's junket to the Granite State, "What took him so long?"

The press corps, already bored with Bush and election post-mortems, tags along. McCain's the darling of the moment, the opinion presses favorite senator, a media-made maverick, who was sedulously courted by both John Kerry and George Bush. McCain, true to form, flirted with them both and sniped at them both, but in the end remained wedded to the GOP, even as the party fell further under the sway of neo-cons and Christian fundamentalists that McCain publicly claims to abhor.

But that's all part of the McCain profile. He is the senator of the hollow protest. McCain is nothing if not a political stunt man. His chief stunt is the evocation of political piety. From his pulpit in the well of the senate, McCain gestures and fumes about the evils of Pentagon porkbarrel. He rails about useless and expensive weapons systems, contractor malfeasance, and bloated R&D budgets.

But he does nothing about them. McCain pontificates, but rarely obstructs. Few senators have his political capital. But he does nothing with it. Under the arcane rules of the senate, one senator can gum up the works, derail a bad (or good, though those are increasingly rare in this environment) bill, dislodge non-germane riders, usually loaded with pork, from big appropriations bills. McCain is never that senator. He is content to let ride that which he claims to detest in press releases and senate speeches.

A recent example. In late October, McCain went on 60 Minutes to decry a footnote in the Defense Appropriations Bill of 2004 that transferred billions of dollars from so-called Operations and Maintenance accounts for US troops in Iraq to porkbarrel projects, such as gold mines and museums, in the states of powerful senators. In his stern voice before the cameras,

McCain made congressional looting sound like a treasonable offense. But what he failed to disclose is the fact that he actually voted for the bill. Not only that, he was personally approached by each senator who wanted just such a transfer of funds and gave it his seal of approval.

McCain the Maverick is a merely fine-honed act. Brand McCain thrives on these kinds of casual hypocrisies.

* * *

In the past couple of years, McCain has been portrayed as one of the doves the senate. It's a stunning transformation and a phony one. Instead, throughout his career in Congress McCain has often been one of the hottest hawks around. During the war on Serbia in 1999, in one rhetorical bombing run after another, McCain bellowed for "lights out in Belgrade" and for NATO to "cream" the Serbs. At the start of May of that year he began declaiming in the US senate for NATO forces to use "any means necessary" to destroy Serbia.

McCain is often called a "war hero", a title adorning an unlovely resume starting with a father who was an admiral and graduation fifth from the bottom at the US Naval Academy, where he earned the nickname "McNasty". McCain flew 23 bombing missions over North Vietnam, each averaging about half an hour, total time ten hours and thirty minutes. For these brief excursions the admiral's son was awarded two Silver Stars, two Legions of Merit, two Distinguished Flying Crosses, three Bronze Stars, the Vietnamese Legion of Honor and three Purple Hearts. The publication *US Veteran Dispatch* calculates our hero earned a medal an hour, which is pretty good going. McCain was shot down over Hanoi on October 26, 1967 and parachuted into Truc Boch Lake, whence he was hauled by Vietnamese, and put in prison. And rightly so. McCain's target that afternoon was a lightbulb factory, a civilian target with no military importance. In other words, McCain was in the midst of committing a war crime when his jet was shot down. McCain sports a chestful of medal, all but one of them deriving from his time as the Pentagon's most useful POW.

A couple of years later he was interviewed in prison camp by Fernando Barral, a Spanish psychiatrist living in Cuba. The interview appeared in the Cuban newspaper *Granma* on January 24, 1970.

McCain's fragile psyche runs on what Barral described "the personality of the prisoner who is responsible for many criminal bombings of the people." Barral went on, "He (McCain) showed himself to be intellectually alert during the interview. From a morale point of view he is not in traumatic shock. He was able to be sarcastic, and even humorous, indicative of psychic equilibrium. From the moral and ideological point of view he showed us he is an insensitive individual without human depth, who does not show the slightest concern, who does not appear to have thought about the criminal acts he committed against a population from the absolute impunity of his airplane, and that nevertheless those people saved his life, fed him, and looked after his health and he is now healthy and strong. I believe that he has bombed densely populated places for sport. I noted that he was hardened, that he spoke of banal things as if he were at a cocktail party."

McCain is deeply loved by the liberal press. As Amy Silverman, a reporter at the Phoenix weekly *New Times* who has followed the senator for years, puts it, "As long as he's the noble outsider, McCain can get away with anything it seems—the Keating Five, a drug stealing wife, nasty jokes about Chelsea Clinton—and the pundits will gurgle and coo."

Indeed they will. William Safire, Maureen Dowd, Russell Baker, the *New Yorker*, the *New York Times Magazine*, *Vanity Fair*, have all slobbered over McCain in empurpled prose. The culmination was a love poem from Mike Wallace on 60 Minutes, who managed to avoid any inconvenient mention of McCain's close relationship with S & L fraudster Charles Keating, with whom the indulgent senator romped on Bahamian beaches. McCain was similarly spared scrutiny for his astonishing claim that he knew nothing of his wife's scandalous dealings.

McCain's escape from the Keating debacle is nothing short of miraculous and it's probably the activity for which he most deserves a medal. After all, he took more than $100,000 in campaign contributions from the swindler Keating between 1982 and 1988, while simultaneously logrolling for Keating on Capitol Hill. In the same period McCain took nine trips to Keating's place in the Bahamas.

When the muck began to rise, McCain threw Keating over the side, hastily reimbursed Keating for the trips and suddenly developed a profound interest in campaign finance and reform.

Yet McCain is legendary among those who have worked with him for a pathologically vicious temper, also for his skill in adopting apparently principled stands which are never exposed to any rigorous test.

The pundits love McCain because of his grandstanding on soft money's baneful role in politics, thus garnering for himself a reputation for willingness to court the enmity of his colleagues.

In fact colleagues in the Senate accurately regard McCain as a mere grandstander. They know that he already has a big war chest left over from the corporations that crave his indulgence, as chairman of the Senate Commerce Committee. Communications companies (US West, Bell South, ATT, Bell Atlantic have been particularly effusive in McCain's treasury, as have banks, military contractors and UPS. They also know he has a rich wife and the certain knowledge that his supposed hopes for an end to soft money spending will never receive any practical legislative application.

* * *

John McCain says he models himself after TR. "I'm a Teddy Roosevelt kind of Republican," McCain told a crowd of about 1,000 people in East Lansing, Michigan. "I believe America needs a strong leader. And most Republicans take in pride in identifying with TR, who believed that second only to the national defense, one of our most important public duties is to wisely husband the country's natural resources. Like TR I'll be the kind of president who will have the courage stand up to the special interests and say no. There are some things they just can't have." The crowd of students plus those elusive Reagan Democrats cheered lustily as McCain raised his arms in his now customary crimped victory salute.

Two days later McCain was in Spokane, capital of Washington's Inland Empire, where the Republican Party is dominated by big timber, big agriculture and the hydro-power conglomerate that includes the aluminum factories, the barge fleets and the pulp mills. Over his 18-year career in the House and Senate John McCain has rarely let them down. He has supported property rights legislation, backed the salvage logging rider, fought measures for stricter control over pesticides and harshly denounced proposals to breach dams on the Columbia and Snake Rivers to save endangered salmon.

Even in that crowd, McCain claimed to be a conservationist: "It's possible for a conservative president to be an environmentalist." So the question is what kind of environmentalist is John McCain?

McCain has confused many observers. Even staunchly Democratic organizations such as the League of Conservation Voters, can't seem to find it in themselves to pin him down on the environment. The League's profile of McCain notes that "on most issues dealing with Arizona, National Park protection and auto-efficiency standards, his record ranges from good to excellent". But the group's own annual ranking (heavily prejudiced against Republicans, it must be admitted) gives the Arizona senator a lifetime rating of only 20 per cent. Several years he rated a zero.

When he's out West, McCain is fond of saying that his political mentor was Barry Goldwater. But McCain is no Goldwater. And that's not a compliment. Goldwater was, essentially, a western populist, a Libertarian version of Mike Mansfield, Lee Metcalf and Frank Church. Goldwater always had a passion for the outdoors and in the end singled out as his greatest political regret his vote to authorize the construction of Glen Canyon dam. McCain is not one for searing self-scrutiny. As with the rest of his political agenda, McCain's environmentalism has always been pointedly opportunistic. Voting for a popular Arizona wilderness bill when he faced a tough election. Introducing legislation at the behest of local businesses to limit overflights of planes and helicopters at Grand Canyon National Park. Perhaps, this is a sign for optimism. After all, he isn't a Wise-Use ideologue.

McCain tends to analyze the polls with an obsessiveness comparable to the Clintons. Of particular interest has been Republican pollster Frank Luntz's work, which shows that upwards of 70 percent of Republicans favor strong environmental laws and increased funding for national parks. The environment, in other words, might be a wedge issue, one that can win over independents, Reagan Democrats, Republican moderates and women. Hence, a recent McCain speech on the environment in San Diego, where he thundered, "Republicans have to do a lot more than they are doing today on the environment." Aside from generic calls to fully fund the Land and Water Conservation Fund (which gets its money from royalties from offshore oil drilling), McCain tends to leave the particulars fuzzy.

Of course, McCain is hardly alone in this regard. Indeed, on a bad day he can even sound a bit like Hillary Clinton. "One area I believe we must focus upon is to ensure that our laws and rules are more performance-based and that we focus better on outcomes rather than means," McCain writes on his webpage. "To that end we should work to instill greater flexibility to employ new approaches to meeting our standards and environmental goals."

His votes in the Senate have gone somewhat beyond "greater

flexibility", embracing takings legislation, which forces the government to pay-off property owners in order to keep them from violating environmental laws, opening of the Arctic National Wildlife Refuge to oil drilling, and Bob Dole's regulatory reform bill, which yanked the teeth out of the enforcement of laws from the Clean Air Act to the National Environmental Policy Act.

When the interests of the military and the environment come into conflict, as often happens in the Western states, there's no question where John McCain stands. In 1993, McCain placed a hold on the nomination of Mollie Beatie, Clinton's choice to head the Fish and Wildlife Service. McCain had been told by his buddies in the Marine Air Corps that the Fish and Wildlife Service planned to halt low-level flights above the Cabeza Prieta National Wildlife Reserve, near Yuma, Arizona. McCain's strong-arm tactics worked. Bruce Babbitt sent the senator a letter pledging that the military fly-bys would not be impeded. With this easy victory conquest of Babbitt under his belt, McCain struck again the following year, when he placed a rider onto the California Desert Preservation Act, allowing military flights over the wilderness areas and national preserves created by the act. Now, McCain shouldn't be forced to shoulder all the blame for that one. His amendment was fondly received by the bill's author, Senator Dianne Feinstein, who had already perverted the bill by permitting mining claims inside in the so-called national preserve.

In 1999 McCain attached a rider to the Defense Appropriations bill that would have permanently transferred to the Pentagon 7.2 million acres of federal wildlife refuge land managed by the BLM and the Fish and Wildlife Service, where they would become used as a bombing range and a testing ground for a new generation of missiles. McCain's rider exempted the military from conducting any environmental review of its programs.

One of the issues that divides the often united Western delegation is the Department of Energy's plan to bury the nation's commercial nuclear waste inside Yucca Mountain, an earthquake prone region on Shoshone lands in western Nevada. The plan, dubbed "mobile Chernobyl", sets up an MX missile system for nuclear waste, with trains shipping the radioactive materials from across the country on a maze of rail routes. McCain, happy to keep the waste out of Arizona, enthusiastically supports the scheme. And he backs the creation of even more nuclear waste by standing forth as one of the nuclear power industry's most reliable allies. "While waste and proliferation issues present unique challenges, nuclear energy can play a key role in reducing pollution emissions and controlling releases of carbon dioxide," said McCain.

"If there's one thing we know about McCain, it's that he can't be trusted", says Roger Featherstone, director of the GREEN, an Albuquerque, New Mexico environmental group. "Anybody who promotes McCain as an environmentalist is either an idiot or a liar." Much of the blame for McCain's reputation can be laid to on our gullible press. Living on Earth, the NPR environmental show, recently produced a puff piece touting McCain as the Senate's most environmentally conscious Republican. Of course, most of McCain's act is scripted for the photo op. When the chips are on the table, McCain can be counted on to do the bidding of industry. Take the issue of subsidies. In 1996, McCain introduced a bill that would have slashed corporate welfare, including millions in subsidies to big timber in form of federally funded logging roads. The measure was enthusiastically received by liberals and the Washington press corps, which wasted no time hailing McCain as a "maverick" and a "renegade Republican". But a few months later McCain had the opportunity to make part of his plan reality, but he defected, voting against a measure offered by then-Senator Richard Bryan, the Nevada Democrat, that would have eliminated the very same timber road subsidies. McCain didn't explain his flip-flop.

McCain played a malignant role in one of Arizona's most controversial issues, the mad scheme by the University of Arizona to erect seven deep space telescopes on national forest lands at the summit of Mt. Graham. Mt. Graham is known as a sky island, a lush montane oasis rising out of the Sonoran desert. In its upper reaches, Mt. Graham is cloaked in a dense alpine spruce-fir forest unique in the world. It is home to more than 18 endangered plants and animals, the most famous of which is the Mt. Graham red squirrel, found nowhere else. Mt. Graham is not only an ecological marvel, it is also a sacred mountain to the San Carlos Apache.

Neither of these factors carried weight with McCain, who was hell-bent on doing favors for the University. He duly introduced legislation exempting the $520 million project from compliance with the Endangered Species Act, Antiquities Act and the Native American Religious Freedom Act.

In the spring of 1989, the Forest Service began to raise questions about the project. Worried about the impacts on the endangered Mt. Graham red squirrel, Jim Abbott, the supervisor of the Coronado National Forest, ordered a halt to road construction at the site. The delay infuriated McCain. On May

17, 1989, Abbott got a call from Mike Jimenez, McCain's chief of staff. Jimenez told Abbot that McCain was angry and wanted to meet with him the next day. He told Abbott to expect "some ass-chewing". At the meeting, McCain raged, threatening Abbott that "if you do not cooperate on this project [bypassing the Endangered Species Act], you'll be the shortest tenured forest supervisor in the history of the Forest Service." Unfortunately for McCain, there was a witness to this encounter, a ranking Forest Service employee named Richard Flannelly, who recorded the encounter in his notebook. This notebook was later turned over to investigators at the GAO.

A few days later, McCain called Abbott to apologize. But the call sounded more like an attempt to bribe the Forest Supervisor to go along with the project. According to a 1990 GAO report on the affair, McCain "held out a carrot that with better cooperation, he would see about getting funding for Mr. Abbott's desired recreation projects". Environmentalists attempted to bring an ethics complaint against McCain, citing a federal law that prohibits anyone (including members of Congress) from browbeating federal agency personnel. The Senate ethics committee never pursued the matter. When the GAO report, condemning McCain, surfaced publicly, McCain lied about the encounter, calling the allegations "groundless" and "silly".

In 1992, Robin Silver and Bob Witzeman went to meet with McCain at his office in Phoenix to discuss Mt. Graham. Silver and Witzeman are both physicians. Witzeman is now retired and Silver works in the emergency room at Phoenix hospital. The doctors say that at the mention of the words Mount Graham, McCain erupted into a violent fit. "He slammed his fists on his desk, scattering papers across the room", Silver told me. "He jumped up and down, screaming obscenities at us for at least 10 minutes. He shook his fists as if he was going to slug us. It was as violent as almost any domestic abuse altercation."

Witzeman left the meeting stunned: "I'm a lifelong environmentalist, but what really scares me about McCain is not his environmental policies, which are horrid, but his violent, irrational temper. I think McCain is so unbalanced that if Vladimir Putin told him something he didn't like he'd lose it, start beating his chest about having his finger on the nuclear trigger. Who knows where it would stop. To my mind, McCain's the most likely senator to start a nuclear war."

March, 2005

Twelve

King of the Hill

Ted Stevens' Empire

T ed Stevens doesn't exploit loopholes, he drills them.

From his aerie in the US senate, the Alaska Republican exerts his power over vast terrains of legislation and budgeting, from the logging of the Tongass National Forest to the development of the Star Wars missile defense scheme.

Since Stevens, the longest-serving Republican in Congress, became the chair of the Senate Appropriations Committee in 1997, his power has magnified. Through his machinations, federal spending in Alaska has nearly doubled in the past eight years. On a per capita basis, Alaska now leads the nation in the receipt of federal money, at nearly $12,000 for each resident and twice the national average. Alaska also now occupies the top spot for so-called earmarked appropriations, special pet-projects in home states of senators and representatives on the appropriations committees. Under Stevens' sway, Alaska now gets more than $611 in federal funds for each Alaskan for these special earmarks. The national average for earmarked pork projects is $19 per capita.

Of course, this money doesn't go directly into the pockets of all Alaskans, but is channeled into projects benefiting the senator's political patrons and in some cases into projects in which the senator and his family own a financial stake.

Among the special earmarks engineered by Stevens: a $2 million project to monitor Alaska's skies for volcanic ash, a provision that ended up as a segment on the TV show "West Wing"; $1 million for an airport on remote St. Georges Island; $2.5 million to train Russian workers for jobs in Alaska's offshore and Arctic oil fields; $15 million to the University of Alaska to study the aurora borealis.

Ted Stevens is a leading foe of the Endangered Species Act. He has tried to demolish the nation's premier wildlife law by cutting funding to enforce its provisions and by intimidating Fish and Wildlife Service personnel. Even so, the senator has shoveled federal money into wildlife projects that benefit friends and backers in Alaska. In 2003, he inserted line items in the mammoth federal spending bill that gave $4 million to study how to aid beached sea lions and $100,000 for a census of Pacific walrus populations. He has redirected millions in federal funding away from the study of salmon stocks in Oregon, Washington and northern California, where the fish are endangered, up to salmon projects in Alaska, where fish populations are relatively stable.

Stevens also used his power to direct a $22 million gift, disguised as emergency relief to four Southeast Alaska towns. The money was supposed to soften the blow from decreased logging on the Tongass National Forest, American's largest temperate rainforest, caused by the closure of two pulp mills. Of course, thanks to Stevens' intervention the logging on the Tongass has continued unabated, despite pleas from scientists and wildlife biologists who charge that the cutting is endangering hundreds of species of wildlife. Still the supposedly timber dependent communities of Sitka and Ketchikan are happy to get the money, since when the mills were operating they saw little flow their way. "We owe Senator Stevens a lot," says Stan Fuller, mayor of Sitka. "For years, we didn't get anything. Flat nothing. It was like we weren't even here."

* * *

Stevens, who portrays himself as a gritty pioneer from Girdwood, Alaska, is actually a Hoosier. He was born in Indianapolis in 1923 and moved to Huntington Beach, California as a teen. During World War II, Stevens served under General Clair Chenault as a pilot in the quasi-private Air Force known as the Flying Tigers, an enterprise which would over the course of a few decades evolve into the CIA's notorious Air America. In China, Stevens ferried Chaing Kai-Shek's KMT fighters over the Himalayas to camps in Burma and Nepal. At the time and for decades to come, the KMT financed their war against the Japanese and Mao's Red Army through the opium trade.

After the war, Stevens returned to southern California, where he got a degree at UCLA. Then it was off to law school at Harvard. From Harvard, Stevens embarked for Alaska to strike it rich. But his private practice soon fizzled in the thinly populated territory. In 1953, he was rescued from these professional doldrums by his friend Fred Seaton, who secured Stevens a position as US District Attorney for Fairbanks. Seaton soon became

Eisenhower's Interior Secretary and he brought Stevens with him to DC to serve as his chief counsel.

The young lawyer divided his time over the next six years between two consuming tasks: securing statehood for Alaska and opening up as much land as possible in the new state to plunder by timber, mining and oil companies. As a reward for his services, Ike elevated Stevens to the position of solicitor for the Interior Department, a position he held for a year until Kennedy gave him the boot.

With his resume fattened up, Stevens returned to Alaska, setting up shop as an oil industry lawyer in Anchorage, where he laid the groundwork for opening the North Slope to the oil cartels. But his time in Washington had fired Stevens' political ambitions. Billing himself as the man who won Alaska's statehood, Stevens was elected to Alaska's House of Representatives in 1964, where he quickly rose to the position of Speaker.

In 1968, Alaska's senator Bob Bartlett died suddenly and the state's governor, Wally Hickle, soon to become Nixon's Interior Secretary, tapped Stevens to fill the empty senate seat. A year later, Stevens held onto the seat in a special election and since then he has never faced a serious challenge.

A fierce party loyalist, Stevens stuck with his patron Nixon even as the president crashed in the wreckage of Watergate. The party rewarded Stevens for his unflinching fidelity. He was handed plum posts in the senate not normally reserved for a senator from a remote and sparsely populated state. He moved from assistant Republican whip to chair or ranking member of the powerful Government Affairs and Commerce committees, as well as the Defense Appropriations subcommittee. And finally he landed the most desired position in Congress: the chair of the Senate Appropriations Committee. By 1985, Ted Stevens was king of the Hill.

It was around this time that Stevens began to gripe publicly about the great financial sacrifice he had made by devoting his professional career to the political stewardship of Alaska. These periodic outbursts, often at town meetings in places such as Seward and Ketchikan, may have been ignited by the rise of his fellow Republican from Alaska, Frank Murkowski. Murkowski, a relative newcomer to the state, had made millions as an investment banker before moving to Anchorage and running for the senate.

But Stevens had also suffered a severe financial reversal in 1986, when a crab-fishing venture that he had sunk more than a million dollars into went bust. Stevens was mired in debt and chaffing about his meager senate salary of $130,000 a year.

Soon thereafter Stevens began to use his position as overlord for $800 billion in annual federal spending to steer government contracts and subsidies to enterprises owned by friends, family members and business associates. Within a few years, Stevens was a millionaire like Murkowski. So too was his wife, his son and his brother-in-law.

Ted Stevens was perfectly positioned to profiteer from these kinds of giveaways devised in the inner chambers of his senate offices and buried in the subtext of spending bills that are hundreds of pages thick. Not only did Stevens control the purse strings of the government, but for years he also chaired the Senate Ethics Committee, which wrote and enforced the rules on conflicts of interest involving senators and family members—rules that proved very lax indeed.

* * *

Like the sons of Trent Lott and Harry Reid, Ted Stevens' son Ben works as a top lobbyist in DC, pulling in big fees by trading on his father's unrivaled position in the senate. For example, in 2000 Senator Stevens earmarked $30 million in disaster relief funds to the Southwest Alaska Municipal Agency. The agency promptly hired Ben Stevens to advise the group on how those funds should be spent.

Dozens of other Alaska companies have sought the services of the senator's son. From 2001 to 2004, Ben Stevens' financial disclosure forms show that he has been paid more than $750,000 in lobbying and consulting fees. Stevens notes that he considers his lobbying business only "part-time" work. That's because his full-time job for most of that time was to head up the Alaska Special Olympics, which his father financed with a $10 million federal appropriation. Ben Stevens was paid $715,000 as director of the organization.

During that time, Ben was also working for VECO, a large oil services company that had built pipelines in Alaska and in southwest Asia. Ben Stevens was paid more than $210,000 by VECO from the late 1990s through 2002. In 1999, VECO had built a $70 million pipeline in Pakistan. When the Pakistan government was slow to pay up, VECO complained to Senator Stevens. Stevens told the Pakistanis that he would a big trade deal with the country until they offered up the money to VECO. The Pakistanis complied and the trade pact was approved.

Ben Stevens' stunning success as lobbyist is remarkable considering the fact that until 1998 he had no experience at all as either a lobbyist or a consultant. Indeed, he had spent the previous 15 years working on a commercial fishing boat in the Bering Sea. But this experience on the icy ocean has also come in handy in Washington.

The senator claims that he rarely speaks to his son about legislative matters, except when they involve commercial fishing. "Ben's an expert on fishing," Stevens told the *Anchorage Daily News*.

Indeed, Ben Stevens gets paid $170,000 from the Alaskan fishing industry to guard their interests in Washington. He soon proved worth the fees. In 2003, as the invasion of Iraq was in high gear, the Bush administration sent an emergency request to Congress for $80 billion to fund the war.

Senator Stevens saw this as a fail safe way to spread a little cheer to his son and his clients. Deep inside the war spending bill, Stevens embedded a provision long-sought by the Alaska fishing industry forcing the Department of Agriculture to classify wild salmon caught in Alaskan waters as an "organic" food. The designation would allow the fishing industry to significantly mark up the price of such certified fish.

Stevens also used the Pentagon funding bill as cover for two more fishing measures: a $45 million subsidy to Alaskan fisheries and a provision requiring the military to purchase only American fish, 80 percent of which comes from Alaska. Later, Stevens promised that his next move on their behalf was a scheme to compel the military to include "salmon jerky" as a part of the basic ration kit for troops in Afghanistan and Iraq.

* * *

In 2000, Stevens engineered and pushed through a measure that amended the Defense Appropriations Act to allow tiny Alaskan Native Corporations to receive no-bid contracts from the Pentagon (and, later, the Department of Homeland Security) worth hundreds of millions of dollars. The tribal entities were under no obligation to actually perform the work. Instead, they could simply subcontract it out to big defense contractors, such as SAIC and Bechtel, at a handsome profit. In essence, the tribal corporations act as cutouts for big companies that don't enjoy the same loopholes in federal contracting provisions.

One of those tribal companies pays $6 million a year to lease an office building owned by Senator Stephens and his business partners. Stephens sees no conflict of interest in the deal. "I'm a passive investor," Stephens told the *Los Angeles Times*. "I don't make the business decisions." Not for the corporation he doesn't, but as the overseer of $800 billion federal discretionary spending he makes sure that those businesses enjoy a generous supply of federal funding.

Of course, while Stevens is willing to exploit the tribes as a cut-out to steer millions to favored projects and businesses, he shows open disdain for the aspirations of the tribes themselves. In the fall of 2003, Stevens took to the airwaves to publicly lambaste the tribes for wanting to assert control over their own lands, tribal members and enterprises. Stevens vowed to use his power to block any federal funding for tribal courts in native villages and accused the tribes of trying to destroy the state.

"The road they are on now is the destruction of Alaska," Stevens warned in a racist diatribe carried on Alaskan Public Radio. "The native population is increasing at a much, much greater rate. I don't know if you know that. And they want total jurisdiction over what happens in a tribal village, without regard to state law and without regard to federal law. If all the villages in Alaska are tribes, more than half the tribes in the United States are in Alaska, and if each one is entitled to a court…uh, you see, it's not going to happen."

Stevens' outburst enraged Alaskan tribal leaders and civil rights advocates. "As an Alaskan native person, I take very strong offense to the statements made by the senator," says Heather Kendall-Miller, an attorney with the Native American Rights Fund. "He talks about it as if it were 'us' versus 'them.' I haven't heard that kind of talk since I don't know when. It's assault on tribalism."

Stevens has been accused of running a kind of legislative protection racket. In 2001, Stevens intervened to save a $450 million military housing contract in Alaska that the Pentagon wanted to cancel. The contract was held by an Anchorage firm run by a longtime friend of the senator. This friend had made Stevens a partner in several lucrative real estate deals. Since 1998, Stevens' initial $50,000 investment in the firm had yielded the senator more than $750,000 in profits.

Of course, it's not all about making money. It's also about self-glorification. In 2001, Stevens implanted $2.2 million in federal money to underwrite the expansion of the Anchorage airport. And what is this new facility called? Ted Stevens International Airport, an honor usually reserved for the dead or at least the retired.

April, 2005

Part Three

The Profiteers

In time of war the loudest patriots are the greatest profiteers.

—August Babel

Thirteen

Sticky Fingers

The Making of Halliburton

There's no more pungent symbol of the corrupt nature of the Bush administration's invasion and occupation of Iraq than Halliburton, the Houston, Texas-based oil services conglomerate, which has raked in billions in revenue from the war even in the face of charges of massive overbilling, shoddy work, official bribery and political influence-peddling.

The remarkable thing is that Halliburton's looting of Iraq and the US treasury happened in broad daylight, right under the nose of the press, the Democrats and the camera lights of Michael Moore, who made Dick Cheney's former company the bete noir of his film "Fahrenheit 9/11." Nothing deterred the company from capitalizing on the war it helped orchestrate.

Even the Pentagon's own team of auditors, who nailed Halliburton red-handed for bilking the government for $108.4 million in overcharges for only "one task order" of its work in Iraq, found their report languishing in a kind of bureaucratic netherland for many months.

The damning investigation by the Defense Contract Audit Agency was completed in early October of 2004 and shipped up the line to Pentagon's dark triumvirate, Douglas Feith, Paul Wolfowitz and Donald Rumsfeld. And there it sat. The Pentagon's civilian leadership mothballed the explosive report for more than five months, until after the election, the inauguration, the State of the Union Address and the Defense Department budget request had all safely transpired.

Even congress was denied a peak at the report's findings until mid-March 2005. The Pentagon rejected 12 separate requests from Congressman Henry Waxman, the California Democrat who has spearheaded the ad hoc congressional inquiry into Halliburton's contract abuse, seeking to examine the internal audits of Halliburton's $2.5 billion contract for fuel supplies and other services to the US military and occupation government in Iraq.

Waxman charged that the Pentagon withheld the damaging reports at the behest of the office of Vice President Dick Cheney, the former CEO of Halliburton.

The Halliburton audits were also concealed from a team of investigators from the United Nations, which is probing profiteering from oil contracts in

Iraq. More than $1.5 billion of Halliburton's $2.5 billion deal was funded by Iraqi oil sales overseen by the UN.

"The evidence suggests that the Pentagon used Iraqi oil proceeds to overpay Halliburton," says Waxman. "And then the company and the Pentagon sought to hide the evidence of these overcharges from the international auditors."

Call it the Oil-for-Contracts scandal. But you didn't hear daily drumbeats about the outrageous rip-off on FoxNews.

When someone finally leaked the audit to Waxman's office, the documents disclosed a thick wad of Halliburton billings that the Pentagon bookkeepers deemed "illogical."

The most peculiar billing found in this limited series of transactions was a $27.5 million charge for shipping cooking gas and heating fuel that the Pentagon auditors valued at $82,000. This single invoice amounted to an overcharge of more than 335 times the value of the liquefied natural gas delivered by Halliburton's subcontractors.

The auditors examined only a single task order in Halliburton's scandal-plagued contract with the Army Corps of Engineers, yet their report lambasted nearly every aspect of the deal, from the no-bid award to the cost-plus [i.e., an open-ended contract with a built-in profit] nature of the contract to the almost total lack of supervision of the work orders and the subcontractors.

From May 2003 to March 2004, Halliburton sent the Corps of Engineers bills totaling more than $875 million for supplies of fuel to US operations in Iraq. For this task order alone, the Pentagon auditors estimated that Halliburton overbuild the government by at least $108.4 million. That's real money, even by Pentagon standards.

But that's only a rough opening bid for the true scale of the looting, in large part because the company's indefatigable stonewalling. The auditor's report accuses Halliburton of misleading the government inspectors at nearly every turn. For example, the auditors allege that Halliburton simply refused to hand over any information on its subcontractors in Kuwait. "Halliburton failed to demonstrate its prices for Kuwait fuel were 'fair and reasonable'", the auditors wrote in their report.

Similarly, Halliburton kept the Pentagon investigators in the dark about the prices it paid for purchasing fuel from Turkey and Jordan.

The Defense Contract Audit Agency report comes on top of previous investigations tagging Halliburton, and its Kellogg, Brown and Root subsidiary, for more than $442 million in "unsupported" billings for its work in Iraq, including charges for meals that were never served, $45 cases of pop, unnecessary heavy equipment, tailoring fees and $152,000 for movie screenings. In all a report prepared by the Democratic Policy Committee estimates that Halliburton's overcharges in Iraq alone exceed $1 billion.

Okay, the Pentagon learned a billion-dollar lesson the hard way, right? Wrong. In July 2005, the Pentagon discreetly let slip that it had awarded Halliburton a fat new contract for yet more logistics work in Iraq. How fat? Try $5 billion. In fact, the contract was secretly handed to Halliburton in May, but the Pentagon kept it under wraps for more than a month. Why? "The Army didn't consider it necessary" to reveal the terms of the deal, a Pentagon spokesman explained to Reuters.

In the ever-expanding universe of Pentagon contracting, cost is never the problem, public exposure is.

* * *

Halliburton, the signature corporation of the Bush-Cheney onslaught on Iraq, didn't start its corporate life on the government dole. In fact, the company patriarch, Erle P. "Red" Halliburton, despised the federal government. His distaste for Uncle Sam was matched only by his ferocious hatred of Mexicans, blacks and labor unionists.

In 1919, Red Halliburton started the New Method Oil Well Cementing Company from his home in Wilson, Oklahoma, a hardscrabble town in the oil patch. Halliburton's big innovation was something called the Cement Jet Mixer. When the oil boom hit Texas, the wildcatters and other drillers quickly began experiencing problems with their deep shafts. The steel pipe funneling the oil up from the Permian basin and other reservoirs of crude would sooner or later develop cracks, allowing groundwater to contaminate the crude. In some cases, the pipes would even explode.

Halliburton's solution, which he unveiled in the oil town of Burkburnett, Texas, was to seal the well-pipes in a sheath of concrete, protecting the pipes from corrosion and precious loads of crude from contamination. He was soon in demand across the oil fields of Texas and Oklahoma. Erle changed the name of the company to Halliburton and raked in millions from his patent. Halliburton continues to garner millions from its drilling technology, from Saudi Arabia to the Amazonian rainforest.

Meanwhile, in that same crucial year of 1919, the other half of Halliburton was also beginning to take shape as two friends from San Marcos, Texas, Herman Brown and Dan Root, formed a road paving company that would eventually become one of the world's largest construction firms. The Brown & Root Company shared Halliburton's antipathy toward organized labor, but realized early on that there was a fortune to be made through outsourced government work.

Brown & Root also understood that government contracts are a lot easier to get if you have a politician on retainer.

* * *

In the late winter of 1937, the imperious Texas Congressman James P. "Bucky" Buchanan, chairman of the House Appropriations Committee, suddenly died in office. Buchanan departed the living with some unfinished business of extreme importance to his political cronies. The congressman, who controlled the federal purse, was in the midst of pushing through congress the Lower Colorado River Project, a scheme to build a network of dams across the Texas hill country that would bring water to the people and millions in federal funds to favored contractors. The centerpiece of this enterprise was the Marshall Ford Dam outside Austin and the company that had won the contract to build the dam was none other than Brown & Root.

The $10 million dam deal was the biggest Brown & Root contract to date. But there were two problems left by Buchanan's ill-timed passing: the money for the dam hadn't yet been approved by congress and the land at the dam-site wasn't owned by the federal government. What had suddenly looked like a sure thing, now found Brown & Root on the unnerving verge of bankruptcy. The company had gone into debt by more than $1.5 million in order to purchase the equipment needed to build the dam.

Brown & Root decided there was no turning back. They began construction on the dam before getting any federal funds and before the feds had actually acquired the land from the state of Texas.

But the company had an ace in the hole in the shape of Lyndon Baines Johnson, the lumbering former schoolteacher who was vying to replace the departed Buchanan. In the spring of that year, young LBJ met several times with Herman Brown, vowing to make congressional approval of the dam project his top priority. Brown sluiced cash into LBJ's campaign and he sailed to victory in a special election on May 13, 1937. LBJ lived up to his obligations. A little more than a week after having arrived in DC, the freshly hatched congressman had engineered congressional approval for both the appropriation and the land purchase.

The Marshall Ford Dam deal launched LBJ's career as a can-do politician without parallel in American politics and it set Brown & Root on course to become one of the federal government's favorite contractors. The apex political fixer Thomas "Tommy the Cork" Corcoran later observed that "LBJ's whole world was built on that dam". So too was Brown & Root's.

LBJ had the good fortune to land on the congressional committee overseeing the operations of the US Navy as it prepared for World War II. When LBJ's fortunes rose on the Hill, so did Brown & Root's. As a brawny member of the Naval Affairs Committee, the ambitious congressman, a key southern supporter of FDR's New Deal and therefore confident of the backing of the White House for almost any pet project, steered as many big contracts to his political financiers as possible.

It was courtesy of LBJ, and his privileged position in the congress, that Brown & Root got into the Pentagon contracting business in a big way. In 1940, the former road paving firm won a huge contract to build the Corpus Christi Naval Air Station, a complex of runways, hangars, barracks and command centers sprawling across 2,000 acres of swamp and scrubland on the gulf coast of Texas. It was a model for things to come.

The Corpus Christi Naval Air Station was one of the first "cost-plus" contracts, a sweet deal where the government simply pays every bill the contractor submits. The initial price-tag was pegged at $23.5 million, with Brown & Root guaranteed a profit of $1.2 million. But within a year, the cost had soared to more than $45 million, with Brown & Root pocketing more than $2.4 million in profits. It was an early lesson in the demented logic of Pentagon contracting: the bigger the cost-overruns, the juicier the profits. In the end, the Naval Air Station cost the Pentagon more than $125 million.

The Corpus Christi deal initiated Brown & Root into the risk-free fraternity of favored Pentagon contractors. The company that had prospered through the Great Depression thanks to federal dam projects was poised to make a killing from World War II, with most of the deal coming courtesy of the US Navy and its congressional overlord LBJ and the powerful congressman from Houston, Albert Thomas. Working together, LBJ and Thomas convinced the Navy to give Brown & Root a lucrative shipbuilding contract, even though, as investigative reporter Robert Bryce notes, up until that point the company "had never built so much as a canoe."

But over the next five years, Brown Shipbuilding, a huge operation on the Houston Ship Channel, would build 355 ships for the Navy, specializing in sub chasers and escorts for destroyers. The company made a cool $500 million from the deal.

As the war drew to a close, Brown & Root went from building ships to melting more than 20,000 surplus airplanes they bought on the cheap from the War Assets Administration. They were soon one of the big players in the aluminum business, much of which they sold right back to the feds, making tens of millions in profits. This neat trick was followed by a huge cost-plus contract to build the US military base on Guam in the south Pacific, a deal that started out with a price tag of $25 million (a huge amount in 1949) but soon ballooned to more than $250 million.

Never say that Brown & Root wasn't grateful. They knew that their fortunes rode on the backs of their political benefactors and they did their best to keep them happy. Unlike many others in Congress during the 1940s, Johnson wasn't rich. He and Lady Bird fretted about money during the early years of their marriage. Then, in the mid-1940s, opportunity came calling when KTBC, Austin's first radio station, went on the market. Using money from Lady Bird's inheritance and generous infusions of cash from Brown & Root, the Johnsons bought the station, made major upgrades in its operations and squeezed federal broadcast regulators into allowing it to expand its output and change its location to a more central place on the dial. Soon the Johnsons were rich. As LBJ said, "Finally, I was a millionaire".

For Johnson, money was the route to political power. From his early days running the Texas branch of FDR's National Youth Administration (NYA), LBJ had set his eyes on landing a seat in the US senate. LBJ got the NYA position, at the age of 29, through the intervention of Alvin Wirtz, the lead attorney for Brown & Root and a noted fixer. As for LBJ, he later said that Wirtz was "like a daddy to me". Brown & Root harbored similar ambitions for their man. They owned a few congressmen, but an obedient senator was the key to a higher order of riches.

* * *

LBJ's first shot at the senate came in 1941, after Texas Senator Morris Sheppard keeled over from a brain hemorrhage. Running as a New Dealer and fueled by cash from Herman Brown, Johnson embarked on a fabulously corrupt campaign against the populist governor of Texas, W. Lee "Pass the Biscuits, Pappy" O'Daniel, a flour magnate and the state's most popular radio personality. He ran on an anti-union and anti-FDR platform that appealed to rural Texas voters.

Ballot boxes were bought by both campaigns. Johnson bought them in San Antonio and southern Texas, while O'Daniel, called the greatest campaigner in Texas history, purchased them throughout east Texas. With 97 per cent of the votes counted, Johnson led the race and seemed assured of victory. Then more ballots mysteriously materialized, and O'Daniel claimed victory by 1,311 votes. The final fix may have been made by a cabal of Texas oil men and ranchers who wanted O'Daniel out of Austin. They figured he could do them less damage in Washington.

Johnson vowed to learn the lessons of his defeat. He shed much of his New Dealer image and reemerged as a Southern populist, touting his votes against an anti-lynching bill, against Truman's bill to outlaw the poll tax, and for the union-busting Taft-Hartley Act. He also courted cash from every corporation and mogul he could find, promising to return their investment tenfold.

When he ran again in 1948, Johnson almost certainly lost the vote, but stole the election, abetted by Brown & Root, the company's lawyer Alvin Wirtz, and newspaper tycoon Charles Marsh.

Once again, Johnson faced a popular and reactionary governor for the Texas senate seat, vacated when Pappy O'Daniel grew bored of living in DC. This time his opponent was Gov. Coke Stevenson, rancher, bigot and anti-communist. In the Democratic primary, Stevenson steamrollered Johnson by more than 70,000 votes; yet in a crowded field, the governor didn't top 50 per cent, forcing a run-off election in the fall. It would become the most expensive political campaign waged in Texas until George W. Bush, underwritten by the descendents of LBJ's backers, defeated Anne Richards in the fierce 1994 gubernatorial campaign.

Stevenson was a wildly popular figure in Texas, but LBJ had an equalizer: a nearly bottomless reservoir of campaign money provided by

Brown & Root and Wirtz's client list of oil barons, including H.L. Hunt and Sid Richardson. LBJ also enjoyed free access to a DC-3, courtesy of Brown & Root, which would rush him across the vast Texan plains for as many as 10 appearances in a single day.

Fifty-two years later, Halliburton offered its corporate jets for use by George Bush and his campaign team during the 2000 campaign and subsequent tumultuous Florida recount. For those flights, the Bush campaign reimbursed Halliburton only the cost of one first class ticket.

In 1948 it was also this same DC-3 that made emergency flights to Austin and Dallas in search of cash from the accounts of Brown & Root. The money was delivered in $100 bills stuffed into grocery bags. The bagman was none other than John Connolly, the future governor of Texas and Halliburton board member. Each haul would net between $40,000 and $50,000 for the Johnson campaign.

Johnson also prevailed upon the Bell Helicopter Company, which would soon relocate to Texas, to loan him a chopper for his campaign. One of the first politicians to use the newfangled machine, Johnson would descend upon his campaign venues with the "Yellow Rose of Texas" blaring from loudspeakers attached to the landing gear—a prelude for the Wagner-screaming choppers in Apocalypse Now.

All of this got LBJ close, but quite not close enough, to assure him of an outright victory. The 1948 election needed to be both bought and stolen.

As the polls closed in the Texas senate race of 1948, the margin was razor thin, with Coke Stevenson running slightly ahead of LBJ. Over the next few days, precincts across the vast state counted and recounted their votes. Five days after the election, an amended return came in from Jim Wells County in the southern outback of Texas. It seems that a certain Luis Salas, following the suggestion of a Brown & Root lawyer, began scouring the courthouse for a missing box of ballots. He chanced upon the infamous Box 13 from the hamlet of Alice, Texas, which contained 220 votes, all for Johnson, which was enough to push LBJ into the lead by 87 votes. (A later analysis by Johnson biographer Robert Caro showed that 220 names had been added to the voters' list after the polls had closed.)

Stevenson rushed to the courts for relief. He won round one. He got a state judge in Texas to place an injunction against the ballots from Alice. Again, the race was ultimately decided by the U.S. Supreme Court by the intervention of a single justice, Hugo Black. Black was a New Dealer elevated to the high bench by FDR. With time running out, LBJ's lawyers Abe Fortas (whom LBJ ultimately rewarded by putting him on the Supreme Court) and Alvin Wirtz, who was also Brown & Root's lead corporate counsel, arranged a secret meeting with Black in his chambers at the Supreme Court. At this *ex parte* conclave, Wirtz impressed upon Black the importance of LBJ's election to the senate, saying that many New Deal programs (he presumably did not mention the gross topic of Pentagon contracts) hinged on the outcome.

On September 29, 1948, Black came through. The justice issued an order overturning the state judge's injunction and also put the brakes on a parallel investigation into vote fraud in Jim Wells County. LBJ was pronounced the winner of the primary by 87 votes and then went on to crush his Republican opponent in November.

True to form, Johnson never tried to conceal the role his corporate sponsors played in securing the 1948 election. Indeed, he bragged about his prowess at securing powerful and deep-pocketed backers, saying that his rise to the senate had been "Brown & Root funded."

Once again, it didn't take LBJ long to pay back his political investors with interest. In the spring of 1949, only months after claiming his senate seat, LBJ, the former New Dealer, launched an assault on Leland Olds, the chairman of the Federal Power Commission. Olds, a former muckraking reporter, was appointed by FDR to head the commission, which set power rates and regulated natural gas prices. His term expired in 1948, and Harry Truman had just announced his intention to reappoint him to the position, enraging the oil and gas industry. On Olds' advice, Truman had vetoed a bill that would have deregulated the natural gas industry.

In addition to Brown & Root, the Brown family also owned the Texas Eastern Transmission Corporation, then the nation's biggest natural gas pipeline company. The Browns were furious at Olds's rulings and pleaded with Johnson to defeat his renomination. LBJ did more than that. He destroyed the man in a set of hearings that would lay the groundwork for the show trials of the McCarthy era.

With the help of his pals Sam Rayburn and Senator Robert Kerr, Johnson, a freshman senator, got himself appointed chairman of the committee overseeing the Federal Power Commission. From this position, he launched into an onslaught on Olds, smearing the former supporter of Herbert Hoover as a "communist" who "travels with those who proposed the Marxian answer." LBJ, who only a few years earlier had used his political muscle to secure the vast public hydropower projects on the Little Colorado with the goal of providing cheap power to the citizens of the Hill Country, now accused Olds of "plotting a course toward confiscation and public ownership".

LBJ's ambush of Olds was scripted by none other than Brown & Root's lawyer, Alvin Wirtz. After this grilling, Olds was rejected by the senate on a vote of 53-15 and left the government a broken man. Johnson, however, flew back to Houston the night after his destruction of Olds on a private jet owned by Brown & Root. A company limousine met him at the airport and whisked away to the Brown & Root suite at the Lamar Hotel, where a victory party was in full swing featuring whiskey, women and the richest oil men in Texas—men who were primed to get a lot richer.

* * *

As the partnership between LBJ and Brown & Root propelled both the company and the politician to new heights of power and wealth, Halliburton was taking a different track: capitalizing on the globalization of the oil industry.

During World War II, Halliburton was called upon to help build the infrastructure for the oil fields of Saudi Arabia, launching a profitable relationship with the petro-kingdom that persists to this day. While the US oil companies were later given the boot by the Saudi royal family, Halliburton continued to prosper, constructing pipelines, refineries and oil terminals.

Soon there were other summonses from the Middle East. In late 1940s, Halliburton began doing business in Bahrain, followed by an equally lucrative contract with the royal family of Kuwait to manage that kingdom's oil fields.

The big prize in the 1950s was Iran, where Halliburton enjoyed tens of millions in contracts which were suddenly placed in jeopardy with election of Mohammed Mossadegh, who had campaigned on a pledge to nationalize Iran's enormous oil reserves. Needless to say, this prospect didn't sit well with Halliburton and the consortium of British and American oil companies exploiting Iran's petroleum wealth.

When Mossadegh moved forward with his plans, the oil companies appealed to President Eisenhower to intervene, who turned the matter over to his National Security Council. As it happened, Halliburton had a man on the inside to press its case in the person of Dillon Anderson. Anderson was a partner in the Houston law firm of Baker Botts, the family firm of James A. Baker, III, which had represented Halliburton for many years. Soon after Eisenhower's election, Anderson, who had funneled more than $200,000 into the Eisenhower-Nixon campaign, was invited to join the administration as a consultant to the National Security Council.

The NSC, with judicious prodding from Dillon Anderson, quickly sanctioned a CIA plan, devised by Kermit Roosevelt, son of Teddy Roosevelt, to overthrow Mossadegh. And so it came to pass. On August 19, 1953, the CIA launched its coup. Mossadegh was arrested and thrown in to jail and Reza Pahlavi was re-installed on the Peacock Throne as the Shah of Iran.

In return, the Shah soon signed over control of Iran's oil resources to a consortium of western oil companies, lead by Exxon, Mobil and Texaco. Halliburton was also back in Iran. Over the next 25 years, the company cashed in on more than $10 billion in contracts with Iran.

As for Dillon Anderson, Ike soon elevated the Yale-trained lawyer from Texas to the position of National Security Adviser, where he served until 1957.

* * *

In 1962, Herman Brown died and his brother, George, began searching for possible corporate suitors who might take over the company. In the summer of that year, George Brown worked out a strange deal with Halliburton, which was looking to diversify its operations. Halliburton agreed to acquire Brown & Root for the bargain basement price of $36.7 million, far below the market value of the company. But in exchange, Halliburton executives agreed to let Brown and his colleagues run the new Brown & Root subsidiary as a quasi-independent arm of Halliburton.

Of course, the acquisition of Brown & Root had another great advantage for Halliburton. The fiercely Republican oil services company, which prospered under Eisenhower, now found many familiar doors in Washington shuttered under the Kennedy administration.

Brown & Root, though, was riding higher than ever thanks to its old political fixer, LBJ, now Kennedy's vice president. At the time of the merger, Brown & Root had just been handed one of its biggest federal contracts, the multi-billion dollar deal to build NASA's Manned Space Center outside

Houston—a complex that would later be renamed the Johnson Space Center.

But the most majestic profits, as always, were to be made during wartime and LBJ gave them a big one. During World War II and Korea, Brown & Root made billions building bases and ships in the US. But Johnson's Vietnam War forever changed the role of Pentagon contractors, and Halliburton's Brown & Root subsidiary led the way.

For the first time, the Pentagon began to privatize construction and logistics operations during wartime in the war zone. In 1965, Halliburton formed a consortium with the Idaho-based firm Morrison-Knudsen to manage big construction projects for the Pentagon in Vietnam. Over the next five years, the contracts would fatten to more than $2 billion. They also followed a familiar contour: the contracts were awarded without competitive bidding and on a cost-plus basis with a built-in profit guaranteed.

Soon Halliburton employees were a common sight across South Vietnam— digging wells, building latrines, managing commissaries, excavating harbors and constructing barracks— from Da Nang to Cam Rahn Bay.

The biggest project by far was its $220 million contract to build the mammoth Air Force Base at Phan Rang, which Halliburton constructed on top of some of the most beautiful Cham temple complexes in Vietnam. Phan Rang, from which US bombers pounded North Vietnam and later Cambodia, gained a little notoriety in December 1967, when Bob Hope brought his Christmas show there featuring a sultry performance by Raquel Welch that nearly caused a riot on the base.

The cost overruns in Vietnam quickly swelled and soon caught the attention of auditors with the General Accounting Office. In 1967, a GAO report on Halliburton's operations in Vietnam skewered the company for abandoning "normal management controls" and for wasting millions of dollars. The GAO disclosed that Halliburton "could not account for the whereabouts of approximately $120 million worth of materials which had been shipped from the US to Vietnam."

The GAO audit should have given the company a black eye and caused the government to reconsider the outsourcing of wartime logistics work, but the prophetic report was buried by the Pentagon and ignored by the press. As a result, Halliburton flourished. Over the course of the Vietnam war, Halliburton's annual revenues nearly tripled and it emerged from the war as the world's second largest construction firm, trailing only Bechtel.

* * *

In the fall of 1979, the Iranian revolution led to the expulsion of Halliburton from the lucrative sinecure it had enjoyed under the Shah's dictatorship.

Not to worry. Halliburton quickly moved to replace those revenues with an equally rich stream from Iran's neighbor and blood enemy, the Baathist republic of Iraq, now under the grip of Saddam Hussein.

Like many other US companies that choose to turn a blind eye to the regime's more sanguinary manifestations, Halliburton had been working in Iraq since the early 1970s, even though the Ford and Carter administrations had both refused to recognize the socialist government.

In 1973, Halliburton won a $120 million contract to build Iraq's two mammoth oil terminals in the Persian Gulf off the coast from Umm Qasr. This contract was to prove immensely profitable over the next three war-plagued decades. For one thing, those big terminals, the Mina al-Bakr and the Khor al-Amaya were inviting targets. With the outbreak of the prolonged Iran/Iraq, those oil terminals, Iraq's main source of getting its crude to global markets, were hit time and time again by Iranian saboteurs. Each time they were bombed, Halliburton was called in to repair the damage. Then thirty years after they were constructed, Halliburton was hired by the Pentagon to take control of the two terminals and get them into working condition in the earliest days of the US invasion.

Because the offshore terminals were such easy targets for Iranian gunboats, in 1981 Saddam signed a $2.5 million contract with Halliburton to build a feeder pipeline from the terminals out into the Gulf where the crude oil could be safely sluiced into wary tankers.

Two years later Saddam hired Halliburton once again. This time the Iraq government contracted with the Houston firm to build a long oil pipeline, that would skirt Iranian bombs, running from Basra to Yanbu on the Red Sea in Saudi Arabia. The deal was worth $2 billion. The pipeline won the approval of the US Undersecretary of State Lawrence Eagleburger, who would later land a spot on the Halliburton board.

Halliburton would continue to work on a variety of projects in Iraq right up until the first Gulf War. Indeed, a few weeks before Saddam sent his tanks into Kuwait, the Iraqi government had paid Halliburton $57 million for its work on the Mina Al-Bakr terminal and a seismographic project to help the Iraqi Oil Exploration Company enhance its exploration technology.

* * *

In 1991, Halliburton was picked by the Pentagon to put out 300 oil well fires in Kuwait, while its subsidiary, Kellogg, Brown & Root, grabbed a big contract to reconstruct the ravaged buildings of Kuwait City.

In 1992, Halliburton won a $3.9 million contract from the Pentagon in the waning days of the George H.W. Bush administration to a develop a scheme for outsourcing to private corporations much of the logistics and construction work previously handled by the US Army Corps of Engineers. The plan came to be known as LOGCAP and Halliburton soon got an additional $5 million just to flesh out the details.

The LOGCAP deal was sanctioned by none other than Secretary of Defense Dick Cheney. Under the initial contract, Halliburton established a plan for housing and feeding 20,000 troops in various hot spots around the globe. In a scenario that would be reprised in the Iraq war, Halliburton soon won the contract to implement the LOGCAP plan that the government had paid it to devise. First stop Somalia, where Halliburton set up shop providing fuel, food, laundry services and even morticians for US troops.

Then in 1995, at the same time Cheney was taking over the reins at Halliburton, the Pentagon handed the company a $550 million contract to provide logistical support for US and NATO's IFOR forces in Bosnia, Croatia and Hungary. Halliburton won another $6.3 million contract to service US troops stationed at the air base in Aviano, Italy, from which US jets launched bombing raids on Yugoslavia.

The contract was another of the notorious cost-plus deals, where Halliburton simply faxed over receipts to the Pentagon and got fully reimbursed, along with a guaranteed 1 percent profit and performance bonuses that went as high as 9 percent of the total costs. It's the contract that keeps on giving.

While Defense Secretary, Cheney defended this kind of military outsourcing as an efficient way to control spiraling costs. In reality, of course, the privatization of military logistics operations was neither cost-conscious nor particularly efficient. But it was politically expedient since it allowed civilian officials in the Pentagon to steer billions into the coffers of favored contractors, such as Halliburton, Lockheed and DynCorp. Far from being the path toward a leaner military, the General Accounting Office pegged the LOGCAP program as an adventure in "high risk government spending."

In 1997, the renewal of the LOGCAP contract was finally put up for competitive bid and, lo and behold, DynCorp snatched the golden egg of Pentagon contracts away from Halliburton. But even the Clinton administration showed mercy to the Republican firm. It cushioned the blow by awarding Halliburton a $405 million no bid deal to provide support for US troops in Bosnia. Two years later, Halliburton won the 5-year renewal of this deal, valued at $180 million.

Then in 1999 Halliburton struck gold once again in the Balkans when Clinton went to war against Serbia over Kosovo. Halliburton got a $200 million cost/plus contract to work in Kosovo. But before the year had ended that contract, covering everything from road construction, vehicle maintenance and power generation to food services, latrines and mail delivery, had generated nearly a billion dollars in revenues for Halliburton.

Of course, the deal had sublime benefits for the Clinton administration as well. By outsourcing most of the logistics work in Kosovo, the Pentagon was able to reduce its deployment by around 8,000 troops, helping Clinton and Albright to sell an unpopular war at home.

The company's Kosovo operations were rife with fraud. Halliburton charged the US Army $85.98 for each sheet of plywood it used in construction projects during Clinton's war on Serbia and its aftermath. A later probe found that the company had bought the plywood for $14 per sheet. A GAO investigation also revealed that Halliburton was billing the Pentagon for cleaning offices in US bases the Balkans four times a day. One former Halliburton employee said that the company had inflated costs on 224 different projects in Kosovo.

There were also numerous allegations of human rights violations by Halliburton workers, including mounting claims of racial discrimination and sexual harassment in the Balkans. Halliburton, which employed thousands of foreign-born subcontractors, even went so far as to operate segregated dining facilities and "Americans Only" bathrooms.

In Iraq, LOGCAP would be a recipe for rampant fraud, even for the provision of basic of services. For example, Halliburton sent the Pentagon a bill for $240 million in dining hall charges for feeding 4,700 troops each day. But a review by Pentagon auditors found that the bill was inflated by nearly 200 percent, since the company never served more than 2,500 soldiers on any single day.

The Clinton years were very good to Halliburton right to the final days. In the fall of 2000, Halliburton won a $300 million contract to build a massive prison at Guantanamo Bay in Cuba. This prison, which serves as the torture and interrogation center for Bush's wars, was originally designed to hold Haitians and, according to some sources, Cubans, in the event of the collapse of the Castro government. Two years later, Halliburton would land the contract to build the other big torture center at Bagram Air Base in Afghanistan.

* * *

In 1995, Halliburton hired Dick Cheney as its CEO. Cheney swiftly announced two goals for the company: make it the top Pentagon contractor and greatly expand its contractual relationships with foreign governments. Speaking of Halliburton's logistics work for the Pentagon in the Balkans, Cheney said, "the first person to greet our soldiers as they arrive and the last one to wave good-bye is one of our employees." Halliburton: the Alpha and Omega of Pentagon contractors.

Cheney didn't have much experience in the corporate world before becoming Halliburton's chieftain and his tenure there shows it. But Cheney was no mere figurehead. At least he didn't see himself that way. Almost immediately, Cheney began poking his fingers into the Halliburton corporate machine, with, it must be said, less than glamorous results. Old hands at Halliburton remember Cheney as arrogant and inept, a clumsy autocrat.

Of course, Cheney did deliver some morsels for the shareholders. Most notably, Halliburton's US government contracts bulged from $1.2 billion to $2.3 billion under Cheney's reign as CEO. Moreover, US government financing for Halliburton projects in the Third World soared soon after the Wizard of Wyoming took control of the company, ballooning from $100 million in the five years prior to Cheney's arrival to more than $1.5 billion during his time at the helm.

Of course, Cheney didn't wrest these deals from the feds alone. When Cheney went to Halliburton he took along some of his old pals at the Pentagon with him, most notably Admiral Joe Lopez, a top Cheney aide during the

Bush I regime. In 1999, Cheney urged Lopez to leave the Pentagon and join Halliburton. He rewarded him with the plum position of vice president for governmental operations, where he got paid nearly a million a year to court members of congress and his old chums at the Pentagon.

Another Cheney veteran worked along side Lopez to keep the government contracts flowing to Houston. Dave Gribbin, one of Cheney's closest aides, left his position as Assistant Secretary of Defense for Legislative Affairs for a slot as one of Halliburton's top lobbyists. He later served as a key figure on the Bush-Cheney transition team.

Yet, even the most forgiving analysis of the Yale dropout's leadership of Halliburton must admit that the Cheney years were marked by a series of staggering false moves and financial missteps that nearly crippled the company. Indeed, it's fair to say that the only life-support for the company during those five years was the nearly inexhaustible tide of cash coming from Halliburton's Pentagon contracts. Nearly every other venture racked up huge levels of debt and legal liabilities.

Witness Cheney's disastrous decision to acquire Dresser Industries, another oil services and engineering company. Cheney pursued a company that no one else really wanted and to compound his blunder he paid an outrageous price for it. Halliburton acquired Dresser for $7.7 billion, which proved to be at least 16 percent more than the company's actual value. In the end, Dresser's workers paid the price. In the immediate wake of the Dresser acquisition, Cheney fired 10,000 of the company's employees. Then for good measure Cheney and his gang looted Dresser's employee pension fund, in an act of corporate theft worthy of the junk bond takeover pirates of the 1980s.

There was another ugly problem with the Dresser deal that somehow escaped Cheney's notice. When Halliburton bought Dresser, it also acquired the company's enormous asbestos liability, a burden which Cheney assured company stockholders would be resolved "without material effect." It's the kind of casual lie covering a metastasizing problem that would become a Cheney signature as vice president.

At the time of the takeover, Dresser was facing more than 66,000 claims for asbestos-related health problems from its subsidiary Harrison-Walker. These claims eventually totaled something on the order of $5.5 billion, an amount that threatened to bankrupt Halliburton.

Yet, instead of firing of Cheney for this calamitous mistake, the

Halliburton board, now ornamented by the rotund figure of former Secretary of State Lawrence Eagleburger, awarded its chieftain a $1.5 million bonus for his decisive role in the doomed acquisition.

Cheney also approved a legally dubious scheme to set up dozens of offshore shell corporations designed to exploit Enron-style accounting hijinks in order to make Halliburton's bottom line seem more robust than it really was. Little wonder where he got the ideas: as he proclaimed in an advertisement, he relied on the accounting firm of Arthur Andersen that went bust in the Enron scandal. These scams didn't lead to an indictment of Halliburton executives, but the SEC did ding the company with a $7.5 million fine for its deviant accounting practices—a slap on the wrist, to be sure, but a black eye for the moral hypocrite Dick Cheney.

Evidence of the systematic accounting fraud at Halliburton during the Cheney years has now been marshaled into a class action suit by Halliburton shareholders that may even yet sink the company.

But those off-shore subsidiaries weren't merely a way of hiding money from corporate auditors, the SEC and the IRS. They were also designed to help Halliburton evade government prohibitions against US-based companies doing business with unsavory regimes.

In 1995, the State Department hit Cheney's Halliburton with a $3.8 million fine for violating the trade embargo with Libya. A similar investigation by the Department of Justice was launched in 2004 into Halliburton's operations in the second-leg of the axis of evil, Iran. Using a subsidiary corporation set up in Cheney time in the Cayman Islands, Halliburton had been doing business with the Mullahs of Iran since 1997, in flagrant violation of the US trade embargo.

In a way then, it's not surprising that Cheney's official biography, posted on the White House's website, forsakes all mention of his career as the commander-in-chief of Halliburton. But Cheney does have the quaint habit of taking this modesty too far. In 2003, he was asked about his financial ties to Halliburton. The vice president demurred, as if the very name of the company was unfamiliar to him. "I have no financial interests in Halliburton of any kind," Cheney said flatly. In fact, at that precise moment Cheney enjoyed options on 43,300 shares of Halliburton stock and was pocketing $162,392 a year in deferred compensation from the company.

* * *

On February 26, 2003, less than a month before the invasion of Iraq, a meeting was convened in the inner sanctum of the Pentagon. The purpose of this conclave was to devise a project that would come to be known as RIO or Restore Iraq Oil. Gathered around that table just down the hall from the office of Douglas Feith were ranking officials from the State Department and the US Agency for International Development (USAID), as well as the Pentagon. The meeting was chaired by Lt. General Carl Strock, a ranking official at the US Army Corps of Engineers.

The top priority on that February morning was to decide which US company would receive the juicy contract to put out the expected oil field fires and to rebuild and manage Iraq's oil infrastructure, from the wellheads to the pipelines to the big oil terminals off the coast near Basra.

In a way, this meeting in the bowels of the Pentagon was all for show, a kind of mating ritual between the government and its favorite contractor. There was little doubt about who was going to land the deal. So little doubt, in fact, that a Halliburton executive had been invited to attend the secret conclave.

Indeed, a few months earlier Halliburton had already been paid $1.9 million to draft a plan for how to implement RIO. The company had essentially written its own job description, a scenario that would make that initial payment mushroom into the billions.

There were several other companies that could have done the job that was given to Halliburton. Fluor-Daniel, Parsons and GSM Services were all just as qualified for the task. Yet, none of these firms were invited to submit a bid or a plan of action. Instead, Lt. General Strock steered the cost-plus contract into Halliburton's hands without the faintest whiff of competition. When his own contract auditors objected, Strock sought to silence them by saying he had determined that "the compelling emergency" in Iraq dictated swift and unilateral action.

Of course, this decision had been set in motion much earlier and by figures far loftier in the power hierarchy of the Bush administration than lowly Lt. General Strock from the bureaucratic outback of the Corps of Engineers.

An Army Corps of Engineers email, uncovered by *Time* magazine, disclosed that the initial decision to have Halliburton draft the RIO plan had been "coordinated" with the office of Vice President Dick Cheney. Over the course of the fall of 2002 and the early winter of 2003, Halliburton executives met on several occasions with Cheney's staff at the White House and at the Pentagon.

At an October 2002 meeting, Michael Mobbs, an assistant to Undersecretary of Defense Douglas Feith, parlayed with Cheney's chief of staff Lewis "Scooter" Libby to personally deliver the jubilant news that Halliburton had gotten the RIO planning contract.

Cheney, as is his natural inclination, continues to deny any involvement, direct or implicit, in the Pentagon deals that have sent billions in no bid contracts to his former company, at the very same time Halliburton continued to sweeten his bank accounts with more than $140,000 a year.

There was another curious hitch to the Halliburton RIO deal. Instead of being administered by Douglas Feith's office at the Pentagon (as were almost all of the other Iraq contracts), the Halliburton RIO contract was pawned off on the Corps of Engineers, a remote outpost of the Pentagon known, to the extent that it is known at all, for the management of locks and dams on American rivers.

Then an unexpected thing happened. Despite a lot of baiting from the US military and the most bellicose voices of in Bush administration, Saddam didn't ignite the Basra oil fields.

For a moment, it looked as if Halliburton might be left out in the cold. But no. As if they were rerouting a river in the Smoky Mountains, the quick-fix generals at the Corps of Engineers simply reconfigured the terms of the Halliburton contract, changing it from putting out oil well fires to hauling fuel for US military operations.

* * *

When it came time to select a space for its corporate offices to oversee the new Iraq contracts, Halliburton decided not to bunker down inside the Green Zone in Baghdad. Instead, the company opted for posh offices at the Khalifa resort on the beaches of the Persian Gulf a few miles from Kuwait City. The spot was sunny, safe and expensive. Halliburton spent more than $73 million a year just to house its executives in Kuwait—that's $73 million a year billed to the Pentagon, plus a two percent profit tacked on for good measure.

It turns out that there wasn't much for these managers from Houston to manage. That's because nearly all of Halliburton's work in Iraq was farmed out to subcontractors. The tricky part was trying to find the right subcontractor. Not necessarily the company that would do the best job, but the one that would charge the most for the work, since Halliburton's built-in profits came as a fixed percentage of the costs. The higher the costs, the bigger the profits.

Several of the subcontracts in Iraq were doled out accompanied by the judicious application of cash bribes. Even here Halliburton benefited. As Halliburton executives and managers dispensed and received millions in kickbacks, the company itself simply wrote the dispensations directly onto the invoices submitted by the subcontractors. Often these bills exceeded the true costs of the projects by 300 or even 400 percent—with Halliburton snagging a built-in profit from the bribe-bloated contracts.

Apparently, Halliburton views these kickbacks and bribes as a kind of a priori cost of doing business across the globe. A pungent example: A team of French investigators unearthed a robust Swiss bank account harboring $5 million, which reportedly derived from bribes involving Halliburton contracts in Nigeria. In June 2004, the company eased out Jack Shanley, chairman of its Kellogg, Brown & Root subsidiary, for having received "improper benefits" from this very account.

A Department of Justice investigation charged that Halliburton bribed the Nigerian officials in order to win a billion-dollar construction contract. Halliburton later discreetly disclosed that it may have paid upwards of $180 million in bribes.

A parallel probe was launched by the Securities and Exchange Commission into an admission by Halliburton that one of its managers slipped $2.4 million into the pockets of another Nigerian official in order to secure illegal tax-breaks for its business in the impoverished African nation.

* * *

In southern Iraq, much of Halliburton's logistics work ended up in the hands of a Kuwaiti firm called La Nouvelle, which handled meals, sanitation facilities and laundry. Before La Nouvelle picked up the subcontract to do the laundry at a US military base near Basra, the monthly cleaning bill had averaged around $62,000. A few months after La Nouvelle took over, the tab soared to $1.2 million a month. La Nouvelle billed $108 for each 15-pound bag of laundry at this base, $80 a bag more than the very same company charged at another base.

Pentagon auditors concluded that La Nouvelle was overbilling for its laundry services alone by at least $1 million a month, with Halliburton enjoying its slice of the profits without even having had to break a sweat. They were quite literally laundering money.

While millions were splurged on opulent accommodations for its executives, bribes and kickbacks and scandalously inflated laundry bills, Halliburton skimped on the maintenance of its vehicles, which were transporting fuel and supplies on the dangerous desert roads from Kuwait to the US bases in Iraq. Only six months into the occupation of Iraq, Halliburton's fleets of trucks began to breakdown due to lack of spare parts and shoddy upkeep. The result was not just a slow down in the delivery of fuel and military supplies, but a greatly enhanced risk to the lives of Halliburton's drivers, who were becoming easily identifiable targets for the growing insurgency in Iraq. By the end of March 2005, more than 65 Halliburton employees had been killed in Iraq and more than 200 injured— the most of any private contractor in the war zone.

Much of the fuel those Halliburton drivers were carrying into Iraq came courtesy of a company called Altanmia, a Kuwait firm with cozy ties to the country's royal family.

Altanmia charged Halliburton a hefty $2.65 per gallon, roughly the price charged at the pump in Washington, D.C. But this rate was nearly three times the 97 cents per gallon that the Iraqi Oil State Marketing Organization was paying to buy oil from Jordan and Turkey.

Halliburton never uttered the meekest protest about the grossly inflated fuel prices. With good reason. It simply passed the bills on to the Pentagon and cashed its reimbursement checks, complete with the 4 percent government gratuity.

In the first six months of the war, Pentagon auditors estimated that Halliburton had overcharged the US Treasury by at least $61 million for its fuel deliveries.

Ironically, Altanmia executives griped that they were forced to charge that hefty amount in order to cover the kickbacks and bribes they were forced to pay to Halliburton officials in order to secure the contract. In an email documenting a meeting between Altanmia executives and officials at the US embassy in Kuwait City an Altanmia manager is quoted as saying that "anyone visiting their [i.e., Halliburton's] seaside villas at the Kuwaiti Hilton who offers to provide their services will be asked for a bribe."

When the price gouging by Altanmia began to draw the attention of Pentagon auditors, the US Army Corps of Engineers, which was responsible for overseeing the implementation of the contracts, came up with an elegant solution. It informed Halliburton that the company no longer had to submit a public record of the fuel purchases.

This bizarre and secret waiver of standard Pentagon accounting practices was signed by the Corps' top contracting officer, Gordon A. Sumner, on December 19, 2003—stymieing the pending congressional and Pentagon investigations in contract fraud by the company.

* * *

In February 2005, the State Department finally weighed in with a damning report on Halliburton's work to rehabilitate the oil fields in southern Iraq. The unusually frank assessment accused Halliburton of undocumented cost overruns totaling tens of millions of dollars and generally "poor performance."

The State Department report pointed out that Iraqi oil production at the beginning of 2005 was lower than it had been during the previous fall. The situation had gotten so dire that the US Embassy in Baghdad, then under the command of John Negroponte, issued what is known as a "Cure Notice," a stark warning to Halliburton executives that if the company's performance didn't improve the $1.2 billion contract would be terminated.

Negroponte followed up his threat by recruiting the Parsons Corporation, Halliburton's archrival, to "execute some of the remaining work in the south." Parsons had previously been awarded the $800 million contract to repair and manage the oil fields around Kirkuk in northern Iraq.

As far as the Pentagon was concerned all of this was written off to carping from the sidelines by busy-bodies and tightwads at the State Department. In the spring of 2005, the Bush administration over-ruled its own auditors and awarded Halliburton a $9.4 million bonus for its work in Afghanistan and Kuwait, operations which the Pentagon described as "excellent."

With the bulk of the Pentagon contracts cashed in and government investigators closing in on all fronts, Halliburton placed Kellogg, Brown & Root on the market, looking to squeeze one final payout from its golden goose.

Now who says crime doesn't pay?

June, 2005

Fourteen

Lockheed and Loaded

The Company that Runs the Empire

Lockheed is headquartered in the Bethesda, Maryland. No, the defense titan doesn't have a bomb-making factory in this toney Beltway suburb. But as the nation's top weapons contractor, it migrated to DC from southern California because that's where the money is. And Lockheed rakes it in from the federal treasury at the rate of $65 million every single day of the year.

From nuclear missiles to fighter planes, software code to spy satellites, the Patriot missile to Star Wars, Lockheed has come to dominate the weapons market in a way that the Standard Oil Company used to hold sway over the nation's petroleum supplies, before being broken up for being a monopoly. And it all happened with the help of the federal government, which steered lucrative no bid contracts Lockheed's way, enacted tax breaks that encouraged Lockheed's merger and acquisition frenzy in the 1980s and 1990s and turned a blind eye to the company's criminal rap sheet, ripe with indiscretions ranging from bribery to contract fraud.

Now Lockheed stands almost alone. It not only serves as an agent of US foreign policy, from the Pentagon to the CIA; it also helps shape it. "We are deployed entirely in developing daunting technology," Lockheed's new CEO Robert J. Stevens told *New York Times* reporter Tim Weiner. "That requires thinking through the policy dimensions of national security as well as technological dimensions."

Like many defense industry executives, Stevens is a former military man who cashed in his Pentagon career for a lucrative position in the private sector. The stern-jawed Stevens served in the Marines and later taught at the Pentagon's Defense Systems Management College, an institution which offers graduate level seminars in how to design billion dollar weapons deals. From the Marines, Stevens landed first at Loral, the defense satellite company. Then in 1993 he went to work at Lockheed, heading its "Corporate Strategic Development Program". There Stevens wrote the game plan for how Lockheed would soar past Boeing, General Dynamics, Northrop Grumman and the others, as the top recipient of Pentagon largesse.

The plan was as simple as it proved profitable. Instead of risking the competition of the marketplace, Lockheed, under Stevens' scheme, would target the easy money: federal contracts. The strategy was also straightforward: flood the congress with PAC money to get and keep grateful and obedient members in power. Those friendly members of congress would also be surrounded by squads of lobbyists to develop and write legislation and insert Lockheed-friendly line items into the bloated appropriations bills that fund the government. It also called for seeding the Pentagon and the White House with Lockheed loyalists, many of whom formerly worked for the company.

"We need to be politically aware and astute," said Stevens. "We need to work with the congress. We need to work with the executive branch. We need to say: we think this is feasible, we think this is possible. We think we have invented a new approach."

The scheme succeeded brilliantly. By the end of the 1990s, Lockheed had made the transition from an airplane manufacturer with defense contracts to a kind of privatized supplier for nearly every Pentagon weapons scheme, from the F-22 fighter to the Pentagon's internet system. Then 9/11 happened and the federal floodgates for spending on national security, airline safety and war making opened wide and haven't closed. Lockheed has been the prime beneficiary of this gusher of federal money.

Since September 2001, the Pentagon's weapons procurement program has soared by more than $20 billion, from $60 billion to $81 billion in 2004. Lockheed's revenues over the same time period jumped by a similar 30 percent. And, despite the recession and slumping Dow, the company's stock tripled in value.

Almost all of this profiteering came courtesy of the federal treasury. More than 80 percent of Lockheed's revenue derives directly from federal government contracts. And most of the rest comes from foreign military sales to Israel, Saudi Arabia, South Korea and Chile. Israel alone spends $1.8 billion a year on planes and missile systems purchased from Lockheed. Lockheed sells its weaponry, from F-16 fighters to surveillance software, to more than 40 nations. "We're looking at world domination of the market," gloated Bob Elrod, a senior executive in Lockheed's fighter plane division.

And there's little risk involved. Nearly all of these sales are guaranteed by the US government.

After 9/11, Bush tapped Lockheed's Stevens to lead his presidential commission on the Future of the US Aerospace Industry, a body which, not surprisingly, wasted little time pounding home the importance of sluicing even more federal dollars in the form of defense and air traffic control contracts to companies such as Lockheed.

But Stevens' position was just the icing on a very sweet cake. Former Lockheed executives and lobbyists toil every day on behalf of the defense giant from the inside the administration and the Pentagon. At the very top of the list is Steven J. Hadley, recently tapped to replace Condoleezza Rice as Bush's National Security Advisor. Prior to joining the Bush administration, Hadley represented Lockheed at the giant DC law firm of Shea and Gardner. Other Lockheed executives have been appointed to the Defense Policy Board and the Homeland Security Advisory Council. Bush's Transportation Secretary, Norman Mineta, and Otto Reich, the former deputy Secretary of State for the Western Hemisphere, both once worked as Lockheed lobbyists.

But the revolving door swings both ways for Lockheed. On its corporate board reposes E.C. Aldridge, Jr. Before retiring from the Defense Department, Aldridge served as the head of the Pentagon's weapon procurement program and signed the contracts with Lockheed to build the F-22, the world's most expensive airplane.

When insiders don't get you everything you need, there's always political bribery. In the US, politicians who serve Lockheed's interests get annual dispensations of corporate swill courtesy of the company's mammoth political action committee. Each year Lockheed's corporate PAC doles out more than $1 million, mainly to members of the crucial defense and appropriations committees.

Overseas, Lockheed has often resorted to a direct bribe of government officials. In the 1970s, Lockheed famously handed out $12.5 million in bribes to Japanese officials (and organized crime figures) to secure the sale of 21 Tristar aircraft to Nippon Airlines. The ensuing scandal brought down Japanese Prime Minister Kakuei Tanaka, who was convicted of being on the receiving end of Lockheed's payola. Even though the imbroglio lead the enactment of the Foreign Corrupt Practices Act in 1977 which set stiff penalties for bribery, Carl Kochian, Lockheed's CEO at the time, defended the practice of handing out covert cash inducements as a cost-effective way of securing billions in contracts for the company. Bribery was just a cost of doing big business.

And indeed the Corrupt Practices Act didn't deter Lockheed from handing out financial incentives to foreign officials to speed things along. In the 1990s, Lockheed admitted to stuffing the pockets of an Egyptian official with $1.2 million dollars in order to grease the sale of three Lockheed-made C-130 transport planes to the Egyptian military.

The clunky old C-130 Hercules continues to bring millions to Lockheed, which sells the cargo plane to Jordan, Egypt and Israel. But the biggest profits continue to derive from sales to the Pentagon, even though the latest model of the transport has been plagued with operational problems and cost overruns. Of course, in the funhouse economics of defense contracts "cost over-runs" simply mean more millions in taxpayer money going into the accounts of the very defense contractors that performed the untimely or shoddy work in the first place.

Since 1999, the Air Force has purchased 50 of the new C-130J prop planes from Lockheed. But none of these planes have performed well enough to allow the Air Force to put them into service. An audit of the C-130 contract by the Inspector General of the Air Force revealed a host of problems with the new plane that had been gilded over by Lockheed and Pentagon weapons buyers.

One of the biggest problems with the plane is an ineptly designed propeller system that keeps the C-130 from being flown in bad weather. The C-130J is powered by six propellers covered in composite material that becomes pitted or even dissolves under sleet, hail or even heavy rain. Ironically, many of the first batch of planes were delivered to an Air Force reserve unit in Biloxi, Mississippi, where they were supposed to function as "Hurricane Hunters," plying through thunderstorms and heavy winds in search of the eye of the storm. The planes proved useless for the task. As a result, most of the C-130Js have been used only for pilot training.

"The government fielded C-130J aircraft that cannot perform their intended mission, which forces the users to incur additional operations and maintenance costs to operate and maintain older C-130 mission-capable aircraft because the C-130J aircraft can be used only for training," the IG audit concluded.

Nevertheless, the Air Force paid Lockheed 99 percent of the contract price for the useless planes.

"This is yet another sad chapter in the history of bad Pentagon weapons systems acquisitions," said Eric Miller, a senior Defense Investigator at the Project on Government Oversight. "For years, the Air Force has known it was paying too much for an aircraft that doesn't do what it's supposed to. Yet it has turned a blind eye. The aircrews who have to fly these aircraft should be very angry. They've been betrayed by the very government that should be ensuring that the weapons they receive are safe and effective."

The profits from the C-130 are a mere pittance compared to what Lockheed stands to make from its contracts to produce the two costliest airplanes ever envisioned: the Joint Strike Fighter and the F-22 Raptor.

The Joint Strike Fighter, also known as the F-35, is slated to replace the venerable F-16. Even though the initial designs for the F-35 proved faulty (there continue to be intractable problems with the weight of the plane), the Pentagon, under prodding from influential members of Congress, awarded the Lockheed a $200 billion contract to build nearly 2,000 of the still unairworthy planes. Lockheed plans to sell another 2,500 planes at a sticker price of $38 million apiece to other nations, starting with Great Britain. Once again, most of these sales will be underwritten by US government loans.

The F-35 contract was awarded on October 16, 2001. Already, costs have soared by $45 billion over the initial estimate with no end in sight.

But the F-22 Raptor stands in a class of its own. With a unit price of more than $300 million per plane, the Raptor is the most expensive fighter jet ever designed. One congressional staffer dubbed it, "Tiffany's on wings." Conceived in the 1980s to penetrate deep into the airspace of the Soviet Union, the F-22 has no function these days, except to keep a slate of defense contractors in business, from Lockheed, which runs the project, to Boeing which designed the wings to Pratt-Whitney which designed the huge jet engines.

The F-22 was supposed to be operational a decade ago. But the latest incarnation of the plane continues to suffer severe problems in fight testing. Its onboard computer system is mired with glitches and its Stealth features haven't prevented the plane from popping up "like a fat strawberry" on radar. Even worse, several test pilots have gotten dizzy to the point of nearly passing out while trying to put the fighter through evasive maneuvers at high altitudes.

Even so, the doomed project moves forward, consuming millions every week, and no one with the power to do so seems to show the slightest inclination to pull the plug.

* * *

By one account, Lockheed garners $228 in federal tax money from every household in the US each year. But when it comes time to paying taxes Lockheed pleads poverty. By taking advantage of a bevy of designer loopholes, Lockheed's legion of accountants has reduced the corporation's annual tax liability to a mere 7 percent of its net income. By comparison, the average federal tax rate for individuals in the US is around 25 percent.

Of course, these kinds of special dispensations don't come cheaply. Lockheed spends more money lobbying congress than any other defense contractor. In 2004, a banner year for the company, it spent nearly $10 million on more than 100 lobbyists to prowl the halls of congress, keeping tabs on appropriations bills, oversight hearings and tax committees. Over the past five years, only Philip Morris and GE spent more money lobbying congress.

With Lockheed, it's sometimes difficult to discern whether it's taking advantage of US foreign policy or shaping it. Take the Iraq war. Lockheed's former vice-president, Bruce Jackson, headed an ad hoc group called the Committee for the Liberation of Iraq. This coven of corporate executives, think tank gurus and retired generals includes such war-mongering luminaries as Richard Perle, Jeane Kirkpatrick, Gen. Wayne Downing and former CIA director James Woolsey. The Washington Post reported that group's goal was to "promote regional peace, political freedom and international security through replacement of the Saddam Hussein regime with a democratic government that respects the rights of the Iraqi people and ceases to threaten the community of nations."

This supposedly independent body seems to have gotten its marching orders from inside the Bush White House. Jackson and others met repeatedly with Karl Rove and Steven Hadley, Condoleezza Rice's number two at the National Security Council and a former Lockheed lobbyist. The group eventually got a face-to-face meeting with the dark lord himself, Dick Cheney. After meeting with White House functionaries, members of the Committee would fan out on cable news shows and talk radio to inflame the fever for war against Saddam.

Jackson has long enjoyed close ties to the Bush inner circle. In 2000, he chaired the Republican Party's platform committee on National Security and Foreign Policy and served as a top advisor to the Bush campaign. Naturally, the platform statement ended up reading like catalogue of Lockheed weapons systems. At the top of the list, the RNC platform pledged to revive and make operational the $80 billion Missile Defense program supervised by Lockheed.

In 2002, the Bush administration called on Jackson to help drum up support in Eastern Europe for the war on Iraq. When Poland and Hungary came on board, Jackson actually drafted their letter supporting an invasion of Iraq. His company was swiftly rewarded for his efforts. In 2003, Poland purchased 50 of Lockheed's F-16 fighters for $3.5 billion. The sale was underwritten by a $3.8 billion loan from the Bush administration.

Lockheed also made out quite nicely from the Iraq war itself. It's F-117 Stealth fighters inaugurated the start of the war with the "Shock and Awe" bombing of Baghdad. Later, the Pentagon stepped up orders of Lockheed's PAC 3 Patriot missile. The missile batteries, designed for use against SCUD missiles that Iraq no longer possessed, sell for $91 million per unit.

After the toppling of Saddam, Lockheed executives saw an opportunity to gobble up one of the big private contractors doing business in Iraq, Titan Corporation. The San Diego-based company was awarded a $10 million contract to provide translators for the Pentagon in Iraq. Two of those translators, Adel Nakhl and John Israel, were later accused of being involved in the torture of Iraqi prisoners at Abu Ghraib prison. Titan translators, who are paid upwards of $107,000 a year, were also implicated in a scandal at Guantanamo prison.

Like Lockheed, after 9/11 Titan jettisoned almost all of its commercial operations and began to focus entirely on government work. By 2003, 99 percent of its $1.8 billion in corporate income came courtesy of government contracts. The firm also went on a buying spree of other smaller defense contractors. Since 2001, Titan gobbled up ten other defense-related companies. The most lucrative acquisition proved to be BMG, Inc., a Reston, Virginia based company that specializes in information collection and analysis for the Pentagon and the CIA. BMG alone held Pentagon contracts worth $650 million.

The abuse scandals didn't deter Lockheed from pursuing Titan. Indeed, Christopher Kubasik, Lockheed's chief financial officer, told the *Los Angeles Times* that the torture allegations "were not significant to our strategic decision."

The merger was later delayed for other reasons by the Justice

Department, which was looking into allegations that Titan executives and subsidiaries paid bribes to government officials in Africa, Asia and Europe in order to win contracts—a method of doing business that Lockheed executives must have admired.

Titan, which was formed amid the Reagan defense build up of the early 1980s, saw itself as a new kind of defense contractor, a weapons company that didn't make weapons. Instead of building missiles or planes, Titan concentrated on developing software and communication packages for Pentagon programs. Its first big contract was for the development of a communications package for the guidance system of the Minuteman missile. Since then Titan has become a major player in the lucrative information technology market.

In recent years, Lockheed has begun to aggressively pursue the same types of "soft defense" programs. In the past decade, Lockheed's Information Technology sales have increased by more than four hundred percent. The bonanza began during the Clinton administration, when Al Gore's "reinventing government" scheme auctioned off most of the data-management tasks of the federal government to the private sector. Now nearly 90 percent of the federal government's Information Technology has been privatized, most of it to Lockheed, which is not only the nation's top arms contractor but also its top data-management supplier.

This opened vast new terrains of the government to conquest by Lockheed. It now enjoys contracts with the Department of Health and Human Services, Department of Energy and EPA. Lockheed also just corralled a $550 million contract to take over the Social Security Administration's database. The privatization of Social Security has already begun.

But even in the IT sector, the big bucks are to be made in the burgeoning surveillance and Homeland Security business. Lockheed now runs the FBI's archaic computer system, which took some much deserved heat for letting the 9/11 hijackers slip through its net without detection. It also won the $90 million contract to manage the top secret computer network for the Department of Homeland Security, a system that is supposed to function as a kind of "deep web", linking the systems of the FBI, CIA and Pentagon.

All of this is a precursor to even bigger plans hatched by Lockheed and its pals in the Pentagon to develop an all-encompassing spying system called the Global Information Grid, an internet system that is meant to feed real time tracking information on terrorist suspects directly into automated weapons systems, manufactured, naturally, by Lockheed.

"We want to know what's going on anytime, any place on the planet," pronounced Lorraine Martin, Lockheed's vice-president for Command, Control and Communications Systems. And eliminate them, naturally.

On the battlefield of defense contractors, Lockheed has now achieved full-spectrum dominance.

May, 2005

Fifteen

Straight to Bechtel

"More Powerful Than the US Army"

O n the second anniversary of the invasion of Iraq, Bechtel, the gargantuan global construction firm based in San Francisco, issued its revenue numbers for 2004. While the situation continued to deteriorate for the US military forces in Iraq, Bechtel reported more fragrant news.

Although the privately-owned company doesn't disclose its profits, Bechtel did announce that its income was soaring to new heights not seen since the 1960s when the company was damming some of the world's most glorious canyons, building some of the most dangerous nuclear plants and constructing military bases for the staging of the war on Vietnam.

For the year 2004, Bechtel brought in more than $17.4 billion, a record haul for the company. That makes two record years in a row. Last year Bechtel chalked up more than $17 billion for the first time. Both records were all the more impressive given the senescent economy.

Much of that robust income stream is coming from its operations in Iraq, where Bechtel is the king of contractors. A few days after the war began, the US Agency for International Development handed Bechtel a $680 million contract for the reconstruction of Iraq infrastructure, a by-invitation-only deal awarded in a secret process. That number has been jacked up twice and now totals more than $1.8 billion and may eventually reach as much as $50 billion.

Under the terms of the deal, Bechtel got $515 million to rebuild Iraq's power generating stations; $33 million for rebuilding roads and railroads; $44 million to dredge the seaport at Umm Qasr; $45 million to rehab the Iraqi telephone network, covering 240,000 phone lines; $52 million for repair of the Baghdad airport; $208 million to rebuild sewage and water treatment plants; and $53 million for the reconstruction of Iraqi schools. All courtesy of US tax dollars and Iraqi oil revenues.

For this initial round of contracts alone, Bechtel was also guaranteed another $80 million for company profits.

The obliteration of Iraq's civic buildings, roads and power plants proved to be a billion-dollar bonanza for Bechtel. To build you must first destroy.

The company won't say how much of its revenue comes from its Iraq contracts, but it probably amounts to about 10 percent of the total haul. "Iraq's a big job for us," says Jude Laspa, Bechtel's executive vice-president. "But not the biggest."

True enough. But most of Bechtel's earnings come with an ironclad guarantee of a profit, a guarantee backed by the federal government. Indeed, more than half of Bechtel's revenues come courtesy of the government, many of the deals awarded without competitive bidding and on a cost-plus basis.

Moreover, when the Bechtel does non-US government business in the Third World, it often enjoys the financial backing of the US in the form of subsidized loans from the Export-Import Bank and insurance from the Overseas Private Investment Corporation.

"Our business is a lumpy business," said Laspa. "Some projects come through that are a billion, some are a mere $200 million." (Note the sly emphasis on "mere.")

One of Bechtel's biggest non-Iraq "lumps" is a $5 billion deal to take over the management of the Hanford Nuclear Reservation, the most radioactive landscape in the Western Hemisphere. The contract at Hanford, where the US government once made plutonium for hydrogen bombs, will provide Bechtel with a steady stream of income over the next five to ten years, cleaning up radioactive debris and chemical waste, and prepping the site for what may become a new generation of nuclear weapons production.

Bechtel also won the choice contract to manage the Nevada Test Site, another multi-billion dollar deal. Bechtel is supposed to rehab the test site, turn part of it into a bizarre tourist destination and, according to some insiders, prepare the grounds for another round of nuclear testing.

Rarely does a big Pentagon construction project surface that doesn't have a role set aside especially for Bechtel. Thus it should surprise no one that Bechtel has gotten a piece of the biggest boondoggle of our time, the $100 billion Ballistic Missile Defense project, AKA Star Wars. In a joint venture with Lockheed, Bechtel got a contract to build and manage the Ballistic Missile Defense test site in the Marshall Islands. Just another juicy lump in the gravy train.

* * *

The origins of the world's largest engineering firm date to 1898, when Oakland businessman Warren Bechtel won a contract to level the grade for railroad beds across California and Oklahoma, using mules and Chinese and prison laborers. The rise of the company is vividly sketched in Leon McCartney's excellent history, *Friends in High Places: the Bechtel Story.*

In 1930, Bechtel joined forces with another Bay Area tycoon, Harry Kaiser, to Boulder Canyon with Hoover Dam, which clogged the Colorado River for 200 miles. At the time this curved monstrosity was billed as the largest construction project since the building of the Great Pyramid at Giza.

In the 1940s, with World War II in full-throttle, Stephen Bechtel, son of Warren Bechtel, teamed up with his college roommate John A. McCone. The Bechtel-McCone partnership specialized in making billions from the war through shipbuilding and military base construction projects. McCone also introduced Bechtel to the lucrative oil services business, an enterprise for all seasons but one which blooms with special vigor during times of war. Soon Bechtel was building oil refineries and pipelines across the world, including a secret Alaska pipeline as part of a project for the War Department. Thirty years later, Bechtel would be the lead contractor for the big Trans-Alaska Pipeline, which sluices crude oil from Prudhoe Bay to the port of Valdez.

Blazing a course that so many future Bechtel executives would canter down, McCone, one of the more sinister characters of the 20th century, left Bechtel for Washington, where he became head of the Atomic Energy Commission and one of the central figures in the instigation of the Cold War. McCone soon introduced his new friend, Allen Dulles, the nation's top spy, to his old partner in the Bay Area, Stephen Bechtel.

Dulles and Bechtel became fast friends and golfing buddies. While slicing drives at Congressional Country Club and shanking irons into the Pacific at Pebble Beach, the two men would discuss the clandestine opportunities for a privately-owned firm like Bechtel in Dulles's shadow world. It is from Dulles that the Bechtel family acquired its obsession with secrecy. Long before the advent of Hollywood stalkers and anarchist pie throwers, the Bechtel family and its top executives traveled with bodyguards. The family has even gone so far as to petition a California court to shield their voter registration cards from public inspection.

More often than not, the talk between Dulles and Bechtel turned to oil and the Middle East. Under Dulles's guidance, Bechtel stepped up its operations in the Persian Gulf region, especially in Saudi Arabia. Bechtel engineered the oil infrastructure for the Standard Oil Company's burgeoning empire in Saudi Arabia, building pipelines, refineries, highways and ports. When Standard Oil's Aramco partnership in Saudi Arabia was nationalized, Bechtel didn't miss a beat. Instead, the company inaugurated a profitable new relationship with the Saudi royal family and went right to work building airports, military bases and an 850-mile long pipeline from Saudi Arabia to Jordan.

Somewhere along the line, the Bechtels encountered Saudi Arabia's largest construction company, which is also a family-run empire, called Bin Laden Construction. Founded by Osama's father, Mohammed Bin Laden, the Bin Laden firm worked on dozens of joint projects with the Bechtel Corporation, which had already perfected the art of subcontracting out hard labor to low-paid workers in the Third World. Outsourcing is a strategy that Bechtel is using in Iraq today, where 92 percent of its work there is subcontracted out to desperate Iraqis. The Bin Ladens and Bechtels remain close to this day. Indeed, the Bin Laden family owns a $10 million stake in the Fremont Group, the Bechtel Corporation's investment subsidiary. Moreover, the BinLaden Group is a doing work on Bechtel's biggest contract, the $20 billion deal with Saudi government to excavate two new ports, in what has been called the most expensive construction project in world history. Well, since the last big Bechtel project.

From Saudi Arabia, Bechtel soon extended its reach in the Middle East to Bahrain, Kuwait, Iraq and Iran. Not all of these countries were as gracious as the Saudi's when American oil companies and their associated firms like Bechtel came calling to drill into their sands. For example, following the 1958 coup in Iraq, one of Bechtel's top executives, George Colley, Jr., was yanked from his car and stoned to death on a Baghdad street, in a scene that eerily foreshadows the abductions and assassinations of US contractors in Iraq today. Of course, Bechtel wouldn't let the killing of an executive stand in the way of making money. After a more compliant regime took control of Baghdad, Bechtel was back, building a pipeline for the Iraq Petroleum Company running from Kirkuk to the Syrian port of Baniyas and helping Saddam himself construct the Bekme hydropower dam near the Iraq border with Turkey. As we shall see, this wasn't Bechtel's only dalliance with the

Beast of Baghdad.

When Iran antagonized US oil companies and the CIA by nationalizing their oil reserves, Allen Dulles and Kermit Roosevelt sought and received Bechtel's assistance in the CIA run coup that overthrew Mossadegh and installed the Shah. Bechtel provided a similar service in 1965 when the CIA instigated the bloody coup that toppled President Sukarno of oil-rich Indonesia and put into place the corrupt and iron-fisted regime of General Suharto.

After Dulles was eased out of the CIA, John F. Kennedy picked Bechtel's old hand, John McCone, to replace him as the nation's top intelligence spook and Stephen Bechtel himself became the CIA's emissary to the Business Council. The Agency and the company have rarely pursued separate interests since then.

* * *

When it comes to governmental relations, Bechtel goes both ways: it penetrates the government and the government penetrates it. Over the past forty years, Bechtel has trawled for executives from the Pentagon, State Department, Interior Department, World Bank, and the West Wing of the White House. It's executives have included Robert Hollingsworth, the former head of the Atomic Energy Commission; Parker T. Hart, former ambassador to Saudi Arabia; Rear Admiral John G. Dillon, head of the Pentagon's construction office; former Senator J. Bennett Johnston, the Louisiana Democrat and oil industry legislative enforcer, was named to the board of Nexant, a Bechtel subsidiary; and Richard Helms, former director of the CIA.

These days Bechtel's top recruit from DC is its executive Vice-President Jack Sheehan. Sheehan, a four-star general who served as head of the Atlantic Command and as NATO supreme, oversees Bechtel's chemical and oil operations, with a particular focus, naturally, on the opportunities in the Middle East and Central Asia. Sheehan has some experience there as well. In the late 1990s, Bill Clinton called upon Sheehan to serve as his special adviser to Central Asia, where he scrutinized oil reserves and pipeline routes in far off places like Turkmenistan and Azerbaijan. Politically, Sheehan is ambidextrous, lending his talents with equal vigor to Democrats and Republicans. Soon after Bush's installation as president, the president and Donald Rumsfeld recruited Sheehan to serve on the influential Defense Policy Board, once commanded by ultra-hawk Richard Perle.

Under the right circumstances, Bechtel is more than willing to loan out some of its corporate stars to the feds—on a temporary basis, of course. In 2003, President Bush named Riley Bechtel, the company's current CEO, to serve on the Export Council, a team of corporate chieftains and economists that sets trade policy, a policy which seems to focus more on exporting jobs than products.

The former head of Bechtel's energy division, Ross Connolly, was named by Bush as the vice president of the Overseas Private Investment Corporation (OPIC). OPIC provides financial backing and underwrites insurance for US companies doing business in places where the indigenous population is often less than thrilled about their presence and economic pursuits, which often takes the unpleasant form of toxic gold mines, power plants, chemical factories, pipelines or hydro dams. Needless to say, Bechtel is a frequent recipient of OPIC's largesse.

Similarly, Bechtel has shrewdly seeded with its executives the upper layers of the Export-Import Bank, which provides government loan guarantees for US companies doing business overseas. In August of 2002, Clinton named Daniel Chao, vice president of Bechtel Holdings, to a coveted slot on the bank's advisory committee. The Ex-Im Bank, which has provided tens of millions in loan guarantees for Bechtel over the years, was once headed by John L. Moore, a former VP at the company, and Stephen Bechtel himself once adorned its advisory board.

It was back in Reagan time, however, when Bechtel seem to reach an apogee of influence over the operations of the federal government. For Defense Secretary, Reagan picked Caspar Weinberger, Bechtel's longtime general counsel. Over at Langley, Reagan enthroned William Casey as director of the Central Intelligence Agency. Casey had been on retainer with Bechtel as a special consultant for many years.

Then there was George Shultz, Reagan's Secretary of State. Prior to joining the Reagan administration, Shultz served as president of Bechtel, where one of the big projects on the drawing board was a long-desired pipeline from Iraq to Jordan.

After the Iranian revolution, Bechtel had been booted from Iran by the Ayatollah. To counter this ungracious exile, Bechtel warmed once again to its old friends in Iraq, then engaged in a bloody war with Iran.

From his desk at Foggy Bottom, Shultz summoned his old pal Donald Rumsfeld for a covert assignment. He appointed Rummy his special envoy to Saddam Hussein and sent him to Iraq in 1983 with the task of convincing the Iraqi dictator to back Bechtel's plan for a pipeline across Iraq to Aqaba in Jordan.

Rumsfeld's trips to Baghdad would prove fateful assignations for all concerned. The fallout would even lead to the appointment of a special prosecutor tasked with looking into the role Attorney General Edwin Meese played in the affair.

Rumsfeld landed in Baghdad in December 1983, where he held a series of meetings with Saddam and Tariq Aziz, the Deputy Prime Minister. This secret conclave occurred at one of the bloodiest moments of the Iran/Iraq war, a war the US tacitly backed as a way to destabilize the revolutionary mullahs of Iran. By this time, it was well known by US intelligence that Saddam had used poison gas against Iranian troops, killing and maiming thousands.

Two decades later, as the Bush administration ramped up the war rhetoric against Saddam, Rumsfeld would claim that his journey to Baghdad was a heroic and virtuous mission, where he chastised the Iraqi strongman to his face for committing crimes against humanity.

Saddam, however, had the foresight to videotape several of the parlays. One infamous clip shows a deferential Rumsfeld smiling and shaking the hand of the Tiger of Tikrit. Later Rumsfeld, like a witness before the Iran/contra committee, would claim he had no clear recollection of pressing the flesh with Saddam.

However, the true motives behind those missions are now coming into focus, thanks to internal Reagan administration documents unearthed through the Freedom of Information Act by the National Security Archives and through the excellent reporting of Jim Vallette. Rumsfeld did not browbeat Saddam over gassing Iranians and Kurds or for his pursuit of a nuclear bomb. He was there to beg the dictator's indulgence on behalf of Bechtel's dream pipeline to Aqaba.

Saddam may have been born in a hut and he may show a peculiar fascination with romance novels, but he was more than an intellectual match for the plodding Rumsfeld. Hussein scrutinized Bechtel's plans and told Rumsfeld that he was interested in finding a new outlet for Iraqi oil but that he was hesitant to sign a $2 billion check over to Bechtel to build a pipeline that ran so near the Israel. Saddam explained to Rumsfeld that he would need assurance that the Israelis would not bomb the pipeline once it began operations. It was a reasonable consideration, given the fact that Israeli MiGs had annihilated Saddam's Osiraq nuclear power plant on June 7, 1981.

Rumsfeld conveyed Saddam's concerns to his boss George Shultz. And here's where the affair slides from sleazy to felonious. Shultz has since claimed that he recused himself from all Bechtel related matters while he headed the State Department. Yet Shultz closely reviewed a top secret State Department cable which spelled out Saddam's fears regarding Israeli sabotage and speculated about ways in which they might be addressed by the Reagan administration. "In response to Rumsfeld's interest in seeing Iraq increase oil exports, including through a possible new pipeline across Jordan to Aqaba, Saddam suggested Israeli threat to security of such a line was major concern and US might be able to provide some assurances in this regard."

Soon the State Department went to work to meet Saddam's conditions. Here the heavy-lifting shifted from Rumsfeld to Under-Secretary of State Lawrence Eagleburger, then Shultz's top deputy for political affairs. Eagleburger, a protégé of Henry Kissinger who now adorns the board of Halliburton, endeavored to find political financing for the pipeline project. Only days after Rummy returned from his parlay with Saddam, Eagleburger fired off a memo to the Export-Import Bank urging them to back the Bechtel project. The December 22, 1984 Eagleburger memo the Ex-Im Bank directors said the loan "would signal our belief in the future viability of the Iraqi economy and secure a US foothold in a potentially large export market."

Stocked as it was with Bechtel loyalists, the Ex-Im Bank didn't need much prodding from above. But Eagleburger's intervention on behalf of Saddam and Bechtel put the project on the fast-track. By June of 1984, the Ex-Im Bank had approved a $485 million dollar loan for the pipeline. This generous dollop of corporate welfare was soon followed by a similar pledge from the Overseas Private Investment Corp., which chipped in with promises of ensuring the pipeline against damages caused by Israeli missiles.

But Saddam still wasn't satisfied, as he explained to Rumsfeld in a second visit. The thorny problem of Israeli sabotage needed to be resolved before he would sign off on the deal with Bechtel.

To vault this final hurdle, the State Department and Bechtel turned to a shady Swiss financier called Bruce Rappaport. Rappaport, who Bechtel offered to make a partner in the deal, was a close friend of Shimon Peres, the leader of the Israel's Labor Party and then Prime Minister. According to Rappaport, Peres, when approached about Saddam's complaint, said that Israel would need to be richly compensated in exchange for writing a pledge not to destroy the Aqaba pipeline.

Under a deal devised by Rappaport, Bechtel and Saddam would give the executive a 10 percent discount on freshets of oil from the pipeline and Rappaport would in turn hand over a portion of that money, estimated to be in excess of $70 million, to Peres's Labor Party coffers.

This convoluted bribery scheme was communicated to the Reagan administration by one of Rappaport's partners, E. Robert Wallach, a DC lawyer with close ties to Edwin Meese, then Reagan's attorney general. In a memo to Meese, Wallach noted that "though it would be denied everywhere...a portion of those funds will go directly to Labor." That memo, among others, would spark the appointment of James McKay as an Independent Counsel looking into allegations of financial corruption and ripe ethical lapses involving Meese and top White House advisor Lynn Nofsinger.

McKay's report makes for illuminating reading on the mutually enriching intersection of politics, diplomacy and transnational corporate villainy. Among other things, we learn that Bechtel also recruited two other luminaries of the US intelligence community, former CIA director James Schlesinger and Reagan's former National Security Advisor William Clark. Schlesinger and Clark worked on Saddam. Clark threw himself into the assignment with such enthusiasm that he even tried to convince the Iraqi dictator that he was an emissary from Reagan himself. In the end Saddam didn't bite and the deal fell through.

Meese, a bit player by any standard, resigned under a cloud and became an object of media ridicule and late night jokes, depicting the pudgy prosecutor of public morality as the James Watt of the Justice Department. But no investigation was ever launched into the truly corrupt machinations of Shultz and his coterie at the State Department. Indeed, Shultz skated through the numerous scandals of Reagan time largely unblemished and emerged as one of the media's favorite "wise old men." Naturally, this exalted reputation as an éminence grise served Shultz and his masters well when he returned to private life and the board of directors of Bechtel.

* * *

Despite the setback after the Aqaba pipeline deal fell through, Bechtel didn't abandon Iraq. In 1988, Bechtel inked a $2 billion deal with Saddam to build and operate a huge petro-chemical plant outside Baghdad. On its foul menu of toxic chemicals, the plant brewed up large batches of ethylene oxide, an ingredient in the manufacture of plastic.

But ethylene oxide also has another use. It is a chemical precursor for the manufacture of mustard gas. Despite prohibitions against providing Iraq with so-called dual use chemicals, Bechtel didn't pull out of the project until the first Gulf War appeared to be imminent.

No sanctions were ever leveled against the company for supplying Saddam's regime with the building blocks for restocking his chemical weapons arsenal. Indeed, when Iraq submitted its much derided inventory of its chemical weapons stockpile to the UN in the fall of 2002, it identified Bechtel as a chief supplier. This embarrassing disclosure, however, was redacted by the Bush administration before the documents were released to the press. It only came to light after the French released the uncensored documents and by then the US press couldn't be bothered to pursue the story.

After the first Gulf War, Bechtel won a $2 billion contract for reconstruction of Kuwait City, a deal which was secured, according some sources, through the judicious application of under-the-table dispensations to key members of the Kuwait royal family. Standard business in Kuwait. Just ask Halliburton.

With the cruel sanction regime imposed on Iraq by the US blocking further Bechtel joint ventures with Saddam, the company began to explore new global opportunities wrenched open by the neo-liberal economic policies of the Clinton administration.

In 1999, heeding to the lash of the World Bank and Clinton's State Department, the government of Bolivia agreed to privatize the public water utility in the city of Cochabamba. Under a bill pushed through the Bolivian parliament in October 1999, the government turned the management of the utility in this arid city to International Water, Inc., a subsidiary of Bechtel. Almost immediately, Bechtel jacked up the price of the monthly water bill to about $20, a staggering amount for citizens of a city where the average monthly income is around $100. Soon thousands of people failed to pay their bills with the predictable consequence of having their water shut off.

The bills and the shut-offs propelled thousands of protesters into the streets. In January of 2000, demonstrators effectively shut down the city for a week, before they were violently suppressed by the national guard, at the behest of Bechtel. Over the course of the next few months, hundreds of thousands of Bolivians took to the streets in solidarity and joined marches to the embattled city. There were general strikes and counterattacks, which left hundreds injured and several dead in the streets. The protests almost brought down the government and eventually the privatization bill was repealed and Bechtel was booted from Bolivia, leaving the good people of Cochabamba with their old water company and a crushing mound of debt.

Naturally, Bechtel didn't leave without firing a parting shot. The company filed a breach of contract suit with the World Court demanding $25 million from this destitute nation.

Similar ventures were launched in the Philippines and India. Indeed, Bechtel is now the world's biggest transnational water works company. But that honor doesn't make their presence any easier to swallow. In India's Tamil Nadu province, Bechtel's role in the privatization of the water and sanitation systems of the city of Tirupur, known as "T-shirt Town" for all the textile plants, sparked violent protests. (Connoisseurs of corporate crime will also recall Bechtel's joint venture with Enron to build and run the $2 billion natural gas power plant at Dabhol in the state of Maharashtra. The operations racked up a cruel litany of abuses from bribery of state officials to land theft, pollution and arrests of demonstrators on trumped up charges.)

Bechtel's experience in the privatization of public resources, while an unhappy one in Bolivia, proved a kind of corporate test-drive for the fire sale that would await the company in the wake of the war on Iraq and the toppling of Saddam's Ba'athist regime.

After the 9/11 attacks, Bechtel executives sensed an opportunity to return to its old haunts in Iraq, unfettered by sanctions or the nitpicking of Saddam. Along with its old emissary Donald Rumsfeld—who, only hours after witnessing the walls of the Pentagon crumple from an attack by a passenger jet commandeered by a Saudi, called for the bombing of Iraq—Bechtel geared up for war on Saddam. For the job, it hauled out the company's old war-horse, George Shultz, then serving as a Bechtel board member and senior counselor.

In early 2002, Shultz, along with Lockheed executive Bruce Jackson, set up an outfit (call it a "war tank") called the Committee for the Liberation of Iraq, which he himself chaired. From this perch, Shultz and his cohort, including Richard Perle and former CIA director James Woolsey, fired off pro-invasion op-eds, lobbied congress and scattered across the cable news talk shows beating the war drums.

With public support for the war showing signs of wavering in the late fall of 2002, Shultz penned an article in the *Washington Post* which called for the ouster of his old friend and business partner Saddam Hussein. In the past, Shultz had dismissed as unavoidable trifles of war the gassing of Iraqi Kurds and Iranian troops in the interest of doing business with the Iraqi dictator. But now, even though his own company had built a dual use chemical plant for Saddam, Shultz begged the public to support an invasion of Iraq to eliminate those very same weapons of mass destruction. "A strong foundation exists for immediate military action against Hussein and for a multilateral effort to rebuild Iraq after he is gone," Shultz wrote. Here multilateral should be translated as multinational, as in multinational corporations, like Bechtel.

And so it came to pass. First the cruise missiles, then the contracts. The first big reconstruction contract was awarded a few days after the start of the war in a secret bidding process headed by USAID administrator Andrew Nastios, who formerly oversaw the "Big Dig" project in Boston, where, yes, Bechtel was the lead contractor. As a bonus, the company was indemnified against all liabilities it might incur doing business in Iraq.

In other words, Bechtel is shielded from suits brought by US workers or by Iraqis victimized by the shoddy work. This may set a new standard in economic colonialism, where n a corporation from an invading country indemnified from damages suffered by the conquered country.

* * *

So over the course of the last two years, Bechtel has been making tons of money from the war on Iraq that its executives helped orchestrate. But two years after the fall of Baghdad and billions later in reconstruction contracts, the daily situation for most Iraqis is worse than it was before the war. The power grid remains unreliable. Hundreds of sewage treatment plants are still inoperable, with millions of gallons of filthy water pouring into the Tigris and Euphrates every day. The phone system is primitive at best. The trains still don't run. The highways are cratered. The Baghdad airport serves only military flights. Schools are splashed with a coat of paint and told to reopen.

When local Iraqi officials object or try to offer advice, they are ignored or bullied. "The impression we get is that Bechtel is more powerful than the US Army," says Dr. Nabil Khudair Abbas, a top official with the new Iraqi government's Ministry of Education.

No one reviews or evaluates Bechtel's work. It's too dangerous and few non-Iraqis give a damn, anyway. Certainly, not the Bechtel executives, operating out of their opulent penthouses in Qatar and Kuwait City.

"If the Americans had given us the money directly, we could have done a much better job," says Abdeel Razzaq Ali, headmaster of the Anbariyn School in a poor, Shiite area of Baghdad. "Why do we need Bechtel? They have done absolutely nothing."

Perhaps someone should tell the Iraqi people about the secret motto of this family run empire as dictated years ago by longtime CEO Stephen Bechtel: "We're more about making money, than making things."

Buyer beware.

April, 2005

Sixteen

The Saga of Magnequench

Outsourcing US Missile Technology to China

Magnequench is an Indianapolis-based company. It specializes in the obscure field of sintered magnetics. Essentially, it makes tiny, high-tech magnets from rare-earth minerals ground down into a fine powder. The magnets are highly prized by electronics and aviation companies. But Magnequench's biggest client has been the Pentagon.

The neodymium-iron-boron magnets made by Magnequench are a crucial component in the guidance system of cruise missiles and the Joint Direct Attack Munition or JDAM bomb, which is made by Boeing and had a starring role in the spring bombing of Baghdad. Indeed, Magnequench enjoys a near monopoly on this market niche, supplying 85 percent of the rare-earth magnets that are used in the servo motors of these guided missiles and bombs.

But the Pentagon may soon be sending its orders for these parts to China, instead of Indiana. On September 15, 2004 Magnequench shuttered its last plant in Indiana, fired its 450 workers and began shipping its machine tools to a new plant in China. "We're handing over to the Chinese both our defense technology and our jobs in the midst of a deep recession," says Rep. Peter Visclosky, a Democrat from northern Indiana.

It gets stranger. Magnequench is not only moving its defense plants to China, it's actually owned by Chinese companies with close ties to the Chinese government.

Magnequench began its corporate life back in 1986 as a subsidiary of General Motors. Using Pentagon grants, GM had developed a new kind of permanent magnet material in the early 1980s. It began manufacturing the magnets in 1987 at the Magnequench factory in Anderson, Indiana.

In 1995, Magnequench was purchased from GM by Sextant Group, an investment company headed by Archibald Cox, Jr., the son of the Watergate prosecutor. After the takeover, Cox was named CEO. What few knew at the time was that Sextant was largely a front for two Chinese companies, San Huan New Material and the China National Non-Ferrous Metals Import and Export Corporation. Both of these companies have close ties to the Chinese government. Indeed, the ties were so intimate that the heads of both companies were in-laws of the late Chinese premier Deng Xiaopeng.

At the time of the takeover, Cox pledged to the workers that Magnequench was in it for the long haul, intending to invest money in the plants and committed to keeping the production line going for at least a decade.

Three years later Cox shut down the Anderson plant and shipped its assembly line to China. Now Cox is presiding over the closure of Magnequench's last factory in the US, the Valparaiso, Indiana plant that manufactures the magnets for the JDAM bomb. Most of the workers have already been fired.

"Archie Cox and his company are committing a criminal act," says Mike O'Brien, an organizer with the UAW in Indiana. "He's a traitor to his country."

It's clear that Cox and Sextant were acting as a front for some unsavory interests. For example, only months prior to the takeover of Magnequench San Huan New Materials was cited by US International Trade Commission for patent infringement and business espionage. The company was fined $1.5 million. Foreign investment in American high-tech and defense companies is regulated by the Committee on Foreign Investments in the United States (CFIUS). It is unlikely that CFIUS would have approved San Huan's purchase of Magnequench had it not been for the cover provided by Cox and his Sextant Group.

One of Magnequench's subsidiaries is a company called GA Powders, which manufactures the fine granules used in making the mini-magnets. GA Powders was originally a Department of Energy project created by scientists at the Idaho National Engineering and Environmental Lab. It was spun off to Magnequench in 1998, after Lockheed Martin took over the operations at INEEL.

In June 2000, Magnequench uprooted the production facilities for GA Powders from Idaho Falls to a newly constructed plant in Tianjin, China. This move followed the transfer to China of high-tech computer equipment from Magnequench's shuttered Anderson plant. According to a report in Insight magazine, these computers could be used to facilitate the enrichment of uranium for nuclear warheads.

GA Powders isn't the only business venture between a Department of Energy operation and Magnequench. According to a news letter produced by the Sandia Labs in Albuquerque, New Mexico, Sandia is working on a joint project with Magnequench involving "the development of advanced electronic controls and new magnet technology".

Dr. Peter Leitner is an advisor to the Pentagon on matters involving trade in strategic materials. He says that the Chinese targeted Magnequench in order to advance their development of long-range Cruise missiles. China now holds a monopoly on the rare-earth minerals used in the manufacturing of the missile magnets. The only operating rare-earth mine is located in Batou, China.

"By controlling access to the magnets and the raw materials they are composed of, US industry can be held hostage to Chinese blackmail and extortion," Leitner told *Insight* magazine last year. "This highly concentrated control-one country, one government-will be the sole source of something critical to the US military and industrial base."

Visclosky and Senator Evan Bayh asked the Bush administration to intervene using the Exon-Florio Amendment to the 1988 Defense Appropriation Act to pry the Chinese money out of the company and force Magnequench to keep its factories in Indiana.

There was precedent for just such a presidential move. In 1990, George H.W. Bush ordered the state-owned China National Aerospace and Export Company to divest its interest in Mamco Manufacturing of Seattle, reportedly because of concern that the Chinese firm could have use Mamco to acquire jet fighter engine technology. The directive came from Bush three months after CATIC had seized control of Mamco. When after six months the Chinese company refused to relinquish its interest in Mamco, Bush ordered the Treasury Department to place the company in receivership and barred the Chinese officials from having any access to its facilities.

Unlike his father, Bush 2 declined to respond to the pleas from Visclosky and Bayh. The Treasury Department, which could have intervened to stop the move, also refused to act. Visclosky says that he also contacted the Pentagon. Its procurement officials admitted to him that Magnequench was the only domestic supplier of the smart bomb magnets (Hitachi holds the other contract), but that it had no idea that company was owned by the Chinese or that it was packing up for Tianjin.

As the doors closed on its Valparaiso plant, a memo came from Magnequench executives advising that its HQ will be soon be relocated from Indianapolis to Singapore. No word on yet whether Cox is moving too.

And yes, when the Republicans made a mountain out of what turned out in the end to be a pretty small molehill concerning transfers of satellite technology to China in Clinton time, they said it might be grounds for impeachment. William Safire wrote lots of columns on the matter. Not a bleat from Safire now.

September, 2003

Seventeen

When War is Swell

The Crusades of the Carlyle Group

Across all fronts, Bush's war deteriorates with stunning rapidity. The death count of American soldiers killed in Iraq increases by two a day, every day, with no end in sight. The members of the handpicked Iraqi Governor Council are being knocked off one after another. Once loyal Shia clerics, like Ayatollah Sistani, are now telling the administration to pull out or face a nationalist insurgency. The trail of culpability for the abuse, torture and murder of Iraqi detainees seems to lead inexorably into the office of Donald Rumsfeld. The war for Iraqi oil has ended up driving the price of crude oil through the roof. Even Kurdish leaders, brutalized by the Ba'athists for decades, are now saying Iraq was a safer place under their nemesis Saddam Hussein. Like Medea whacking her own kids, the US turned on its own creation, Ahmed Chalabi, raiding his Baghdad compound and fingering him as an agent of the ayatollahs of Iran. And on and on it goes.

Still not all of the president's men are in a despairing mood. Amid the wreckage, there remain opportunities for profit and plunder. Halliburton and Bechtel's triumphs in Iraq have been chewed over for months. Less well chronicled is the profiteering of the Carlyle Group, a company with ties that extend directly into the Oval Office itself.

Even Pappy Bush stands in line to profit handsomely from his son's war making. The former president is on retainer with the Carlyle Group, the largest privately held defense contractor in the nation. Carlyle is run by Frank Carlucci, who served as the National Security advisor and Secretary of Defense under Ronald Reagan. Carlucci has his own embeds in the current Bush administration. At Princeton, his college roommate was Donald Rumsfeld. They've remained close friends and business associates ever since. When you have friends like this, you don't need to hire lobbyists.

Bush Sr. serves as a kind of global emissary for Carlyle. The ex-president doesn't negotiate arms deals; he simply opens the door for them, a kind of high level meet-and-greet. His special area of influence is the Middle

East, primarily Saudi Arabia, where the Bush family has extensive business and political ties. According to an account in the *Washington Post*, Bush Sr. earns around $500,000 for each speech he makes on Carlyle's behalf.

One of the Saudi investors lured to Carlyle by Bush was the BinLaden Group, the construction conglomerate owned by the family of Osama bin Laden. According to an investigation by the *Wall Street Journal*, Bush convinced Shafiq Bin Laden, Osama's half brother, to sink $2 million of BinLaden Group money into Carlyle's accounts. In a pr move, the Carlyle group cut its ties to the BinLaden Group in October 2001.

One of Bush Sr.'s top sidekicks, James Baker, is also a key player at Carlyle. Baker joined the weapons firm in 1993, fresh from his stint as Bush's secretary of state and chief of staff. Packing a briefcase of global contacts, Baker parlayed his connections with heads of state, generals and international tycoons into a bonanza for Carlyle. After Baker joined the company, Carlyle's revenues more than tripled.

Like Bush Sr., Baker's main function was to manage Carlyle's lucrative relationship with Saudi potentates, who had invested tens of millions of dollars in the company. Baker helped secure one of Carlyle's most lucrative deals: the contract to run the Saudi offset program, a multi-billion dollar scheme wherein international companies winning Saudi contracts are required under terms of the contracts to invest a percentage of the profits in Saudi companies.

Baker not only greases the way for investment deals and arms sales, but he also plays the role of seasoned troubleshooter, protecting the interests of key clients and regimes. A case in point: when the Justice Department launched an investigation into the financial dealings of Prince Sultan bin Abdul Aziz, the Saudi prince sought out Baker's help. Baker is currently defending the prince in a trillion dollar lawsuit brought by the families of the victims of the 9/11 attacks. The suit alleges that the prince used Islamic charities as pass-throughs for shipping millions of dollars to groups linked to al-Qaeda.

Baker and Carlyle enjoy another ace in the hole when it comes to looking out for their Saudi friends. Baker prevailed on Bush Jr. to appoint his former law partner, Bob Jordan, as the administration's ambassador to Saudi Arabia.

Carlyle and its network of investors are well positioned to cash in on Bush Jr.'s expansion of the defense and Homeland Security department budgets. Two Carlyle companies, Federal Data Systems and US Investigations Services, hold multi-billion dollar contracts to provide background checks for commercial airlines, the Pentagon, the CIA and the Department of Homeland Security. USIS was once a federal agency called the Office Federal Investigations, but it was privatized in 1996 at the urging of Baker and others and was soon gobbled up by Carlyle. The company is now housed in "high-security, state-of-the-art, underground complex" in Annandale, Pennsylvania. USIS now does 2.4 million background checks a year, largely for the federal government.

Another Carlyle subsidiary, Vought Aircraft, holds more than a billion dollars in federal contracts to provide components for the C-117 transport plane, the B-2 bomber and the Apache attack helicopter. Prior to 2001, Vought had fallen on hard times. Just before the 9/11 attacks, Vought announced that it was laying off more than 1,200 employees, more than 20 percent of its workforce. But business picked up briskly following the airstrikes on Afghanistan and the war on Iraq.

In 2002, Carlyle sold off its biggest holding, United Defense. The sale may have been prompted by insider information leaked to Carlucci by his pal Rumsfeld. In early 2001, Carlyle was furiously lobbying the Pentagon to approve contracts for the production of United Defense's Crusader artillery system, an unwieldy and outrageously expensive super-cannon. Rumsfeld disliked the Crusader and had it high on his hit list of weapon systems to be killed off in order to save money for other big ticket schemes, particularly the Strategic Defense Initiative.

But, as detailed in William Hartung's excellent book, *How Much Are You Making in the War, Daddy?*, Rumsfeld didn't terminate the Crusader immediately. Instead, he held off on a public announcement of his decision for more than a year. By that time, Carlucci and Baker devised a plan to take United Defense public. The sale to unsuspecting investors netted Carlyle more than $237 million. Six months later, Rumsfeld closed the book on the Crusader. By then the gang at Carlyle had slipped out the back door, their pockets stuffed with cash. United Defense was able to petition the Pentagon to compensate them to the tune of several million for cancellation of the contract. Even when you lose, you win.

So the men behind the Carlyle Group drift through Washington like familiar ghosts, profiteering off the carnage of Bush's disastrous crusades, untroubled by any thought of congressional investigation or criminal prosecution, firm in the knowledge that the worse things get for the people of the world, the less secure and more gripped by fear the citizens their own country become, the more millions they will reap for themselves. Perpetual war means perpetual profits.

Let's leave the last word to Dan Broidy, author of *The Iron Triangle*, an illuminating history of the Carlyle Group: "It's not an exaggeration to say that September 11 is going to make the Carlyle investors very, very rich men."

May, 2004

Eighteen

Boeing and Nothingness

1. Onward and Downward
Book Cooking at Boeing

In the early summer of 2004, a top Wall Street stock picker issued a glowing report about Boeing: buy, buy, buy. The unusually rosy assessment for the troubled company had nothing to do with the need to replenish the Pentagon's arsenal of cruise missiles depleted by the Iraq war or the Bush administration's drive to implement Star Wars, both of which will net Boeing billions. No, this analysis, written by Heidi Wood, a vice-president at Morgan Stanley, pointed to "a no risk" risk deal with the federal government to lease 100 Boeing-767 tanker aircraft.

According to Wood's report, the deal would generate $2.3 billion in revenues for Boeing. To put this in perspective, that's about as much profit as Boeing reaps for the sale of 1,033 of its 737 commercial airliners. From Boeing's perspective, the great part of the tanker deal is that the company has few obligations, yet the government is locked into the leases, even if it proves that the Pentagon doesn't need the planes. Boeing is guaranteed a 15 percent profit on each plane it delivers. "There's substantially less risk than is common in the commercial aircraft market," Wood wrote.

Wood should know what she's talking about. The *Wall Street Journal* calls her the top stock analyst in the Aerospace / Defense sector and she also serves as a Bush appointee to the Commission on the Future of the US Aerospace Industry.

Under the deal approved by the Pentagon in July 2003, Boeing will convert 100 B-767s into military refueling tankers. It's quite a coup, because many Air Force generals have said that the planes aren't needed, an assessment backed up by a General Accounting Office investigation.

There are currently 545 KC-135 tankers in the Air Force fleet. More than 400 of them are new, fully upgraded "R" models. The other 134 tankers are older "E" models that some inside the Pentagon and the Congress are anxious to replace with the leased planes from Boeing.

On the surface, the Boeing proponents appear to have an argument: the

E tankers are aging. Most of the planes are 35 years old. However, the Air Force primarily assesses the life span of planes based not on age but on flight hours. The engines for the "E" model has a projected life of 36,000 flying hours. A 1995 GAO report revealed that the majority of the "E" tankers have accumulated about 13,000 hours. The report projected that not one of the tanker planes in the fleet would reach its limit until 2040. The new plan is to begin replacing the E tankers with the Boeing planes in 2006.

Even if the Air Force decided it needed to upgrade the engines on the E planes sooner, because of added usage and stress from the wars in Afghanistan and Iraq, it would be much cheaper to simply upgrade the engines instead of entering into a lease arrangement with Boeing. The GAO estimates that the entire fleet of "E" tankers could be upgraded with "R" engines for about $3.6 billion. This is more than seven times cheaper than the $26 billion the Air Force will have to fork out for the Boeing commercial tankers.

Despite the fact that Boeing famously fled Seattle to set up its new headquarters in Chicago, the tanker lease deal was engineered through the tireless work of the Washington State congressional delegation, led by Sen. Patty Murray and Congressman Norm Dicks. Wood, who demonstrates a sophisticated understanding of the political economics of the Beltway, cautions investors that Boeing may need to demonstrate its gratitude to the Washington delegation by agreeing to locate some of its manufacturing plant for the new 7E7 commercial jet in Seattle rather than in a more corporate friendly environs.

"A subtle negative may be the payback required considering political capital BA [Boeing] has expended to land the tanker deal," Wood warned. "Now the company is somewhat beholden to its hard-working Washington constituency. This may limit some of the latitude the company would probably like to have in deciding where to build the 7E7, adding pressure to keep some of the 7E7 work in expensive, union-dominated Seattle."

Of course, the congressional delegation couldn't have prevailed on its own. Boeing got some vital help greasing this deal from the inside as well in the form of Darleen Druyun, a top Air Force official who called herself the Godmother of the C-17—the troubled air transport plane made by Boeing. According to Pentagon sources, she helped craft the tanker deal, fought off skeptical Pentagon accountants and auditors, worked the appropriations committees and, finally, when it all seemed nicely tied up, retired from the Pentagon and joined Boeing as an executive vice-president, where she now supervises the company's interests before congress and the Pentagon.

Druyun is not the only Pentagon powerbroker to be recruited into Boeing's corporate hangar. Recently, Boeing's board has boasted both former Defense Secretary William Perry and John M. Shalikashvili, at one time the chairman of the Joint Chiefs of Staff. In 2001, Boeing also hired Rudy De Leon, Clinton's Deputy Secretary of Defense, to run its Washington office. Although De Leon is known as a hawk and a masterful dealmaker, his hiring may have been a rare misstep for Boeing, since congressional Republicans howled that the company should have picked one of their own kind from the Pentagon's rolls.

It's just this kind of zealous devotion to political payback and behind-the-scenes influence peddling that has landed Boeing in a rare spot of trouble. According to a one paragraph item in Reuters from early June 2004, the Inspector General of the Air Force has opened an investigation into Boeing whether or not Boeing should be debarred from bidding on contracts with the federal government. The probe stems from allegations that Boeing executives received proprietary information from Lockheed concerning bids on Pentagon contracts.

The Lockheed affair is not Boeing's only transgression. The Project on Government Oversight, a DC-based Pentagon watchdog group, reported last year that since 1990 Boeing has committed more than 36 violations and has been forced to pay more than $350 million in fines, penalties, restitution and settlement. Among the more recent allegations:

- Boeing placed defective gears in Chinook helicopters;

- Company officials offered bribes to officials of the Bahamas government as a means of securing a contract;

- Produced a defective safety system for the Apache helicopter;

- Misrepresented the progress of clean-up at Rocky Flats nuclear weapons site; Charges from the State Department that Boeing violated the Arms Export Control Act and International Traffic in Arms Regulations-more than 100 instances are cited;

- Accused of civil rights violations in hiring and salary practices toward blacks and women;

- Routinely mistated labor costs and exaggerated overhead costs.

These are serious charges of criminal and civil malfeasance, some of which Boeing didn't even dispute. Yet, despite the rap sheet, Boeing has not been suspended or debarred from bidding on contracts since 1990. Federal contract guidelines require that contractors to the government sanction violators and only award contracts to "responsible" contractors with a record of "integrity and business ethics".

Of course, Boeing is hardly alone in getting a pass from these high-minded rules. In the past decade, out of the top 50 defense contractors the Pentagon has only suspended the contract privileges of only one major company, General Electric Avionics Division, and that lasted for only five days.

Even so, some in Congress aghast at the mere possibility of a crackdown on cheating contractors make haste to loosen the rules even further. At the behest of Boeing and other big contractors, Rep. Tom Davis, the Virginia Republican who chairs the House Government Reform Committee, has just introduced legislation that will unravel many of the key provisions governing the regulation of Pentagon contracts.

One of the changes proposed by Davis is for the Pentagon to shift to so-called Time and Material and Labor Hour contracts, where the weapons firms would get paid for how much time they spent working on a project rather than by such standards as to whether they completed it on time or according to code. This amounts to a blank check without any incentive to ever finish the job. Davis even includes a provision that would prohibit government auditors from examining the contractor's billing records.

The congressman, who once won a Harvard rock trivia contest by correctly identifying the Blues Magoos as the group that performed the 1966 hit "(We Ain't Got) Nothin' Yet, also wants to expand the use of Share-in-Savings Contracts, a kind of Enron-style financial speculation that allows contractors to be lavishly reimbursed for investments in infrastructure upgrades, such as computer systems. The companies are allowed to charge the government for "efficiency savings" over the lifetime of the contract. But even the Bush administration is skeptical of such claims. In hearings before Congressman Davis's committee in 2003, Angela Styles, the chief procurement analyst for the White House, testified that her office had examined dozens of the contracts and "we have seen no real savings."

The program is so ripe for fraud that one expert in defense contracts compared it to the savings-and-loan scandal. "Share-in-Savings" contracts could propagate problems similar to those that accompanied deregulation of the government-insured savings-and-loans institutions or procurement of defense spare parts in the 1980s by sole-source contracts," says Charles Tiefer, a professor at the University of Baltimore School of Law.

The biggest prize for the defense contractors is Davis's plan to scrap key provisions in two hated laws: the Truth in Negotiations Act and the Cost Accounting Standards Act. Back in the late 1960s, Senator William Proxmire teamed with Admiral Hyman Rickover to standardize accounting procedures for defense contractors during the spending frenzy of the Vietnam War. They also set up a board to oversee the enforcement of the standards and deflate the complex accounting tricks of the defense contractors which were costing the government more than $6 billion a year.

The Truth in Negotiations Act forced weapons manufacturers to come clean with the true basis of their pricing and cost data. Under current guidelines, defense contractors must comply with TINA for any contract over $550,000. Davis's measure would effectively gut the bill by making the reporting requirements apply only to contracts involving more than $200 million.

After the defense industry consolidation frenzy of the 1990s, many Pentagon contract offerings now receive only one bid. To allow the defense companies to set their own accounting and pricing rules in this sole-source environment is to invite the kind of runaway fraud last seen in the procurement scandals of the 1970s and 1980s. It's one way to jumpstart the economy. No wonder Wall Street's bullish on Boeing.

July, 2004

2. Pentagon, Inc.

How the Godmother of Boeing Made a Soft Landing

The C-17, the unwieldy transport plane that did much of the heavy lifting during the roll up to Bush's war on Iraq, was forced on reluctant Air Force pilots by Boeing's Pentagon contact, Darlene Druyun. The plane's past performance had gotten mixed reviews at best, but as chief acquisitions officer at the Air Force, Druyun pushed relentlessly to have more of those cargo planes bought and at a premium price. As a kicker, Druyun drafted a quaint provision that would have inoculated the C-17 contract from any pesky government oversight over the likely runaway costs of the program.

Druyun's unceasing efforts at the Pentagon to push this sweetheart deal on behalf of Boeing eventually prompted an internal investigation by the Defense Department's Inspector General and even roused a rare public rebuke from Defense Secretary Donald Rumsfeld.

Druyun recently left the Pentagon, but now she has made a soft landing at the very company she had labored for so zealously in public office: Boeing.

In a January 3, 2003 company press release, Boeing executives gloated that Druyun will head up the company's missile defense division headquartered in Washington, DC. This is one of the more plum positions in town. Boeing is the prime contractor for what the Pentagon calls the Ground-based Midcourse Defense Segment and serves as the lead contractor for the Missile Defense National Team's Systems Engineering and Integration program. These contracts have already generated billions in revenues for Boeing, but much more is on the way. The company expects to do a brisk business now that Bush has officially jettisoned the ABM Treaty and given the greenlight for the rapid deployment of the latest version of the Star Wars scheme. Druyun's duties at Boeing will also include hawking the Airborne Laser program and the Patriot anti-missile system, which seems likely to get another big boost in sales to Israel and Kuwait with the upcoming war on Iraq.

"Darleen Druyun helped drive acquisition reform within the Air Force," said James Evatt, Boeing's senior vice-president for its Defense programs. "Her 'Lightning Bolt' initiatives, which jump-started the reform process. Her personal passion and drive are well known within the defense industry, and we expect her to be a key player in our future success."

Pentagon watchdogs have a somewhat different recollection of Druyun's tenure at the Air Force. They say that the Godmother's initiatives favored the defense contractors, while looting the treasury and putting Air Force pilots in relatively untested and even unsafe planes. The C-17 affair is perhaps the most brazen example of her labors on behalf of the weapons lobby.

In 1990, Congress approved an Air Force plan to buy 120 C-17s from Boeing for $230 million apiece. That contract runs out later this year. In the fall of 2000, the Air Force said it wanted another 60 planes. But Boeing wanted to sell them many more. And they engaged in a bit of blackmail to get their way. Boeing officials claimed that they couldn't afford to keep the C- 17 in production unless they built a minimum of 15 planes each year. Yet, even the Air Force admitted it didn't need that many planes. And the General Accounting Office contends that the Air Force actually only requires about 100 heavy transport planes, 20 fewer than it has already got. With other big ticket items like the F-22 and the Joint Strike Fighter on the Air Force's wish list, the C-17 seemed unlikely to survive congressional scrutiny.

So a plan was hatched to make the new fleet of planes quasi-private. Under this scenario, some of the C-17s would essentially be rented out to private haulers, who would then be in a position to receive financial kickbacks for using the aircraft. According to Pentagon sources, the idea to reclassify the C-17 contract from a military to a commercial project originated with Boeing. It's not hard to figure out what office they went to with the idea. This scheme contained another nifty prize for Boeing. By reclassifying the deal as a commercial operation, it alleviated many of the detailed reporting requirements that go along with defense contracts.

Druyun seized on the idea and wrapped the program in the then ripe rhetoric of the Clinton/Gore reinventing government scheme. "This program is very appealing to all parties involved: the Air Force, the commercial operators, the manufacturers and the American taxpayer," Druyun boasted in December of 2000. In a sign of things to come, this quote appeared in a Boeing press release.

Druyun also raved that the new contract would enable Boeing to employ "streamlined processes" in the production of the plane—never a welcome sign when it comes to building military aircraft, at least from the pilot's point of view.

All this prompted the Pentagon's chief testing official to object to the plan as a potentially hazardous operation. "Policies and procedures flowing from the push toward commercial acquisition are leading the C-17 down a risky path," wrote Philip Coyle, then director of the Defense Department's Operational Test and Evaluation Division. "A lack of fiscal, technical, and testing realism may be creating fleets that cannot meet effectiveness, sustainability, or interoperability requirements."

After the scheme was exposed by the Project on Government Oversight and by a subsequent report in *CounterPunch*, the C-17 plan fell apart. When the dust finally settled, Druyun cashed in her chips and found employment with Boeing. She soon went to work stalking bigger game: missile defense, a multi-billion dollar bonanza for defense contractors, with Boeing at the head of the trough.

"Ms. Druyun is now officially an employee of the company whose interests she so ardently championed while she was supposedly representing the interests of the taxpayers," says Danielle Brian, executive director of the Project on Government Oversight. "This is one of the most egregious examples of the government revolving door in recent memory."

Of course, plucking operatives from the halls of the Pentagon is nothing new for Boeing. Over the years, the company has festooned its corporate board and the halls of its lobby shop with a bevy of top brass.

But by adding the Godmother of the C-17 to the company's DC hangar, the defense contractors seems to be well on the road toward making amends and, naturally, fattening Boeing's bottom line courtesy of the federal treasury.

January, 2003

3. Inside Tankerscam

The Fallout of from 767 Deal

For Boeing, it seemed like the deal of the new century, a no-risk $30 billion contract with the Pentagon to lease a refurbished fleet of 767 passenger jets to serve as refueling tankers for the US Air Force.

It didn't matter that the Air Force, by its own admission, didn't particularly need any more tankers. It also didn't matter that the aging Boeing 767s weren't the best plane to serve in the role of refueling tankers. In fact, there were serious technical shortcomings with the Boeing planes. It also didn't matter that the lease arrangement, promoted as a low-cost upgrade for an aging tanker fleet, would in the end cost the government at least $2 billion more than if the Air Force had simply bought the planes outright.

All of that was inconsequential. The real objective of Tankerscam was to pour billions into the corporate coffers of Boeing in the company's desperate hour of need. In the autumn of 2001, Boeing's financial fortunes were slumping. The domestic airline industry was slow to recover from the 9/11 attacks. Boeing had lost big deals to Airbus and Lockheed. And it had alienated many of its shareholders and political patrons by its abrupt decision to relocate its headquarters from Seattle to Chicago.

The tanker deal, the most costly government lease ever, was designed to rescue an ailing company. The contours of the scheme first formed at a meeting in late September 2001 between Boeing executives and Darlene A. Druyun, then Deputy Assistant Secretary of the Air Force, and Major General Paul Essex, then head of the Air Force's bizarrely-named Global Reach Program.

A week later Druyun's boss, Air Force Secretary James Roche, was on board. Roche fired off a letter to key senators and congressmen urging Congress to quickly sanction the deal, even though the Air Force had yet to conduct a legally-required review of alternatives to the plan. In fact, that review would never take place thanks to Roche. He ordered a halt to just such a review in August 2003, when a Michael Wynne, then a senior procurement officer at the Air Force, had asked Airbus, Boeing's arch-rival, to submit a competitive bid. In a blistering email to Wynne, Roche wrote: "Mike, you must be out of your mind!!! We won't be happy with your doing this!"

Around the same time, Roche sent an email to an executive at Raytheon disparaging the European Aeronautic Defense and Space Company, which owns Airbus. "Privately between us: Go Boeing!" Roche wrote. "The fools in Paris and Berlin never did their homework."

When Roche's letter endorsing the tanker lease deal with Boeing went out to congress, it landed on the desk of one senator was very glad to see it, Ted Stevens of Alaska. In fact, according to Winslow Wheeler, a longtime top level senate staffer on defense matters, it was Stevens who set the entire scheme into motion.

Stevens is a more archaic personality than James Roche. He disdains email and its lingering evidentiary traces. The senator prefers to simply pick up the phone and make his pleasure known directly in his crusty Alaskan growl.

Since the retirement of Henry "Scoop" Jackson, the Washington Democrat known as the Senator from Boeing and the father of the neocons, Ted Stevens has toiled as Boeing's point man on the Hill.

According to Wheeler, Stevens placed a call to Druyun's office at the Air Force shortly after 9/11 urging her to develop a plan using "creative financing" to use 100 Boeing 767s as replacements for the Air Forces fleet of KC-137 tankers. Stevens explained that by "creative financing" he meant that the Air Force should lease the refurbished planes from Boeing rather than purchase them outright. In Stevens' view, the deal served all concerned. Boeing would get a $30 billion stream of revenue and would be able to keep its line of 767s in production despite the downturn in domestic air travel.

Even though the Pentagon didn't need the planes, Stevens suggested it had nothing to lose since by leasing the planes from Boeing it would be paid for in an off-budget appropriation, meaning that it wouldn't mean the slightest reduction in the Air Force's other procurement funds, which could be poured into other mammoth boondoggles such as the F-22 and the Joint-Strike Fighter. In an added twist of legislative showmanship, Stevens, with Druyun's help, sculpted the language of the deal so that it evaded the scrutiny of the tightwad accountants at the Office of Management and Budget.

One question is: did Stevens come up with this scheme on his own or was it implanted in his mind by Boeing executives? There's some tantalizing evidence that the senator was playing the role of errand boy. A few weeks after he made his call to Air Force headquarters, the senator from Anchorage turned up in Seattle for a fundraiser in his honor sponsored by the Boeing

Company. At this event, Stevens pulled in more than $22,000 in campaign contributions from Boeing executives in charge of the company's 767 division. Stevens, of course, denies any connection between Tankerscam and the campaign slush from Boeing. But it's a fine line between a payment for services rendered and a routine political gratuity.

Soon Stevens proved himself to be a master of the appropriations process. He placated the only two senators who stood in the way of the deal, John McCain and Phil Gramm, and then negotiated the measure through the treacherous shoals of the Senate-House conference committee. By the second week of December 2001, the Boeing deal had been approved by both Congress and President Bush.

Then it all began to unravel.

The first crack opened when Darlene Druyun announced that she was retiring from her post as the Air Force's top procurement officer and taking a $250,000 position with Boeing, as a deputy vice-president for the company's Missile Defense Program Unit. It would soon emerge that Druyun had negotiated her new job as she was putting the finishing touches on the Boeing tanker deal.

Then came a flood of leaks to congress and the press by Pentagon whistleblowers exposing the soaring costs of the deal and corrupt means by which it was executed. One particular thorn in the side of the Boeing gang was Michael Wynne, the Pentagon auditor. Wynne's analysis of the true costs of the tanker deal infuriated Boeing's top lobbyist Paul Weaver, who wrote an email to the Secretary of the Air Force, James Roche, complaining that Marvin Sambur, the Air Force's acquisition chief, was "getting beat up" by Wynne over the deal. Roche fired back an email telling Weaver not to worry. "It's time for the big guns to quash Wynne!" Roche wrote. Roche later denied under oath to the Senate Armed Services Committee that he had ever tried to silence Wynne.

Roche's emails, as well as dozens of others, were revealed in a 270-page investigation into Tankerscam by the Air Force's inspector general. The report was publicly released in June by the office of Senator John McCain, although it was heavily censored by the Bush White House. Among the juicy items blacked out by the White House censors were all references to involvement in the deal by White House staffers, top level Pentagon aides (i.e., Rumsfeld and Wolfowitz) and members of congress. In other words, two-thirds of the Iron Triangle had been redacted.

As the deal began to fray, Roche became increasingly agitated. He blamed Boeing for not putting enough pressure on key members of congress. He fired off an email to Michael Sears, Boeing's Chief Financial Officer, and company CEO Phil Condit. "Gee, Mike," Roche wrote. "When I knew you and Phil, I had the sense you wanted to make money. Guess I was wrong."

Rarely have the workings of the Iron Triangle been expressed with such vivid candor by someone from the inside. Following Roche's proddings, Boeing pressed for a meeting at the White House. They got one with Andrew Card, Bush's chief of staff. Card emerged from the session full of promises to salvage the deal.

Even as they tried to save the tanker leasing program, both the Pentagon and Boeing began to look for a patsy to blame if it all went down in flames. By all accounts, Druyun had few friends. During her 15 years at the Pentagon, where she eventually became one of the most powerful women in the history of the Air Force controlling the fate of more than $50 billion in contracts a year, she became know for her abrasive and autocratic personality, burning dozens of colleagues on her rise to the top. Though she was in the Air Force, Druyun cussed like a sailor. "Her mouth," one colleague told me, "was filthier than Ty Cobb's."

When a grand jury was convened to investigate the circumstances around the awarding of the Boeing contract, Druyun was offered up as the sacrificial lamb. She was an easy target. Druyun had negotiated her job with Boeing while she was overseeing Boeing's contracts with the Air Force. This was a clear violation of federal law, although it happens nearly every day in the bowels of the Pentagon and the law against it is rarely enforced. Exactly who turned her in remains something of a mystery. Both Boeing and the Pentagon may have had reasons to cut their losses.

Within a few weeks of her indictment, Druyun, facing the prospect of a daunting stint in the federal penitentiary, began to negotiate a plea with federal prosecutors. In exchange for a guilty plea on one count of conspiracy to violate federal contracting laws, Druyun agreed to cooperate with the prosecutors. Her tale of corruption emerged slowly. At first, Druyun refused to rat out any others. But after two failed polygraph exams, she finally began to spill the beans.

The story Druyun finally told is equal parts personal pettiness and government and corporate corruption on a grandiose scale. By Druyun's own account, she had begun to weary of her job at the Air Force in the summer of 2001 and began looking for a high paying position with a defense contractor. The first offer came from Boeing's rival, Lockheed. Druyun negotiated a tentative deal to take a position with Lockheed in 2002. But when word came from Senator Stevens instructing her to proceed with the Boeing tanker lease scheme, Druyun sensed a more robust opportunity.

After all, Boeing had been very responsive to previous employment requests from Druyun. In 2000, Druyun contacted her longtime friend Michael Sears, Boeing's Chief Financial Officer, requesting that he find a job for her daughter's fiancé, Michael McKee. Sears quickly complied, hiring McKee for a position at Boeing's big facility outside St. Louis. Two months later, Druyun was on the phone to Boeing again, this time with a request for the company to hire her daughter, Heather. Again Boeing complied. It was decision that some in the company quickly regretted. Heather was not up to the task. Her job performance ratings were abysmal and superiors wanted to fire her. Druyun intervened again, demanding that her daughter's job be saved and her performance ratings upgraded. With the fate $30 billion in Pentagon contracts in Druyun's hands, it didn't take long for Boeing executives to comply with her demands.

When Druyun wanted to send her own employment request to Boeing, she deployed Heather as her intermediary. In an email to Michael Sears, Heather said her mother desired a top level job at Boeing, "along the lines of Chief Operating Officer…something that would blow her out of the water." Heather also conveyed to Sears that her mother had selected Boeing from among her many suitors for the company's "honest values."

In a move that would prove fatal for his career, Sears responded eagerly to Heather's advances on behalf of her mother. Sears contacted Druyun at the Air Force in early 2002 and began negotiations for a $250,000 a year position as deputy director of Boeing's Missile Defense unit, which was sucking up billions a year in Star Wars-related contracts from the Pentagon. Sears would plead guilty to a single count of "aiding and abetting illegal employment negotiations." He was sentenced to four months in federal prison.

Druyun explained to prosecutors that Tankerscam was only the last of a slate of Air Force contracts that she had steered to Boeing, often inflating the price or helping the company rig its bids. Two stand out. Druyun said she personally secured a $4 billion contract for Boeing to upgrade the Air Force's fleet of C-130 cargo planes. She also admitted that she was able to get Boeing the $100 billion NATO contract for AWACS, which she knew was grossly inflated. Before leaving her Air Force position, Druyun said she also tweaked the contract on the tanker lease to inflate the cost as a "parting gift" to Boeing.

Druyun was sentenced to nine months in federal prison.

As the IG report, even its censored condition, makes clear, Druyun was but one of many crucial players in Tankerscam. The Boeing bailout was sought by her direct superiors in the Air Force, the highest levels of the Pentagon, including Rumsfeld and his undersecretary for acquisitions Pete Aldridge, senior members of congress and the Bush White House itself. In fact, Druyun wasn't even the only government figure who enjoyed a fiduciary relationship with Boeing at the very moment the deal was being hatched.

Take Richard Perle, the portly Beelzebub of the neocons. At the time of the Boeing deal, Perle served as a top advisor to Pentagon, sitting on the powerful Defense Policy Board. When questions began to surface about the soaring costs of the lease-arrangement, Perle, after meeting with Boeing executives, penned an op-ed in the *Wall Street Journal* defending the deal. But Perle declined to disclose the fact that Boeing had just committed itself to sinking $20 million into Perle's venture capital firm, Trireme Partners, which invests in defense and homeland security related technologies.

In the summer of 2004, Donald Rumsfeld personally intervened to quash a request for hundreds of pages of documents related to Tankerscam from the Senate Armed Services Committee. Rumsfeld had good reasons to be nervous. The document, which would later form the backbone of the IG report, would reveal that the paper trail in the scandal extended far beyond Druyun, the designated fall person, and into the highest levels of the Pentagon, including his very own office.

Although the White House censored most references to the personal involvement of Rumsfeld and his top deputy Pete Aldridge, a couple of incriminating emails and notes escaped the black marker. For example, in July 2003, as congressional attacks on the deal were gaining force, Air Force Secretary James Roche records that he had just heard from Rumsfeld who instructed him "not to budge on the tanker lease proposal."

Around the same time, Pete Aldridge, the former McDonnell-Douglas executive tapped by Rumsfeld to become Undersecretary of Defense for weapons acquisitions, received an email from Ronald G. Garant, a top auditor in the comptroller's office at the Pentagon, warning that the tanker deal was a transparent scam. "We all know that this is a bailout for Boeing," Garant wrote. "Why don't we just bite the bullet" and demand that Boeing trim its costs. Garant warned that unless the deal was altered it would "screw the taxpayer." Aldridge ignored the frank warning from his auditors.

As the deal began to fall apart, Rumsfeld appears to have gotten personally involved in the hunt for a scapegoat. During a Pentagon meeting shortly after Boeing canned Druyun, Rumsfeld is recorded as saying, "in light of that should we take a second look at her involvement in any tanker lease related matters in order to deflect possible criticism from the Armed Services Committee and unfavorable publicity." Note the emphasis here on "deflection."

The tanker deal seemed to corrupt nearly everyone it touched. When word of the rising costs of the deal began to leak out, the White House Office of Management and Budget was forced to evaluate the program. That tasked fell to Robin Cleveland, an associate director of OMB. Ms. Cleveland let Air Force Secretary Roche, a former executive at Northrop Grumman, know that she was inclined to approve the deal but that she wanted a favor in return. Her brother had just applied for a job at Northrop Grumman and she wanted Roche to put in a good word with his former colleagues. Within the hour, Roche had sent a personal message to Northup executives urging them to hire Cleveland's brother. He followed this up with a cheerful email to Ms. Cleveland: "Be well. Smile. Give tankers now! (Oops, did I say that?)"

There is, of course, a continuity to Pentagon scandals, from the great Lockheed C-5A swindle in the 1960s to the bid-rigging schemes of the Reagan era that came to be known as Operation Ill Wind. What gives the Boeing deal a certain unique cachet is that it was made possible by Pentagon reforms that were supposed to curtail contractor fraud. Tankerscam has its ideological origins in the Clinton administration and Al Gore's reinventing government scheme, which proved to be a thinly disguised plan to outsource Pentagon work to the private sector. All in the name of cutting red tape. Of course, at the Pentagon red tape is often the only thing keeping the lid on soaring costs.

So how did it all end? Druyun and Sears landed in prison. Phil Condit, once Boeing's golden boy, lost his job. Roche and Sambur resigned their positions with the Air Force. Undersecretary of Defense for Acquisitions

Pete Aldridge, who approved Tankerscam, discreetly retired and executed a deft landing onto the board of Lockheed.

Boeing got a black eye, but the company wasn't barred from bidding on future Air Force contracts and remains in the running for supplying the Air Force with those very same tankers in the near future. And Ted Stevens, the prime mover of Tankerscam, didn't even have to sweat an ethics inquiry. Those are the kinds of indulgences you enjoy when you're the King of the Hill.

June, 2005

4. Harry Stonecipher's Fear of Flying

Making Love, War and Profits at Boeing

A few days after the Defense Department announced that it was once again probing irregularities in other Air Force contracts with Boeing, the company axed its new CEO, Harry Stonecipher.

The early exit came only a few months after former CEO Phil Condit resigned in the wake growing scandals involving cheating on Air Force projects that got the company banned from work on a missile launching program and landed two top executives in federal prison.

This time the illicit relationship didn't involve a backroom assignation with the Pentagon. Instead, Stonecipher was ousted because he had an affair with a female executive at the beleaguered company. Stonecipher is married; the female executive is divorced.

Stonecipher, who had returned to Boeing in 2003 after a few years of retirement on the golf courses of Florida to rehabilitate the company's reputation after the resignation of Condit, began his dalliance with an unnamed woman executive "several levels down" the corporate ladder in January of 2005. The affair flourished over a few fervid weeks this winter. But it wasn't the sexual relationship alone that did him in, according to the head of Boeing's board. There were no charges of sexual harassment or misappropriation of funds. So the real reason for his ouster remains unclear.

"It wasn't the affair," explained Lewis Platt, chair of Boeing's board of directors. "It was the circumstances surrounding the affair. We thought there were issues of poor judgment that impaired his ability to lead going forward."

Platt didn't disclose the lapses of judgment that cost Stonecipher his $1.5 million a year post. "We simply felt that if certain details were disclosed it would embarrass the company," offered Platt, rather obliquely.

Company rules do not prohibit affairs between co-workers. In fact, inter-office romances are something of a tradition among Boeing executives. Stonecipher's predecessor, Phil Condit, married his secretary and later launched a torrid affair with a Boeing receptionist in the months before he resigned.

When Stonecipher took the helm at Boeing in 2003, he held a defiant press conference were he boasted that his job was to convince Wall Street investors, Pentagon procurement officers and congressional appropriators that Boeing wasn't "run by a bunch of crooks."

He was referring to the procurement scandal involving the leasing of Boeing-owned tankers to the Air Force that resulted in jailing of two Boeing executives and the resignation of Condit. In January 2005, Michael Sears, the former chief financial officer at the company and long-considered a front-runner for the CEO post, was sentenced to four months in federal prison for his role in illegally brokering a job for Air Force procurement official Darleen Druyun, who had steered numerous contracts to Boeing, including the tanker deal. Druyun is serving a nine-month sentence.

At the same time, Boeing had also been caught cheating in another bid for a Pentagon contract. In that scandal, the Pentagon's Inspector General discovered that Boeing had used documents stolen from Lockheed-Martin to aid its attempt to win a rocket-launching contract. As punishment, the Air Force barred Boeing from bidding on new rocket-launching contracts for 20 months, although Stonecipher later prevailed upon the Pentagon to reduce the penalty to a period of a few short months.

Stonecipher, a native of Tennessee who refers to himself as a Hillbilly executive, spoke of himself as a kind of corporate sheriff who would show no tolerance for ethical breaches by subordinates.

"After the ink was dry on my appointment here, I said, OK we are going to have a dedication to a value system," Stonecipher said. "If you are going to work here, you must comply with the Boeing Code of Conduct."

That code of conduct was written for Boeing by the pious Warren Rudman. Rudman, the former senator and Iran/contra cover-upper, has been dubbed the "white Andrew Young" for his history of providing, for a lofty fee, ethical nostrums for unsavory corporations. Under Stonecipher's regime, each Boeing employee was forced to sign the Rudman code.

But the Rudman rules say nothing about affairs. And Stonecipher's tenure as CEO had been very good for Boeing's bottom line. Despite losing commercial plane business to Airbus, Boeing's stock had soared to new highs under Stonecipher's leadership, largely as a result of defense contracts. This has led to speculation inside and out of the company that Stonecipher was shown the door for something more substantial than a mere consensual affair with a female executive, who was not relieved of her position. It's not common practice in corporate America for a board to can a CEO who made millions for their company. Especially when the executive didn't commit a felony or even violate company rules.

This has prompted speculation that Stonecipher may have been forced out in advance of a widening probe into Boeing's contracts with the Pentagon. In late February, Michael Wynne, the acting chief of Pentagon acquisition programs, announced that a recent review of Boeing defense contracts had found irregularities in four contracts ranging from $62 million to $1.5 billion each. Among the Boeing contracts being reviewed are a $1.5 billion award for depot maintenance of the Air Force's KC-135 aerial refueling aircraft; an environmental satellite system worth up to $400 million; a C-40 lease and purchase program worth about $244 million; and a C-22 replacement program worth about $62 million.

The value of the tainted contracts totaled more than $2.2 billion. Wynne ordered the Pentagon's inspector general to begin a more detailed inquiry. A parallel investigation is being conducted by the Defense Science Board. It is slated for release in late 2005.

We do know that Stonecipher was undone from the inside. On February 28, Platt received a packet of information on the affair from a Boeing whistleblower. The dossier included a memo and included copies of emails between Stonecipher and his lover, as well as other evidence of sexual banter. Similar packets were sent to heads of Boeing's legal and ethics departments.

The whistleblower alleged in the memo accompanying the documents that Stonecipher had given a boost to the career and salary of his paramour.

Platt immediately confronted Stonecipher with the accusations from the anonymous tipster. Stonecipher admitted the affair, but denied giving his lover any preferential treatment.

The Boeing board was meeting that week in Huntington Beach, California. As the board members sat down to dinner, Platt broke the news of their CEO's erotic escapades. The board was split on how to handle the situation. Apparently, most board members thought that a mere reprimand would do the trick. After a few hours of heated debate, the board ordered an investigation by an outside law firm from Los Angeles. The inquiry took a week and Stonecipher was fired and removed from his position as board member soon after the lawyer's report was handed to the board. The findings of that report have not been made available.

Few Boeing workers are shedding tears over the fall of Stonecipher.

He was widely considered a pompous and abrasive executive, who had built his career by slashing jobs and moving production overseas. Many Boeing workers were still seething over Stonecipher's ruthless handling of the strike in 2000 by Boeing's engineers. At the time, Stonecipher was Boeing's chief operating officer. His drive to crush the union prompted striking workers to plaster his portrait on portable toilets along the picket lines with a sign reading, "Outsource Harry."

Their wishes finally came true.

March, 2005

Nineteen

How the RAND Corporation Concocted the Colombian War

We've been saying it all along. The war in Colombia isn't about drugs. It's about the annihilation of popular uprisings, by the FARC, the ELN or Indian peasants fending off the ravages of oil companies, cattle barons and mining firms. A good old-fashioned counter-insurgency war, designed to clear the way for American corporations to set up shop in Colombia, with cocaine as the scare tactic. Now we have obtained copies of two Defense Department commissioned reports that starkly outline the same narrative of ongoing military intervention under the cover of the drug war and urge the Bush administration to drop the pretext of counter-narcotics and get on with the business of wiping out the insurgents.

In 2000, the US Air Force hired the RAND Corporation to prepare a review of the situation in Colombia. RAND submitted its 130-page report, called the *Colombian Labyrinth: The Synergy of Drugs and Insurgency and Its Implications for Regional Stability*, in early June 2001. The other report is a paper written by Gabriel Marcella, titled *Plan Colombia: the Strategic and Operational Imperatives*. Marcella is a former chief adviser to the Commander-in-Chief of the US Southern Command who now teaches on national security matters at the US Army War College.

Together, the two reports reach the same conclusion: the US needs to step up its military involvement in Colombia and quit cutting off options by limiting its operations to counter-narcotics raids. But along the way, the reports make a number of astonishing admissions about the paramilitaries and their links to the drug trade, human rights abuses by the US-trained Colombian military and the irrationality of crop fumigation.

The RAND group piously condemns Colombia as "a failed state," where the central government has lost authority, the economy has caved in, and the social systems are in free-fall. In fact, according to RAND's neo-Spenglarian model, Colombia never really developed into a full-fledged "state" at all. The study notes mournfully that "lack of national integration and a large degree of regional autonomy have characterized the Colombian political environment. None of Colombia's regions has been strong enough to dominate the others; as a result a dominant center has not emerged."

This terminal diagnosis serves as a prescription for US military intervention and subsequent restructuring of Colombian society by global financial institutions, such as the IMF and World Bank, whose complaints about the "fragmenting" nature of the nation's economic and political systems are liberally spliced throughout the report.

In fact, the RAND study relies heavily on a December 2000 report by the World Bank, titled "Violence in Colombia: Building Sustainable Peace and Social Capital," which concludes that the quid pro quo for Colombia getting any future large infusions of international financial aid will depend on their successful suppression of the FARC and other rebel groups. Another World Bank memo describes the FARC's fundraising strategy as a "loot-seeking" assault on "primary commodities": cattle ranches on the eastern plains, commercial agriculture in Urabá, oil in Magaldena, gold mines in Antioquia and the coca fields of Putumayo.

Initially, RAND reports, the FARC distanced itself from the drug trade, which it considered to be counter-revolutionary. But RAND says the FARC altered its strategy at its 7th Conference in 1981. And since then the FARC has expanded its base amongst the peasant workers of the coca fields and cocaine labs. While the FARC peasant army has doubled over the past decade, it still only numbers about 7,000 fighters—2,000 fewer than the paramilitary death squads.

It is this move toward taxing "commercial enterprises" by the revolutionaries, which has caused something of a panic in Washington. RAND cites a former CIA analyst as saying that the FARC has invested its "taxes" on these industries into "a strategic financial reserve", which will enable them to "sustain an escalation of the conflict."

RAND alleges that the FARC is stepping up it plans to wage cyber-warfare, citing the recent success of the Zapatistas. Already, RAND says, the FARC has used the Internet to hoodwink US and European environmental, religious and human rights groups into doing its bidding in the "net wars." As evidence it rather feebly trots out an email "pen letter" from the Spring of 2000 where greens, unions and human rights groups joined in a "call for peace in Colombia." RAND also takes the opportunity to chide the head of the New York Stock Exchange for attending a FARC conference last year, a trip which, RAND says, "enhanced the guerrillas perceived legitimacy, diminished the stature of the government in Bogotá and complicated the Colombian government's ability to secure international support."

And the FARC is not the only threat to capital investment in Colombia. The Cuban-inspired National Liberation Army (ELN) operates in petroleum rich northeastern Colombia, where, the RAND report snears, it makes its living from "funds extorted from international oil companies." To date even RAND admits that the ELN has resisted involvement with cocaine, instead pursuing "an economic strategy" consisting primarily of raids on the power grid and the "communications infrastructure."

Much time is spent savaging the "unresponsible macroeconomic management" of Colombia's economy, a situation, RAND warns, that is only made more perilous by the FARC's incursions into Colombia's oil and coffee producing regions. In actuality, the Colombian economy, long the most stable in South America, began to collapse in the mid-1990s, shortly after the wholesale privatization measures instituted by the Gaviria administration, under the lash of the IMF and World Bank.

Both RAND and the World Bank point to the horrifying level of "social intolerance killings," which for men aged 14-44, reached a level of 394 deaths per 100,000 last year. In all, Colombia sees 30,000 annual murders, double the number for the entire United States in 1998. Slightly more than 23,000 murders have been linked to "illegal armed organizations" since 1988. The implication is that the FARC is responsible for these killings and you have to dig deep into the RAND analysis to discover otherwise. In fact, according to statistics compiled by the Colombian government about 3,500 people were killed by the guerrillas and 19,652 by paramilitaries and "private justice" groups.

The leader of the AUC, the central command for the 19 paramilitary "fronts," is a nasty piece of work named Carlos Castaño, who supervises a killing program that sounds as if it came right off the pages of the CIA's Phoenix Program's operations manual. The RAND report details how Castaño's AUC routinely executes "suspected guerrilla sympathizers" in order "to instill fear and compel support among the local population." When that strategy fails to deliver, the AUC simply launches an all-out attack on the villages and massacres the inhabitants. RAND dispassionately notes that the AUC justifies these atrocities, in language that even Bob Kerrey might admire, as a legitimate way to "remove the guerrillas' supply network."

The robust ties between the paramilitaries and the Colombian military (not to mention the CIA and the Pentagon) is cursorily dispensed with by RAND in a brisk few sentences, concluding that such ties are only natural given the circumstances. RAND fails to note that many of the leaders of paramilitary groups where once officers in the Colombian military, some of them trained at the School of the Americas. Although there are nearly as many paramilitary fighters as there are guerrillas, there is a gross and telling disparity between the numbers of paramilitaries (76) versus guerrillas (2,677) killed by the Colombian military. RAND dismisses this as evidence of collusion between the Castaño and the Colombian military, saying that "the results could hardly have been different, given that the guerrillas are much more likely to seek confrontation with the armed forces than are the self-defense forces."

The RAND study takes pains to delegitimize the role of the paramilitaries, sneering that "the term paramilitaries is an unsatisfactory rubric to describe the *autodefensas*, although it has gained widespread currency [so widespread, in fact, that it is used throughout the RAND report]…It has no particular descriptive value in referring to the autodefensas and (perhaps intentionally) might convey the implication of quasi-political status." Despite the murders and the drug trafficking, RAND attempts to portray many of the paramilitaries as performing necessary self-policing functions in the absence of strong state authority, a kind of benign civic group "based on the neighborhood watch concept."

Although 20 pages are devoted to discussion of the FARC's ties to the drug trade, the RAND report spends only a single paragraph on the links of the paramilitaries and the narco-traffickers. But it is as damning as it is brief. RAND grudgingly admits that Castaño's group derives "a considerable extent" of its income from the drug trade and notes that eight of the AUC's 19 death squads also serve as protection gangs for the cocaine industry.

Castaño himself has boasted of his relationship with the drug lords to CNN's International Division. He said that 70 percent of the funds for the AUC come from the drug trade. The remaining 30 percent, the RAND report notes in a stark parenthetical, "coming largely from extortion."

The Colombian government under Pastrana (though not the Colombian generals) takes the public position that the paramilitaries are at least as big of a threat as the FARC and the ELN and is moving, rhetorically, at least, to suppress them. RAND, however, condemns this approach as "unwise and shortsighted." Better, RAND concludes, to mimic the Peruvian model and empower the death squads into "a supervised network of self-defense organizations."

Of course, the Peruvian model was created and implemented by the recently imprisoned head of Peruvian intelligence, Vladimir Montesinos. Montesinos, a longtime CIA asset, won kudos for his bloody tactics against the Shining Path rebels but was undone when it came to light that he had organized a shipment of arms from Jordan to the FARC.

According to Peruvian sources, the shipment of guns from Jordan by Montesinos to the FARC, which got the CIA so enraged they brought him down, was actually a originally intended for the paramilitaries in Colombia (arranged with full CIA approval of course) which the wily Montesinos sold for a higher price to the FARC. This story rings true—Jordan is essentially a US colony, so its much more likely that weapons shipment from there would have to be for an approved customer.

Even more menacingly, RAND suggests that the Colombians could reconfigure the paramilitaries into roving National Guard units that will hunt-and-kill guerrillas. RAND suggests, rather cagily, that this may already be under way with US help. The report discloses the existence of a relatively obscure multi-million dollar contract given by the Pentagon to the Military Professionals Resources, Inc., a group of retired US military and CIA officers and retired FBI assistant director, Joseph Wolfinger. In yet another example of the privatization of US military aid to Colombia, the MPRI is supposed to "assist in the modernization of the Colombian armed forces."

There's no question that the Colombian military, under the eye of US advisers, is taking a more aggressive tactic, employing hunt-and-kill squads supervised by School of America-trained officers. The RAND analysts were particularly thrilled with the results of Operation Annihilator II, a bloody raid on FARC strongholds in Sumapaz. RAND notes approvingly that the body count from Colombian military strikes rose from 364 in 1999 to 506 in 2000.

Plan Colombia is inadequate to the task of eradicating cocaine or the FARC, RAND warns. Moreover, RAND advises that the US contribution, $862.3 million a year, to the effort is too paltry to make much of a difference. Much of the money goes to fund the purchase of 16 Black Hawk attack helicopters and 20 Huey transport helicopters that may not even arrive on the ground for several and which won't have any spare parts.

In addition, RAND ridicules the requirement for human rights training and monitoring, which is attached to the US aid package. "There is a question of the practical limitations on the Colombian government's ability to prevent human rights violations in the context of an armed insurrection," the RAND analysts contend. To buttress this assessment, RAND points to the US experience in Vietnam, arguing that the slaughter of civilians is simply a cost of doing business during wartime and that "even with disciplined troops, the chain of command will ultimately break down at times under the stress of combat."

Of course, most of the US massacres in Vietnam were the result of troops carrying out official policy, such as Phoenix missions, and not the actions of crazed grunts going on killing sprees. The same is true in Colombia, where in the past two years alone where 477 police and military officers have been found guilty of human rights abuses by civilian courts.

The thrust of Plan Colombia's cocaine suppression campaign–and the bulk of US aid—is aimed at Colombian troops seizing coca fields under FARC control in the Putumayo district. This "southern strategy", RAND admits, is a thinly veiled effort to rechannel anti-drug efforts into a full-blown assault on a major FARC stronghold, with US helicopters doing the brunt of the air assaults and US advisors providing aid to the fledgling Colombian military in this riverine region and "for improved radar, airfields and intelligence collection."

But RAND warns that by targeting coca production, particularly with the widespread use of toxic fumigants, the Colombian military, and its US advisors, may actually end up bolstering the FARC's public standing in the region. "According to the governor of Putumayo, about 135,000 of the district's 314,000 inhabitants depend directly on the coca crop for their livelihood. Intensified coca irradication would probably be resisted by the local population, which generate a serious social conflict, further delegitimize the Colombian government among the populace and strengthen support for the FARC."

RAND rightly notes that the aerial fumigation of coca crops is backfiring politically. "Absent viable economic alternatives [such as crop substitution and infrastructure development], fumigation may simply displace growers to other regions and increase support for the guerrillas.

In the end, RAND says that the major flaw in Plan Colombia is that it contains "no clear link to a military strategy", which it largely blames on the US's insistence that its aid must be couched in terms of the drug war. It argues that the drug war approach is on the brink of not only failing, but spilling over into a wider conflict that might require the insertion of US troops. "If the Pastrana administration falters, either in its counter-narcotics or counter-insurgency approach, the US would be confronted with an unpalatable choice. It could escalate its commitment to include perhaps an operational role for US forces in Colombia, or scale it down, which would involve some significant costs, including a serious loss of credibility and degradation of the US's ability to muster regional support for its counter-narcotics and political objectives. At the same time, Bogotá has essentially adopted a US version of the problem, which focuses on narcotic eradication, as the centerpiece of its strategy. As a result, it has gained access to substantial US resources, but at the cost of a loss flexibility to design and implement its own solutions."

RAND concludes that the only solution is the elimination of the threat to the stability of the region posed by the FARC and the ELN. It also advises the Pentagon that "the Colombian government, left to its own devices, does not have the institutional or material resources to reverse unfavorable trends." One of those trends is the resurrection of the domino theory, called here the "spillover effect." RAND suggests that if the US doesn't intervene the Colombian situation "will metastasize into a wider regional upheaval." It is up to the US to act as the "deus ex machina" in this conflict.

Several scenarios are put forth, including that the FARC might "move into Panama in a major way and threaten the Canal and other US interests." RAND suggests that Venezuela, with its oil reserves topping 73 billion barrels, is another "critical US security interest" put at risk by its "guerrilla-infested border" with Colombia, which is daily invaded by "undesirable elements." Further complicating matters, RAND contends, is the rise to power of Hugo Chavez, who has forbidden overflights of Venezuelan territory by US anti-narcotics aircraft. RAND also suspects that Chavez may be secretly "giving aid and comfort" to the FARC and ELN.

Aside from stepping up direct military aid to Colombia, RAND urges the Pentagon to expand the US military presence in the bordering nations as well, including "helping Panama fill the security vacuum in its southern provinces."

The Marcella paper is a more distilled version of the RAND report. Marcella, a specialist in South American matters at the Army War College, suggest that the future US role in Colombia become more like US operations in El Salvador than Vietnam—which, we surmise, means the deployment of death-squads-by-proxy. Hardly a comforting notion, especially when seasoned with the fact that the firm of Cheney, Powell and Rumsfeld has lately reassembled the old gang that did directed such mayhem and misery in Latin America during the 1980s: John Negroponte, Otto Reich and Elliott Abrams. Marcella approvingly invokes the Thatcherite English theorist John Dunn: "there cannot be political control without the without the capacity to coerce."

That's the kind of thinking that could spell a very bloody decade ahead for the people of Colombia.

July, 2001

Part Four: Larcenies

Grand and Grander

War is the statesman's game, the priest's delight, the lawyer's jest, the hired assassin's trade.

—Percy Bysshe Shelley

Twenty

Tiffany's on Wings

The F-22: Believe It or Not

Tiffany's on wings. That's how one senate aide refers to the Pentagon and its contractor's latest dream weapon: the F-22. "It's showy, unimaginably expensive, fragile and utterly useless", the aide tells us. "But there's no stopping it."

The F-22, known to its press agents as the "Raptor", has been on the drawing board since 1981, at which time the Air Force announced that it wanted a generation of new tactical fighter planes to replace the F-15. In 1986, Lockheed was picked to lead the development of this plane, then known as the Advanced Tactical Fighter.

Across the next 15 years, billions of dollars have been poured into the project with little to show for it. Indeed, the F-22 has enjoyed the longest coming out party of any plane in the history of the Pentagon. And, according to Pentagon analysts, it's still nowhere near ready to go into production. Indeed, some argue that the plane, designed to attack an enemy that no longer exists, is already obsolete, both technologically and strategically.

But don't expect these trifling details to stand in the way of the Pentagon, Air Force brass, Lockheed and the F-22's two other prime contractors, Pratt/Whitney and Boeing. These parties are now rushing to put the troubled plane into what's called "initial low rate production" at a date as close as March 30 of this year. Unless the Bush administration intervenes, the Air Force will be saddled with at least 10 of these technological relics and billions more will flow into the coffers of the contractors.

The F-22 was supposed to have completed 1,500 hours of flight testing before going into production. As of early February 2001, it has only tallied 850 hours. But apparently that's not a problem for the Air Force. They've decided to simply reduce the planned test hours. "We are finding test efficiencies in this process", Air Force Brig. Gen. Michael Mushala, program director for the F-22, told *Defense Daily*. "We don't have to have extra flight test time because of the capabilities of the airplane."

In other words, the Pentagon is saying that it can purchase and test these experimental aircraft simultaneously, correcting any problems as it goes along. This is a hoary defense department con called "concurrency." Along with the V-22 Osprey, the F-22 presents a case study for the Pentagon's procurement pathology: call it the buy-before-you-fly syndrome. "One of the oldest tricks is putting off testing until production has begun," says Danielle Brian, director of the Project on Government Oversight, a Pentagon watchdog group. "As a result, the contractor gets paid twice: once to make a flawed system and once to fix it."

When the Air Force first announced plans for the F-22, the Pentagon claimed it was going to be a cheap buy, relatively speaking. In selling the idea to Congress, the plane's pitchmen said it could be produced for $35 million a plane, roughly the cost of an F-15. They were lying, as all witting parties were well aware. "Everyone knew this wasn't going to be a $35 million plane", an Air Force colonel said in 1988. But of course it is a cardinal rule of Pentagon procurement to do and say whatever it takes to sell the project and once these programs get started they build up a political momentum that makes them nearly impossible to shutdown regardless of the cost. It's a kind of bait and switch operation that's been used again and again.

But even by historical standards the escalation in the price-tag for the F-22 has been jaw-dropping. Originally, the Air Force said it was going to purchase 880 planes for around $40 billion. Within a few months, the price doubled to $80 billion. In 1991, the Pentagon's Selected Acquisitions Review looked at the F-22 and decided that fewer planes should be built, scaling the order down to 680 planes for $64.2 billion. Then the 1997 Quadrennial Defense Review cut the number of planes even further: 339 aircraft for the same price. The $35 million fighter has now turned into a $190 million plane, four times the cost of an F-15.

But that's not all. When the GAO looked at the mounting cost-overruns, they estimated that $64.2 billion cap will only enable the Pentagon to buy 254 planes, 630 hundred fewer than originally advertised. Rep. John Murtha, the Pennsylvania Republican, is even more circumspect. He predicts that only 150 fighters will be bought. In other words, the planes could cost as much as $350 million apiece.

None of this troubles Lockheed, as long as the entire $64.2 billion is spent. Indeed, the fewer "limited edition" F-22s Lockheed unloads on the Pentagon, the more "copies" it will sell to Israel, Germany, Chile and Indonesia.

The hemorrhage of billions into F-22 research and development, testing and production recalls the financial follies of the B-2 bomber. Originally, the Air Force announced its intent to purchase 135 of the stealth bombers for $40 billion. In the end, they spent $40 billion for only 20 of the nearly useless machines.

But what has all that money bought? Not much when compared to the F-15 and F-16. Even the Pentagon's top testing officer disagrees with the performance status of the F-22. In a December 20, 2000, memo to the Under Secretary of Defense for Acquisition, Technology and Logistics, Phillip Coyle, director of Operational Testing and Evaluation for the Pentagon, concluded that the problems with the F-22 were so overwhelming that a decision on putting the plane into production should be delayed indefinitely.

Coyle's memo disclosed a litany of problems with the plane, ranging from testing delays, cost overruns, mechanical failures, and serious problems with the avionics system. Coyle warned that the plane couldn't begin operational testing without encountering "unacceptable risks".

Despite Gen. Mushala's testimonials about efficient testing, the F-22 hasn't proved all that safe to fly either. In one of its first test flights, the F-22 began to wobble uncontrollably as it attempted to land, finally smacking into the runway without landing gear, then skidding for 8,000 feet before it caught fire and partially burned. The third test flight was cancelled because the hydraulic gearing didn't work. In March 2001, the Air Force was forced to suspend test flights for six weeks after a review found problems with the plane's brakes, landing gear, environmental control systems, avionics software, missile launch detector, plus cracks in the cockpit canopy.

The Air Force touts the F-22's supposed stealth capabilities as a point of superiority compared with the aging but durable F-15. But the F-22 hasn't proved to be all that invisible, after all. From one discreet angle, the F-22 slips past radar screens. But from other apertures and latitudes, the plane, in the words of a Senate staffer, "lights up like the Budweiser blimp."

Because it's a fighter intended for aerial combat with other fighter planes, the F-22 will be restricted largely to daytime flights. But the plane is so large—partially because the designers put the missiles inside the fighter in order to lower its profile to enemy radar systems—that it will be easily detectable to the naked eye. It's five times the size of the F-16.

"The only way to make the F-22 stealthy is to tear the eyes out of enemy pilots' heads," says retired Air Force Col. Everest Riccioni. Riccioni is one of the three so-called "fighter mafia", who, along with the late Col. John Boyd and Pierre Sprey (now the director of Mapleshade Records), helped to design the F-16, probably the best fighter plane ever produced. Colonel Riccioni is now one of the F-22's most savage critics.

"The US has no realistic future air superiority problem facing it", says Riccioni. "A sane US will not war with India, China or Russia. Nor will we war with France, England, Japan and Germany. None of these nations will attack the US. Other countries are not threats." But, of course, the Air Force lists all of these as potential adversaries. Even Canada has been singled out as a possible enemy. In fact, Riccioni argues that the Air Force has been pursuing foreign sales of its fighters in order to "conjure up" potential threats in order to "artificially sustain the arms industry". In other words, the Air Force is in an arms race with itself. "If sales of US aircraft really pose a threat", Riccioni says, "some decision-makers should be processed for incompetence or subversive intent."

The F-22 was designed to penetrate 400 miles into Soviet airspace, supposedly cruising for most of this distance at supersonic speeds of Mach 1.6. But it turns out that the plane is a gas-guzzler. The fighter is plagued by a low-fuel fraction (the ratio of overall weight to weight of fuel load), which severely hampers its ability to fly at supersonic speeds. One estimate based on early testing suggests that that it might only be able to maintain its Mach-plus speeds for as little as 50 miles, or less than the distance across the Los Angeles basin.

An even more intractable problem involves the F-22's complex and unwieldy avionics system, being developed by Boeing. "The avionics for the F-22 was obsolete before the plane even went into production", a Pentagon analyst told me. That's because the computer systems that act as the plane's brain are powered by five-volt silicon chips. These went out of date in 1992 when Intel introduced the 3.3 volt Pentium chip. Now most computers run on the even faster Pentium III, a 1-volt microchip. "Imagine if this plane ever joins the fleet and is running on computer systems that are already 10 years out of date and will be 30 years out of date in the future," a senate staffer said. "It will be like trying to run a spreadsheet with an abacus."

Just to keep the planes maintained the Pentagon will have pay Boeing and Lockheed to keep open old plants to make the archaic parts for the F-22. The Pentagon has already set aside a billion dollars to address the problem of obsolete parts, a problem that will only get more bothersome over the lifetime of the plane. "It'll be like the Pentagon's version of the blacksmith shop at colonial Williamsburg," the senate staffer told me.

Even in the unlikely event that the F-22's technical and mechanical problems can ultimately be resolved, the plane still won't meet the Air Force's stated goal of rejuvenating an aging fleet of fighter planes. In fact, it will only exacerbate the problem. Under the F-22 program, the Air Force will find itself with fewer fighter planes with an older average age. This problem didn't just sneak up on the Air Force overnight. It was predicted as far back as 1991 report by Pentagon analyst Franklin Spinney.

In 1999 Republican congressman Jerry Lewis of California led a successful effort to cut off funding for the opulent fighter jet. The measure passed by an overwhelming margin: 334-45. But Lewis and his colleagues underestimated the Pentagon's power. In a budgetary sleight of hand, the $2.9 billion annual appropriation was simply reallocated by the House/ Senate conference committee from procurement accounts to that gold mine of the defense contractors: research and development.

A year later Rep. Peter Defazio, the Democrat from Oregon, went back on the attack. In July 2000, Defazio denounced the F-22's cost as obscene and offered an amendment to the defense appropriations bill which would have knocked down funding for the F-22 by $932 million. This blasphemy roused into action Rep. Randy "Duke" Cunningham, a California Republican and a fighter pilot in the Vietnam War.

Cunningham rushed to the floor of the House to defend the honor of the Air Force and its contractors. "Our liberal and socialist friends would tell us the Cold War is over and there is no threat," Cunningham blustered. "Our kids are going to die, and its amendments like this that have stopped our military from surviving and put us in a situation where we have got 21 ships along a pier that cannot be deployed because they are down for maintenance." When Defazio denounced Cunningham's tirade as "bizarre", Cunningham screamed that he had visited the Democratic Socialists of American website and discovered a link to the website of the Progressive Caucus, headed by Defazio.

The combined lobbying might of the Pentagon and its contractors is more overwhelming than any weapons system. It's a lesson many politicians learn the hard way. "I sat on Defense Appropriations for many years, and I can tell you, when they come in with all those charts and movies and all those things", recalls former Senator Dale Bumpers. "They scare the life out of you. You just feel like you're a traitor if you vote against whatever it is they're promoting that particular day."

The funding of a big ticket defense system usually hinges on where it's being built. For optimum appropriations, the factories must be located in congressional districts with political clout. The F-22 fits this bill nicely: the engine is being built by Connecticut-based Pratt Whitney, the troubled avionics system is being developed by Boeing in Seattle and the whole bag of tricks is being put together by at Lockheed's plant in Marietta, Georgia. This brings together a powerful cocktail of political powerbrokers, including Democrats Joe Lieberman and Christopher Dodd, Norm Dicks (D-W), and Zell Miller (D-GA).

The ornate fighter also had a friend in Bill Clinton. As part of his final budget, Clinton included $2.5 billion for the production and purchase of 10 F-22s in 2001. It was the centerpiece of his $60 billion procurement plan. Lockheed was represented on the Hill by Peter Knight, Al Gore's closest friend and finance chair of the Clinton/Gore 1996 reelection campaign. During Clintontime Lockheed poured more than $2.1 million into DNC accounts.

There was some early hope that Dick Cheney or Donald Rumsfeld might rein in the program, especially if it freed up money for an even bigger spending spree: the new Star Wars scheme. Cheney has a history of bucking Pentagon brass. In 1991, as secretary of defense, he pulled the plug on the Navy's A-12 attack plane, a $57 billion boondoggle. He also tried to terminate the V-22 Osprey, a flying deathtrap, but was undermined by his own department and the Osprey's frontmen in Congress.

But similar boldness with the F-22 seems unlikely. When the F-22 was under attack from a coalition of Republicans and Democrats, including Lewis and Defazio, on the Hill, Cheney and Rumsfeld both came to its rescue, signing a letter touting it as a vital component of the new military. Of course, these days Cheney and Rumsfeld keep talking about the modernization of US military hardware, a code-word for billions in expenditures for R&D programs and new high-tech systems—hence Bush's $310 billion defense budget.

A GAO report in 1994 concluded that it would be cheaper and perhaps even more effective from a military point of view to stick with the F-15. "Instead of confronting thousands of modern Soviet fighters, the US air forces are expected to confront potential adversary air forces that include few fighters that have the capability to the challenge the F-15—the US frontline fighter. Our analysis shows that the F-15 exceeds the most advanced threat system expected to exist. We assumed no improvements will be made to the F-15 but the capability of the 'most advanced threat' assumes certain modifications. Further, our analysis indicates that the current inventory of F-15s can be economically maintained in a structurally sound condition until 2015 or later."

So what's behind the F-22? The project's driven in large measure by what some Pentagon analysts call "the cult of stealth". In the mid-80s the Air Force, struggling to stay relevant, realized that "stealth" was a great marketing tool. The public was fascinated by those black, oddly configured, "invisible" airplanes and so were members of congress. It didn't matter if the stealth bomber was just as visible to most Russian radar systems as the B-52 and cost 50 times as much to produce.

"The F-22 is not going to be a fighter-versus-fighter airplane," says Riccioni. "And if you want that capability, you can get it if you don't design for stealth. And if you don't design for stealth, you can make it affordable. And if it's affordable, you can get the numbers you want." Riccioni's right, of course, except for the fact that the Air Force doesn't even need a new fleet of planes because there's no existing fighter threat, hasn't been one since the Korean War, and there's none in the foreseeable future.

Some high-ranking Republicans are beginning to shake their heads at the Pentagon's incessant begging for ever-larger budgets and more expensive weapon systems, like the F-22, even in the face of epidemic cost over-runs. "The Pentagon does not know how much it spends", said Senator Charles Grassley, the Iowa Republican who now heads the Senate Armed Services committee. "It does not know if it gets what it orders in goods and services. And the Pentagon, additionally, does not have a handle on its inventory. If the Pentagon does not know what it owns and spends, then how does the Pentagon know if it needs more money? Ramping up the Pentagon budget when the books are a mess is highly questionable at best. To some it might seem crazy."

March, 2001

Twenty-One

Haywire

The New Navy Fighter Bombs Tests

This will provide scant comfort to Iraqis, who are even now refamiliarizing themselves with the quickest route to the nearest Baghdad bomb shelter, but a recently leaked memo from Pentagon's top weapons inspector warns that the Navy is deploying for battle "an increasing number" of combat systems that may be seriously flawed.

Thomas Christie, director of operational testing and evaluation for the Department of Defense, sent his memo to Gordon England, the Secretary of the Navy in the fall of 2002. The memo was leaked to the Project on Government Oversight, a Washington-based Pentagon watchdog group.

"I am concerned about an apparent trend by the Navy to deploy an increasing number of combat systems into harm's way that have not demonstrated acceptable performance," wrote Christie. "I strongly recommend that you adopt a policy of deploying new combat systems after they have demonstrated appropriate performance during adequate operational test and evaluation."

Christie cited the weapons systems used by the Navy's F/A-18E/F Super Hornet fighter as being the most suspect. The Super Hornets are the Navy's top fighter aircraft in the Persian Gulf and Arabian Sea. In an all-out war against Iraq, the Super Hornets, based on the US aircraft carrier Abraham Lincoln, are expected to lead the Navy's air campaign against Iraq.

When the big new weapons systems fail their testing, instead of asking the contractors to fix the problem, the Navy, ever anxious to have the newest and latest hardware, simply "dumbs down" the test. It's like lowering entrance exams for high-yield explosives. Christie's memo says this happened with two classified weapons systems for the Super Hornet, one is unnamed and the other is a shared reconnaissance model called SHARP, which is supposed to allow pilots to see images up to 50 miles away at altitudes of 50,000 feet in all kinds of weather.

Christie also warned that the Super Hornet's infrared missile targeting system, known as ATFLIR, failed to measure up to expectations during a round of operational testing in April 2002. The AFLIR uses a small visible light camera to detect, classify and track both air-to-air and air-to-surface targets. In the April test of laser-guided bombs, however, the AFLIR system only worked two out of seven times.

An even more widespread problem was encountered when the Navy installed the Joint Standoff Weapon (JSOW) on the USS Stennis aircraft carrier. The JSOW is a guidance system for the Navy's new generation of "smart bombs" and is slated to be used not only on the Super Hornet, but also on the F-16 fighter and B-52 and B-2 bombers. Christie says that the JSOW has yet to demonstrate "acceptable performance" in operational testing.

All of this brings back memories of the first Gulf War, when the Pentagon hailed its new technological prowess, featuring its integrated arsenal of AWACS, Stealth fighters and bombers and smart bombs. Well, it turned out that these new systems didn't turn out to be very efficient or very smart. The stealth systems didn't work in cold weather or heavy winds. The smart bombs hardly lived up to their advanced billing or the daily Pentagon videos of missiles dropping into Iraqi smokestacks. In fact, post-war bombing assessments showed that the smart bombs hit their targets only about 30 percent of the time. Needless to say, we didn't get to watch Gen. Schwarzkopf explain with a telestrator what went wrong when the smart bombs missed their targets and hit neighborhoods filled with Iraqi women and children.

In the end, even the Pentagon figured out that the war couldn't be fought with the smart bombs and resorted to old-fashioned carpet bombing with B-52s. More than 90 percent of the bombs dropped on Iraq were conventional ordinance. Similarly, the sleek and expensive new fighter planes gave way to old war-horses, such as the A-10, which most independent defense analysts credit with destroying the entrenched Iraqi tank divisions in Kuwait and southern Iraq.

The mad rush to get these unproven systems operational before the bombing of Baghdad gets under way has a simple explanation. The Pentagon always wants new and more expensive war toys and its contractors make sure that congress appropriates the money to make that desire a reality. The Super Hornet is built by Boeing. The Navy has already ordered 222 of these fighters, at a price tag of $57 million per copy. And it wants to buy 300 more. There's 29 billion reasons to move as quickly as possible—test scores be damned.

The Pentagon, of course, views Iraq as the ultimate testing ground for its menu of new bombing systems. Given Iraq's decimated air-defense system and inept air force, there's little risk of US planes being taken down through the failure of any of these systems. And, given the tight constrictions on press coverage that have been in place since the first Gulf War, there's also little chance that the flaws in these multi-billion dollar systems will come to light during the impending war.

But when one of these missiles misses its target and slams into a house or marketplace because of a glitch in the new Boeing war technology, it means that more innocent Iraqis will die, unwitting victims of the "operational testing" of a technology which will have only proven its capacity to kill without discrimination.

September, 2002

Twenty-Two

Flying Blind

Predator Prowls the Sky

F ew things are as predictable as the excited bleats of Pentagon flacks touting the killing efficacy of new weapons systems every time the US begins a military operation. During the Gulf War, the press was dazzled with reports of smart bombs and Scud-blasting Patriot missiles. The bombing of Sudan and Afghanistan in 1998 saw the Pentagon and representatives from Boeing boast about the advent of new cruise missiles. The war on Serbia witnessed the use of Stealth bombers and the Predator Unmanned Aerial Vehicle, which the Pentagon portrayed as being the unsung hero of the Kosovo air war.

It is equally predictable that many of these claims fall on their face after the bombing ceases and a final assessment is down. Those precision-guided weapons were laughably inaccurate. The Scud missiles launched by Iraq evaded the Patriot interceptors with ease. The stealth bomber has proved to be so thin skinned that in cold weather it performs with all the agility of a flying ice cube.

Now comes the Predator UAV, which the media, clinging to every word of Pentagon press releases, has hailed as the "revolutionary" reconnaissance aircraft of the future. In recent days, the press has begun to speak of this aircraft, now puttering over Afghanistan, as the key to the war on the Taliban. Bill O'Reilly even suggested that it "may turn out to be Osama bin Laden's worst nightmare."

The Predator drones are 27-feet long with a wingspan of approximately 49 feet. They crawl along at the leisurely pace of about 84 miles an hour, scouting for targets. The drones are made by the San Diego-based General Atomics Aeronautical Systems, which describes its creation as the Pentagon's "eyes in the sky." Going price: $25 million per copy.

But a newly unearthed report by Thomas Christie, the Pentagon's top systems testing officer tells a much different story. Christie is director of Department of Defense's Director of Operational Test and Evaluation division. According to Christie's report, "the system's limitations have a substantial negative impact on the Predator's ability to conduct its missions," and that "poor target location accuracy, ineffective communications, and limits imposed by relatively benign weather, including rain, negatively impact missions such as strike support, combat search and rescue, area search, and continuous coverage."

In sum, this revolutionary new weapon doesn't work right when confronted with wind, cool temperatures, rain, snow or cloud cover—a resumé of incompetence that makes the B-2 bomber look like a model of efficiency by comparison and certainly must make bin Laden and his harem sleep sounder at night. Christie's devastating report sat dormant for months until it was finally excavated by one of the Pentagon's biggest pains in the neck, the Project on Government Oversight.

Here's a sampling of other problems with the Predator that the mainstream media and the Pentagon aren't telling the public.

- According to Air Force sources, since 1995, an estimated 17 of the 50 Predator aircraft sold to the Pentagon have crashed during testing. Another five drones are believed to have been shot down during military operations. At $25 million per drone, hundreds of millions have been squandered during testing alone.

- The Predator lacks the ability to fly in winds any stiffer than that which might be encountered outside the confines of the Astrodome.

- When flying in the rain, the Predator becomes disoriented, locks onto the wrong targets and stops communicating with the Air Force computers that are meant to control its flight.

- There is mounting concern inside the Air Force that the Predator is highly vulnerable to being shot down, even by lightly armed forces such as the Taliban, because it must fly at such slow speeds, at low altitudes and in broad daylight. This avian Predator is no owl. It is useless when flying at night, according to the Pentagon's own review

In other words, the Predator is essentially a sitting duck and, when it flies, it flies blind. "The system is not operationally suitable," the report concludes in the torturous syntax of Pentagon-speak, "because of the serious deficiencies in reliability, maintainability and human design factors."

Osama and O'Reilly take note.

October, 2001

Twenty-Three

Use 'Em or Lose 'Em

Tiny Nukes Are Better Nukes

Make the desert glow for ten thousand years. Wipe them off the face of the Earth. Pulverize them into ashes and glass. Such is the unrestrained blood lust that masquerades as military punditry these days. The *Washington Times* has called on the Bush administration the use of nuclear weapons against Afghanistan and Iraq. Absurd? Dick Cheney and Donald Rumsfeld had the question put to them directly and neither would rule out the use of nuclear bombs as an option. Rumsfeld's deputy, the blood-thirsty, Paul Wolfowitz has warned that the Pentagon is poised to unleash "a very big hammer", a hammer capable of "ending states that support terrorism." (Rumsfeld says the Pentagon has identified nearly 60 such states.)

We now find ourselves closer to the unthinkable possibility of launching a nuclear first strike than at any time since the thawing of the Cold War. What is important to understand is the fact that there are people inside the Pentagon and the nuclear labs who have been urging just such a posture, even before the events of 9/11. There won't be any run-up time or re-targeting necessary. They are ready, fingers on the button, awaiting just a nod from President Bush.

A few years ago the Pentagon came to a remarkable conclusion with regard to the nuclear weapons: smaller is better. These days the Wizards of Armageddon are palpably anxious to develop a new class of nuclear weapons, the so-called "deep penetrator" warheads. These are relatively low-yield weapons, packing warheads as small as 10 kilotons. Rear Admiral George P. Nanos excitedly refers to this new breed of nukes as "hard target killers."

During testimony before the House in May 2001, General John A. Gordon, director of the National Nuclear Security Administration, groused that for the past decade the Pentagon had not been able to actively pursue new weapons designs. He said he wanted to "reinvigorate" planning for a new generation of "advanced nuclear warheads."

"This is not a proposal to develop new weapons in the absence of requirements," Gordon told the committee in a gem of Pentagon doublespeak. "But I am not now exercising design capabilities, and because of that, I believe this capacity and capability is atrophying rapidly."

Gordon wasn't being entirely truthful. In fact, the Pentagon and its weapons designers have been crafting a variety of new weapons over the past decade, right under the nose of the snoozing press. Indeed, although the Clinton administration generated a lot of hoopla by supporting the comprehensive test ban treaty (which it promptly violated with a string of subcritical tests), the Department of Energy and the Pentagon were busy developing new breeds of weapons. In 1997, they unveiled and deployed the B61-11, described as a mere modification of the old B61-7 gravity bomb. In reality, it was largely a new "package", the prototype for the "low-yield" bunker blasting nuke that the weaponeers see as the future of the US arsenal.

But there's no question that the nuclear priesthood is salivating at the prospect of a new generation of nukes, and new infusions of cash, under the Bush regime, which has been stockpiled with nuclear hawks, ranging from Richard Armitage and Paul Wolfowitz to Assistant Secretary of Defense Jack Couch, who a couple of years ago wrote that the US should consider dropping a small nuke on North Korea to teach them a lesson.

The Pentagon, of course, isn't the only one pushing new bombs. So are the nuclear labs and their legions of contractors. "There's an overwhelming desire to develop new nuclear weapons and there are a lot of rationales put forward to justify the expenditure and the risks," says Don Moniak, an organizer with the Blue Ridge Environmental League in Aiken, South Carolina. "For example, the nuclear labs have said they make new design weapons if only to maintain design expertise." Moniak monitors weapons production and plutonium storage and reprocessing at the Department of Energy's Savannah River Site, which Moniak says is being geared up to begin producing plutonium pits, the triggers for hydrogen bombs.

In the spring of 2001 the nuclear labs made their annual big pitch for the Bush administration to completely overhaul the nation's nuclear policy. The plea came in the form of a white paper by Paul Robinson, the director of the Sandia National Labs in Albuquerque. Robinson titled his essay "Pursuing a New Nuclear Policy for the 21st Century." It begins with a strangely unsettling premise: "I recently began to worry that because there were few public statements by US officials in reaffirming the unique role which nuclear weapons play in ensuring US and world security, far too many people (including many in our own armed forces) were beginning to believe that perhaps nuclear weapons no longer had value."

Remember that during the 2000 election campaign, Bush came off as more dovish than Gore, arguing for unilateral cuts in the nuclear arsenal, while Gore, who wanted to keep the stockpile robust and enhanced with new weapons, countered that Bush was a softie on defense. Robinson clearly aimed to set Bush straight, urging him to reject the advice of people like Rumsfeld and Powell who are advocating "extreme reductions in nuclear weapons" in favor of "precision-guided conventional weapons."

Robinson doesn't want to let go a single part of the nuclear arsenal. He even argues that Russia remains a threat, although he inverts the alleged source from that of an opposing superpower to that of a disintegrating nation. As backup for this rationale he quotes US National Security Advisor Condoleezza Rice: "America is threatened less by Russia's strength than by its weakness and incoherence." This stretch is used to justify an upgrading of the most destructive and expensive weapons in the US arsenal, the so-called Category I strategic weapons capable of incinerating large-scale cities.

Robinson also sees no reason to scale-back the US stockpile of Category II weapons, the kind of all-purpose nuclear missile that Robinson dubs the "To Whom It May Concern Force." Robinson hedges when identifying exactly who the targets of these weapons might be, but he eventually concedes that they include the other nuclear and near-nuclear nations, China, India, Pakistan, North Korea, Iran and, presumably, France, though definitely not Israel.

These weapons, primarily low-yield single rocket missiles, would mainly be an investment in the Navy's submarine-launched arsenal to give the US the all-important "forward-basing" advantage—which mainly means that the US wouldn't have to worry about the touchy diplomatic issue of launching nuclear bombs over the territory of non-combatants. (Apparently, this good neighbor policy hasn't infected the Bush Star Wars team, which is toiling away on a contraption that would, if it works, knock incoming missiles down and onto the fields of Poland, Germany, Canada and France.)

But Robinson's real passion is for the Category III weapon, the bunker-busting nuke that is designed for the assassination of the leadership of "rogue regimes", a not so subtle code word for Iraq, although it really does serve as a stand-in for any troublesome non-nuclear nation. Robinson, in a scenario that perhaps even Edward Teller himself may not have envisioned, wants the Bush administration to publicly change it's policy to target heads of state with nuclear bombs. "I believe it will be important to make a part of our declaratory policy that the United States' ultimate intent, should it ever have to unleash a nuclear attack against any aggressor, would be to threaten the survival of the regime leading the state," Robinson writes. "Unless that state's leaders are deterred from the acts we are seeking to deter, our war aims would be single-minded—to destroy that leadership's ability to govern."

Robinson seems to be suggesting that unless the US eventually uses a nuclear bomb against another nation it will somehow lose credibility as the sole imperial power. What better nation to drop such a weapon on than Iraq, which remains an international bad boy. "Because it is so important that this [i.e., using nuclear weapons] never be just an idle boast, which would undercut deterrence, I believe it is essential for us to preplan our targets for any likely contingency…those who would advocate that we should not be allowed to consider deterring chemical or biological attacks with our nuclear arsenal must first show how such attacks might be deterred by other means."

For nuclear hawks like Robinson, the object isn't to merely test these weapons. It's to use them.

"Such actions would collectively imply the abrogation or devaluation not just of the Nuclear Nonproliferation Treaty but the entire fabric of humanitarian law that constrains the violence of war," says Greg Mello of the Los Alamos Study Group, a watchdog group based in Albuquerque, New Mexico. "Under this scenario, one day we might wake up and find ourselves having nuked a city full of real families near a military facility in Iran, let's say, to prevent a possible nerve gas attack on our soldiers, who were sent there to secure an oil field."

November, 2002

Twenty-Four

Patriot Gore

Collateral Damage and the Patriot Missile

Once the rockets are up
Who cares where they come down?
That's not my department
Says Wernher Van Braun.

"Wernher van Braun" by Tom Lehrer

This time around it was going to be different. This time around the Patriot missile was going to live up to all the hype, unlike in the first installment of the Gulf War when the missiles nearly struck out against Iraqi Scuds, the softballs of the ballistic missile world.

There was a lot riding on the Patriot missile system's success. Not just the safety of American and British troops and journalists or Kuwaitis and Israelis, who fear they might have been targets of Iraqi Scud missiles (assuming the regime had any left.) The new and improved Patriot missile also was going to demonstrate the efficacy of the Bush administration's mad rush to deploy a revamped Ballistic Missile Defense System, the Star Wars of Reagan's fantasy. Billions in defense contracts were riding on the backs of those missile batteries.

As in the first Gulf War, the initial press reports on the new Patriots were breathlessly glowing. As missile sirens went off in Kuwait, embedded reporters ritually donned their chemical gas masks, descended into bunkers, then emerged minutes later to announce that they'd been saved by the mighty Patriot missile.

The mobile missile batteries supposedly knocked down several Iraqi Scuds headed toward US Army positions and Kuwait City. Later, it turned out that the missiles weren't SCUDs, but smaller rockets, and they may have simply landed short in the Kuwait desert on their own volition and were not struck down by US missiles.

Then came the really bad news. On March 24, 2003, a Patriot missile battery near the Kuwait border locked onto a British Royal Air Force Tornado G-4 jet that was returning from a raid on Basra. Four Patriot missiles were fired and one hit the jet, destroying the plane and killing two British pilots.

Two days later, the radar for another Patriot missile battery zeroed in on a US F-16. The pilot of the fighter jet drew a bead on the radar dish and destroyed it before he was hit by the killer missile.

Then on April 2 an U.S. Navy F/A-18 Hornet was shot down by another Patriot missile, killing the pilot.

"They're looking into a software problem," said Navy Lt. Commander Charles Owens. "They're going to check everything out. When they do find a fault, they'll put it out to the rest of the world."

But Pentagon watchers aren't holding their breath. Based on past experience, it's more likely that Pentagon brass will attempt to obscure the cause rather than reveal a fatal design flaw in a revered centerpiece in the Army's new arsenal of smart weapons.

Indeed, there's plenty of evidence that the Pentagon and the Patriot's contractors (Raytheon and Lockheed) have known for nearly a decade that the missile has difficulties discriminating incoming missiles from friendly aircraft.

The target discrimination problem was first revealed during testing at Nellis Air Force Base in 1993. During that test an U.S. aircraft simulating a return home from a mission was flying in a corridor reserved for friendly aircraft but still would have been "shot down" by the Patriot were it a combat situation.

Over the years, billions had been poured into the program with little sign of improvement in this fundamental and lethal defect. Subsequent exercises and tests have revealed that the Patriot radar discrimination problems were not fixed, according to Philip Coyle, former Director, Operational Test and Evaluation, the Pentagon's independent testing office. Coyle says the problems were identified in so-called Joint Air Defense Operations/Joint Engagement Zones exercises during the mid-1990s.

Despite this, the Pentagon pushed to increase production of the Patriot III in the months leading up to the invasion of Iraq. In November of 2002, Lt. Gen. Ronald Kadish, the head of the Pentagon's Missile Defense Agency, told Congress that the Army needed to dramatically step up production of the new Patriots, not only for use in Iraq but also "to counter threats in North Korea, Iran and Libya."

"My recommendation is to buy PAC-3s as fast as we are able to buy them," Kadish said. When asked about problems with the system, Kadish brushed them off, saying they were merely "minor" and "annoying."

Congress, ever anxious to peddle Pentagon pork, consented, boosting Patriot missile production by more than 10 percent.

As usual with the Pentagon, cost is no object. But the Patriot is a very expensive system and it's getting costlier all the time. Raytheon and Lockheed originally promised to deliver the new Patriot system for $3.7 billion dollars. Now the cost has soared to $7.8 billion. Each Patriot missile unit costs about $170 million. In the first Gulf War, an average of four missiles were launched against a single incoming Scud.

The old PAC-2 is seriously flawed. But the new version of the Patriot has struggled through field testing, although this didn't deter the Pentagon's rush to increase production. Through the summer of 2002, the new Patriot missile had failed more than half of its field tests.

From the beginning there were signs of serious glitches in the software program that guides the missile. The program was two years behind schedule and the costs soared from $557 million to $1.1 billion for the software alone. And its still never worked right. By 2001, the cost overruns for the system had topped $10 million a month.

You simply can't trust the Pentagon to be honest about the performance of its big ticket items. During the first Gulf War, the generals crowed about the success of the Patriot, saying that it hit more than 80 percent of its targets. In fact, the missile scarcely hit any incoming missiles, as was revealed in a General Accounting Office investigation. The GAO audit concluded that the Patriot missiles hit less than 9 percent of the Iraqi Scud missiles that were launched during the first Gulf conflict.

"The results of these studies are disturbing," said Theodore Postol, the MIT scientist who studied the Patriot missile's kill rate in the first Gulf War. "They suggest that the Patriot's intercept rate during the Gulf War was very low. The evidence from these preliminary studies indicates that the Patriot's intercept rate could be much lower than 10 percent, perhaps even zero." The Pentagon went after Postol with a vengeance, accusing him of using classified documents for his conclusions on the ineptitude of the Patriot missile system.

What's more disturbing is that the Pentagon knew all this and covered it up. So did the Patriot's prime contractor, Raytheon. In the immediate aftermath of the Gulf War, the US Army issued two assessments on the Patriot missile system's performance: one on Patriot Scud kills in Israel and another in Saudi Arabia. Initially, the Pentagon claimed a success rate of 80 percent in Saudi Arabia and 50 percent in Israel. A few months later, the Pentagon scaled those back to 70 percent and 40 percent. A year later, the Pentagon admits that it had a high degree of confidence in only "ten percent" of the kills.

Why the slow comedown? American wars have served as live fire arms shows. The hype on the Patriot, which the US media eagerly gobbled up, was designed to help market the missile system to other nations. In the immediate aftermath of the first Gulf War, more than a dozen nations placed orders for Patriot missile systems. The contracts were signed before the purchasers (including Turkey, South Korea, Kuwait and Saudi Arabia) learned of the Patriot's weak batting average.

There were lethal consequences to the Patriot's failures during the first Gulf War, which the Pentagon glossed over. On February 25, 1991, a Patriot missile battery in Dharan, Saudi Arabia missed an incoming Iraqi Scud. The Scud hit an Army barrack housing US soldiers. The rocket attack killed 28 people and injured more than 100 others.

In other words, the Patriot missile has almost certainly cost more lives of US military than it has saved of civilians.

The Patriot missile is based on 1970s technology and was originally designed for use as an anti-aircraft weapon, a role it reverted to with tragic consequences in the latest Gulf War. In the 1980s, the Patriot was modified to serve as anti-ballistic missile system for use against short-range rocket attacks.

"The Pentagon has known for a decade that the Patriot cannot distinguish its targets from our own aircraft," says Danielle Brian, Executive Director of the Project on Government Oversight, a Pentagon watchdog group. "It is an outrage that they have not fixed this fundamental flaw, yet continue to buy it and sell it to our allies, and have the gall to promote this weapon in both Gulf Wars as a star when they've known it is a dud."

April, 2003

Twenty-Five

Attack of the Hog Killers

Why the Generals Hate the A-10

It's ugly. It's lumbering and it's old. But the A-10 Warthog almost certainly remains the best performing airplane in the Air Force's fleet. The 30-year-old attack plane is safe, efficient, durable and cheap. GI's call it the friend of the grunt, because it flies low, showers lethal covering fire and greatly reduces the risk of friendly fire deaths and civilian casualties.

While the high-tech fighters and attack helicopters faltered in desert winds, smoke-clotted skies and in icy temperatures, the A-10 proved a workhorse in Gulf War I, Kosovo, Afghanistan and the latest war on Iraq.

Naturally, the Air Force brass now wants to junk it.

On May 27, 2003 the *New York Times* ran an op-ed by Robert Coram describing the Air Force's plot to retire the A-10. Coram, author of the highly regarded *Boyd: the Fighter Pilot Who Changed the Art of War*, revealed that in early April 2003, Maj. General David Deptula of the Air Combat Command, ordered a subordinate to write a memo justifying the decommissioning of the A-10 fleet. Remember, this move came at one of the most perilous moments in the Iraq war, when the A-10 was proving its worthiness once again.

Why does the Air Force want to junk its most efficient plane? Coram says that the Air Force never liked the A-10 because it cut against the grain of the post-WW II Air Force mentality, which is fixated on high-altitude strategic bombing and the deployment of smart weapons fired at vast distances from the target. Indeed, the A-10 was rushed into development only because the Air Force feared that the Army's new Cheyenne attack helicopter might cut the Air Force out of the ground support role, and hence much of the action (and money).

The A-10, built in the 1970s by Fairchild Industries, skims the ground at lower than 1,000 feet in altitude, can nearly hover over the battlefield, and spews out almost 4,000 rounds of armor-penetrating bullets per minute. (These are also the weapons coated with depleted uranium that have irradiated so much of Iraq and Afghanistan.) Pilots love the plane because it is easy to fly and safe: the cockpit is sealed in a titanium shell to protect the pilot from groundfire, it has a bulky but sturdy frame, three sets of back up controls and a foam-filled fuel tank.

Of course, the most damning prejudice against the A-10 in the eyes of the generals is the fact that it is old, ugly and cheap—especially cheap. The Air Force generals are infatuated with big ticket items, new technology and sleek new machines. The fastest way to a promotion inside the Air Force is to hitch your name to a rising new weapons system, the more expensive the better. When it comes time to retire, the generals who've spent their careers pumping new weapons systems are assured of landing lucrative new careers with defense contractors.

So each time the A-10 proves itself in battle, the cries for its extinction by Air Force generals become more intense and hysterical. Since the first Gulf War, where the A-10 outperformed every other aircraft even though the Stealth fighter got all the hype, the Air Force has been quietly mothballing the A-10 fleet. During the first Gulf War, the A-10s destroyed more than half of the 1,700 Iraqi tanks knocked out by air strikes. A-10s also took out about 300 armored personnel carriers and artillery sites. At the end of the war there were 18 A-10 squadrons. Now they've been winnowed down to only eight.

In place of the A-10, the Air Force brass is pushing the congress to pour billions into the production of the F/A-22 (at $252 million per plane) and the F-35 fighter (at a minimum of $400 million a copy. These are planes designed to fight an enemy that doesn't exist and probably never will.

The generals are trying desperately to convince skeptics that the F-35 fighter jet can perform the kind of close air support for ground troops that is the calling card of the A-10. As Coram notes, the F-35 will be so expensive and so vulnerable to enemy fire (it can be taken down by an AK-47 machine gun) that Air Force commanders are unlikely to allow it to fly over hostile terrain below 10,000 feet.

But before they can consign the A-10 to the scrap heap, the Generals must first silence the plane's defenders, many of them inside the Pentagon. The witch hunt has already begun.

A few hours after Coram's article appeared, Lt. General Bruce L. Wright, Vice Commander of the Air Combat Command, at Langley Air Force Base, in Virginia, fired off a scathing memo ordering his staff to begin a search-and-destroy mission against the whistleblowers who leaked information to Coram.

"Please look your staffs in the eye and offer that if one of our officers is complicit in going to Mr. Coram, without coming to you or me first with their concerns," the General sniffled. "They ought to look hard at themselves, their individual professionalism, and their personal commitment to telling the complete story."

General Wright then reminded his directors that it was their duty to "constantly look at upgrading our aircraft and weapons systems" and instructed them to promote the "good news" about the "B-2, F/A22, the F35 and even the UCAVs."

The problem for General Wright and his cohorts in the upper echelons of the Air Force is that the new generation of high-tech planes have returned from the last three wars with less than stellar records and lots of bullet holes from lightly armed forces with no functioning air defense system.

Take the Army's vaunted Apache attack helicopter, which the Army generals are touting as a multi-billion dollar replacement for the A-10. During the Kosovo war, 24 Apaches were sent to the US airbase in Albania. In the first week of the war, two choppers crashed in training missions and the remainder of the helicopters were grounded for the duration of the air war.

In Afghanistan, during Operation Anaconda, seven Apaches were sent to attack Taliban forces in the mountains near Tora Bora. All got hit by machine gun fire, with five of them being so shot up that they were effectively destroyed.

In Iraq, according to an excellent account in Slate by Fred Kaplan, 33 Apaches led the initial attack on Republican Guard positions in Karbala, where they encountered heavy machine gun fire and a few rocket-propelled grenades. One was shot down; it's crew taken as prisoners. The other Apaches soon turned tail, with more than 30 of them sustaining serious damage.

But instead of rehabbing the fleet of A-10s, the Pentagon persists in promoting budget-busting new systems that are dangerous to pilots and civilians and ineffective against even the most primitively-armed enemy soldiers.

"For more than 20 years, the Warthog has been a hero to the soldiers whose lives depend on effective air support," says Eric Miller, a defense investigator at the Project on Government Oversight. "The A-10 works and it's cheap. But for some reason that's not good enough for the Air Force."

For the courtiers at the Pentagon, the battles of Afghanistan and Iraq are mere sideshows to the real and perpetual war: the endless raid on the federal treasury. It is a war that only the defense contractors and their political pawns will win. Everyone else, from pilots and taxpayers to civilians, will be collateral damage.

June, 2003

Twenty-Six

My Corporation, 'tis of thee...

The General, GM, and the Stryker

On December 10, 2003, two Strykers, the Army's newest armored personnel carrier, were patrolling near Balad, Iraq, when the embankment beneath them collapsed and the vehicles plunged into a rain-swollen river. Three soldiers died and another was severely injured. Three days later, another Stryker rolled over a roadside bomb south of Baghdad. The explosion left one soldier injured and the vehicle in flames.

It was an inglorious combat debut for the Army's first new personnel carrier in thirty years. But it confirmed the worst fears of some of the Stryker's critics that the vehicle is unsafe and its crews untrained for using it in combat conditions. One former Pentagon analyst described the 8-wheeled vehicle as "riding in a dune buggy armored in tinfoil."

The Stryker Interim Armored Vehicle is billed as the Pentagon's latest weapon in its new high-tech Army, a fast moving carrier designed for the urban battlefield and unconventional wars. In the fall of 2004 the Army deployed 300 Stryker vehicles and 3,500 soldiers to Iraq's notorious Sunni Triangle, the Iowa-sized area in central Iraq where the most intense guerrilla fighting is taking place.

But internal documents reveal that Pentagon weapons testers had expressed serious reservations about whether the Strykers were ready for battle. The Pentagon's chief weapons tester, Tom Christie, warned in a classified letter to the Secretary of the Defense that the Stryker is especially vulnerable to rocket-propelled grenades and improvised explosive devices. These are, of course, precisely the kinds of threats faced by the Stryker brigades now in Iraq.

Advertised as rapid deployment vehicles, the Stryker brigades could in theory be rushed anywhere in the world within 96 hours by C-130 transport planes. But numerous internal studies have questioned whether the Stryker can be deployed by C-130s at all. Moreover, a General Accounting Office report scolded the Pentagon for a host of other problems with the carrier, which was meant to replace the much-maligned Bradley Fighting Vehicle. The GAO report points to serious problems with the Stryker's design and maintenance and discloses deficiencies in training for its use.

Even Defense Secretary Donald Rumsfeld wanted to delay funding of additional Stryker brigades until more testing and training could be completed. But congress, ever an anxious to spread the pork around to as many districts as possible, didn't heed the warning and approved the additional purchases.

The Stryker is a joint venture of two of the mightiest industrial corporations in America: General Dynamics and General Motors. These companies waged a fierce two-year long lobbying battle, stretching from Capitol Hill to the halls of the Pentagon, to win the $4 billion contract to build 2,131 Strykers, which was awarded in November 2000.

The first Strykers, which cost $3 million a piece, more than 50% above projections, rolled off the assembly line in April 2002. Presiding over the ceremony at the Stryker rollout in Alabama was former Army Chief of Staff Eric Shinseki. The Stryker was a key component in Shinseki's plan to upgrade the Army, a scheme he outlined in a 1999 paper titled "Army Vision." In that report, Shinseki called for the development of an interim armored brigade featuring "all-wheel formation". This was a thinly veiled hint that the contract would be awarded to General Dynamics. The Stryker is a wheeled carrier, as opposed to the tank-like vehicles built by United Defense which run on tracks.

During Shinseki's speech in Alabama, he pointedly singled out for special thanks David K. Heebner. Heebner, a former Army Lt. General, had been one of Shinseki's top aides, serving as Assistant Vice Chief of Staff for the Army. As such, he played a key role in pushing for funding for Shinseki's projects, including the Stryker. In November 1999, General Dynamics issued a press release announcing that they had hired Heebner as an executive at the company. The announcement came a full month before Heebner's official retirement date of December 31, 1999. The timing of the announcement is curious for several reasons. Most glaringly, it's clear that the Army was leaning toward handing a multi-billion dollar contract to General Dynamics at the very time Heebner may have been in negotiations with the company for a high-paying executive position.

Federal conflict of interest laws prohibit government employees from being engaged "personally or substantially in a particular matter in which an organization they are negotiating with, or have an agreement with for future employment, has a financial interest." It's not clear if Heebner recused himself from the negotiations with General Dynamics over the

Stryker contract.

However, it's obvious that the Stryker deal, despite the reservations raised by Pentagon weapons testers and the GAO, proved to be very lucrative for both Heebner and General Dynamics. Off the strength of the Stryker deal, Heebner quickly rose to the rank of Senior Vice-President for Planning and Development for General Dynamics, the conduit between the nation's number two defense contractor and the Pentagon. By the end of last year, Heebner amassed more than 13,600 shares of General Dynamics stock valued at more than $1.2 million.

Nice work, if you can get it. Of course, the condolence letters to the newly minted Gold Star moms of sons and daughters mangled in the Stryker's frail confines might get tiresome after a few months.

January, 2004

Twenty-Seven

Hey, Brother, Can You Spare a Million?

How Neil Bush Succeeded in Business Without Really Trying

Now, that ain't workin'
That's the way you do it
Get money for nothin'
And your chicks for free.

Dire Straits, *Money for Nothing*

H is mother still calls him Neilsie. He refers to his dad, the former president, as Gampy. Neil Bush may be the black sheep of the Bush family, but his relatives have never let him down. Whenever he's been mired in financial, legal or marital imbroglios, someone in the Bush family entourage has always reached out a helping hand and often that hand has slipped Neil a fat check.

Neil Bush, the fourth child of George and Barbara, was long thought to be the rising star of the family. He had the looks, the convivial demeanor, middle-of-the-road politics and, although suffering from a severe case of dyslexia that made him the laughing stock of St. Albans, the stuffy DC prep school that groomed Al Gore, the brainpower. At least he seemed brighter than Jeb or George Jr. And, most important of all, he was the favorite son of Barbara Bush, the Agrippina of American politics.

All those lofty political aspirations came to a fatal crash in the fall of 1988, at the precise moment his father was poised to ascend to the presidency, when the Silverado Savings and Loan went belly up with Neil in the driver's seat.

In these days of multi-billion dollar financial crimes by the likes of Enron, Tyco and WorldCom, the failure of a relatively small Colorado thrift may not seem like much. But Silverado came to symbolize the entire savings and loan debacle, which ended up costing the government more than $150 billion in bail out money. Many of these companies exploited the newly deregulated financial markets to lavish unsecured loans to company insiders or political favorites and rewarded company officers and directors with ostentatious salaries and benefits. When the thrifts collapsed, the directors and executives walked away unscathed, while small investors and account-holders were left out in the cold. Appropriately, the looting of the savings and loans hit Texas harder than most other states.

At the time, Neil Bush claimed that he was being made a political scapegoat for Silverado's troubles. He said he was only a bit player in the S&L with no real decision making power, a figurehead and little more. Of course, there was some truth to this. But Neil Bush was not an entirely passive director. Indeed, he used his position as director to steer unsecured loans to his business partners, including at least one project, a scheme to drill for oil in Argentina, in which he had a direct financial stake.

The US Office of Thrift Supervision, which scrutinized the implosion of Silverado, determined that Bush had engaged in numerous "breaches of his fiduciary duties involving multiple conflicts of interest." A couple of years later, Bush and his cohorts in Silverado settled a $200 million civil suit brought by the Federal Deposit Insurance Corporation for $49.5 million dollars. The FDIC had charged the executives and directors of Silverado with gross negligence. Bush forked out $50,000 of his own cash for his part of the settlement, with most of the money coming from insurance companies.

It wasn't supposed to be this way. Bush had moved to Denver in 1980 with his new bride, Sharon. He was to set up a base of political operations in the Rocky Mountain state, with his eyes on the governor's mansion or a senate seat. But first there was a fortune to be made.

In 1983, Neil started an oil company, naturally, called JNB Exploration. The seed money for the operation came in the amount of $150,000 from a Colorado real estate mogul named Bill Walters, the self-proclaimed Donald Trump of Denver. Another early investor in JNB was Walter's friend Ken Goode, also a real estate baron, who arranged $1.75 in million credit for Bush's company from a bank controlled by Walters. For his part, Neil Bush kicked in $100 to the JNB Exploration kitty.

It wasn't long before JNB began to list. A bail out was arranged with money coming from Silverado Savings and Loan, where Bush now served as a director.

Meanwhile, Bush continued to receive favors from Ken Goode. In the mid-1980s, Goode gave Bush $100,000 in investment funds, chips to play with in the stock market. Bush ended up losing all the money, but never paid a cent back to Goode.

Bush did, however, steer millions in Silverado loans Goode's way. In

1986, Bush prevailed upon the Silverado board to approve more than $34 million in loans and credit to Walters and Goode, unsecured by anything other than Bush's word.

Neil also urged the board to loan another of Goode's companies, Goode International, $900,000 to finance an oil drilling operation in Argentina. In his pliant letter to the board, Neil conveniently elided the fact that he was a silent partner in this deal. Indeed, the Argentina oil scheme was his idea, predicated on familial ties to the corrupt of junta of generals then clutching the country in a murderous grip. Silverado was a pyramid scheme of financial self-dealing.

After Silverado crashed, Neil briefly became the poster boy for the S&L crisis. He was mercilessly mocked by the great Texas populist Henry Gonzales, during his hearings on the S&L scandal. Neil Bush's political ambitions were mortally punctured, but his business career was just starting to take off. After all, his father was now president and there was a global network of connections to exploit.

In 1989, a few months after the expiration of Silverado, Neil was offered the chance to run another company that had been created just for him, Apex Energy. The $2.3 million in start up funds came courtesy of Bush family confidant Louis Marx, heir to the Marx toy fortune. Bush pulled down $150,000 a year as CEO. Within two years, Apex Energy took a nosedive into bankruptcy.

But Neil Bush moved on, this time to TransMedia Communications, a cable TV venture headed by Bill Daniel, a longtime funder of Neil's father's political campaigns, who had been lobbying furiously for the deregulation of the telecommunications industry. For his services, Neil was remunerated to the tune of $60,000 per year, even though TransMedia's president, Dick Barnes, later admitted that the younger Bush knew nothing about the cable business.

It was around this time that Neil struck up a friendship with Nigal Fares, son of Issam Fares, then deputy Prime Minister of Lebanon and another longtime friend of the Bush family. Fares hired Neil to negotiate global deals involving the sale of covers for oil storage tankers. This partnership inaugurated Neil's lucrative ventures in the Middle East, leading to fruitful relationships with oil sheiks from Qatar to Dubai, Kuwait to Saudi Arabia.

But Neil didn't just dabble in oil. He also scouted for opportunities to cash in on the new opportunities in the booming markets of Asia. In 1994, he started a company called InterLink with Tom Bridewater, a Utah tycoon and rightwing politician. The plan called for Neil to act as an intermediary to help grease deals between US and Asian companies. According to disclosures in his divorce settlement, Neil earned from $180,000 to more than a $1 million a year from InterLink alone. In fact, it is alleged that Neil was paid $1 million to arrange a private meeting in New York City between Taiwan's president Chen Shui-bian and a US official. The charge was leveled by James Soong, leader of Taiwan's opposition party. Bush admitted to meeting Chen, but denied that he received any money from the Taiwanese leader. Meetings between officials of the US and Taiwanese governments have been prohibited since 1979, when the US normalized relations with Beijing.

The windfalls kept coming his way. On July 19, 1999, Neil experienced one of his greatest triumphs. He made $171,000 in a single day by buying and selling shares of the Kopin Corporation, a display panel company, which on that very afternoon announced a surprise deal with Japanese electronics giant, JVC, causing the stock to soar. While Neil denies profiting from any insider knowledge, the exquisitely timed transaction has all the hallmarks of a Martha Stewart-style deal in reverse. Instead of stemming losses as she may have done with a quick sale, Neil Bush made a quick killing. Kopin had been one of Interlink's early clients and Neil had recently arranged a deal where Telecom Holdings, a Hong Kong company, invested $27 million in Kopin. As a reward, Neil received stock options in the newly beefed up firm. It was merely a coincidence, Neil told the Associated Press earlier this year, that he exercised those options on that July morning and sold them later in the same afternoon, following the momentous JVC deal. Just another fortuitous coincidence.

Neil Bush's escapades across Asia came to the attention of the Grace Semiconductor Management Company, which recruited Bush onto its board of directors. Despite the fact that Neil admitted he knows nothing about semiconductors, the Chinese company recompensed Bush with $2 million in stock and $10,000 per board meeting. Grace is controlled by Taiwanese tycoon Winston Wong and Jiang Mianheng, son of Jiang Zemin, former president of China.

Another of Neil's rich friends is Jamal Daniel, a Syrian-American multimillionaire. When Neil and Sharon griped that their family didn't get to spend very much time in Kennebunkport, Daniel shelled out $380,000 to buy them a cottage next to the Bush compound.

Jamal Daniel also put Bush on retainer for his Crest Investment firm, paying him $60,000 a year to help broker deals in the Middle East. One of Daniel's most recent ventures is New Bridge Strategies, a kind of financial influence peddling outfit whose main endeavor these days is to help companies win contracts for the reconstruction of Iraq. What one brother destroys, another rebuilds.

In May of 2002, Neil Bush found himself alone in his hotel room in Dubai, where he was trying to secure financing for his new company Ignite! Learning, an educational software company geared to exploit his brother's No Child Left Behind education strategy. Neil sat before his laptop computer and pounded out a long email to his wife of 23 years, informing her that he wanted a divorce. Oddly, given his track record of financial coups, Neil's ungentlemanly missive wallows in concerns about the family's frail bank account.

"Your comments at our pool-side dinner with the kids that you and I should race to see who could make a million dollars faster, your belief expressed in different ways that I have not made enough money, your belief that it was easy to make money, and that Jamal Daniel's plotting or Dad's influence will be the magic answer to our financial woes all cause me consternation and reflect the bitterness and anger that has come from the loneliness you described Friday," Neil wrote. "It is very clear that we are failing to meet each other's core needs. We're almost out of money and I've lost my patience for being compared to my brothers, for being put down for my inability to make money, and tired of not being loved. I'm sure you have felt abandoned and a deep sense of loneliness."

Of course, in his e-confessional Neil Bush didn't feel compelled to come clean about the sexcapades with the Asian hookers or reveal the fact that he'd fallen in love with Maria Andrews, the wife of Houston oil baron, Robert Andrews, a woman Sharon Bush would later denounce in public as "Neil's Mexican whore."

At the very moment Neil hit the send button on this brutal adieu, he was sending Maria breathlessly written love letters, pining for the time when they would be both be freed from the shackles of their marriages.

"My heart is breaking with solitude," Neil wrote his lover. "I can't wait to be free to dedicate all of my passion to love you. I hurt to have you in my arms, to make love with you and be a part of your life." Yet another testimonial to Bush family values.

According to Neil, the two met in 2001 when Maria was working as a volunteer in Barbara Bush's office, but things didn't start to get amorous between them until January of 2002 when they found themselves together at a Houston fundraiser for Jeb Bush. A few weeks later Neil showed up at the Andrews's $4 million mansion, known to the neighbors as Swankienda. He came on a mission to raise money for his new project, Ignite! Robert Andrews was an oil tycoon who had made his millions largely through a fruitful alliance with one of Mexico's most notorious moguls, Carlos "Slim" Helu, the billionaire who controls the Grupo Carso conglomerate that includes TelMex.

That spring day, Neil walked away with $100,000 from Robert Andrews for his company and a new companion. As his mother said, Neil's quite the smooth talker. A few weeks later, Maria and Neil absconded to Mexico together, ostensibly to search out new investors for Ignite! They returned with a lucrative production deal courtesy of Slim Helu and a pledge to seek divorces from their respective spouses. Neil soon fired off his parting email to Sharon and, upon returning to Texas from Dubai, moved into a Houston apartment owned by his Syrian business partner, Nijad Fares. In a harmonious display of their new fidelity, Neil and Maria filed for divorce on the same day, August 26, 2002.

When Sharon Bush learned of the affair with Maria Andrews, she launched a pre-emptive battery that would have impressed the Iraq war planners. First, she announced plans to write a tell all book about the Bush clan, hinting darkly about revealing the truth of the Silverado scandal and George W. Bush's boozing and carousing. Then she let slip the fact that she had been spilling family secrets to Kitty Kelley, who was desperately trying to complete her exposé of the Bush family before the 2004 elections.

Then Sharon turned her sights on her rival, the vivacious Maria Andrews. She dramatically confronted the couple at a Houston smoothie shop where Maria and Neil were dining together and called her Neil's "Mexican whore." Then she made allegations that Neil and Maria had been sleeping together for several years and that Maria's youngest child had not been fathered by Robert Andrews but by Neil. Andrews struck back with an $850,000 libel suit. Sharon won the first round when a Texas judge approved her demand for DNA samples from Andrews and the child. But she lost on appeal. And so it goes.

The Neil v. Sharon Bush divorce papers provide the most titillating bed-table reading since the footnotes of the Starr Report. For example, the divorce depositions detail Neil's dalliances with prostitutes in Asia. While Neil was doing Interlink business in Thailand and Hong Kong, he enjoyed the exotic experience of hearing an urgent knocking on his hotel room door. Upon opening the door, Neil was confronted by a beautiful young woman who said she wanted to have sex with him. On at least three difference occasions, Neil accepted the hospitality of his hosts. He admitted to the sexual encounters in his bizarre deposition during his divorce proceedings. The deposition was released in early 2004. Here's a sample of the back and forth between Bush and his wife's lawyer:

Marshall Davis Brown (lawyer for Sharon Bush): Mr. Bush, you have to admit that it's a pretty remarkable thing for a man to just got to a hotel room door and open it and have a woman standing there and have sex with her.

Neil Bush: It was very unusual.

Marshall Davis Brown: Were these prostitutes?

Neil Bush: I don't…I don't know.

Neil's lawyer, John Spalding, counterattacked by charging that Sharon Bush tried to manipulate her husband through the use of voodoo spells. Spalding claims that Sharon clipped strands of Neil's hair and wove them into a bizarre doll that she hid under his bed.

Sharon tartly dismissed such allegations as lawyerly hokum. She admitted to collecting strands of Neil's hair, but not for the purpose of practicing the dark arts of Haiti. Instead, Sharon confessed that she wanted to have Neil's hair tested for the presence of cocaine. "He was looking thin and acting weird," Sharon said. Apparently, a taste for primo powder runs deep in the Bush family.

On March 6, Neil and Maria finally tied the knot. The wedding ceremony took place in Jamal Daniel's palatial home in Houston. Most of the Bush clan was there to toast the new couple, although George and Laura discreetly made other plans for the weekend. After a brief honeymoon, the couple moved into Maria's new home, a multi-million dollar mansion just down the road from Bar and Gampy.

In the charmed world of Neil Bush, it doesn't matter what you do or

even how badly you botch the job, it all works out very well in the end.
    Roger Clinton eat your heart out.

September, 2004

Twenty-Eight

It's a Family Affair:

Uncle Bucky Makes a Killing

Back in 1991, shortly after the depleted uranium-flaked dust had settled some from the first Gulf War, there was a minor tempest in the press over influence peddling by members of the president's family, including his son Neil and his brother Prescott, Jr. Both Neil and Prescott, neither of whom had proven to be exceptionally talented businessmen, had made millions trading on their relationship to the president.

Seeking to distinguish himself from his more predatory relatives, William Henry Trotter Bush, the younger brother of Bush Sr. and an investment banker in St. Louis, gave an interview to disclaim any profiteering on his own part. Indeed, he sounded downright grumpy, as if his older brother hadn't done enough to steer juicy government deals his way. "Being the brother of George Bush isn't a financial windfall by any stretch of the imagination," huffed William H.T. Bush.

Well, perhaps being the brother of the president didn't generate as much business as he hoped, but having the good fortune to be the uncle of the president certainly appears to have padded the pockets of the man endearingly known to George W. Bush as "Uncle Bucky."

A few months before W.'s selection as president, Bush's Uncle Bucky quietly joined the board of a small and struggling St. Louis defense company called Engineered Support Systems, Incorporated (ESSI). Since Bush joined the team, ESSI's fortunes have taken a dramatic turn for the better. This once obscure outfit is now one of the top Pentagon contractors. By 2006, ESSI's revenues will top $1 billion, nearly all of it derived from defense contracts with the Pentagon or with foreign militaries financed by US aid and loan guarantees. Even sweeter, most of these contracts have been awarded in no bid, sole source deals.

True to form, Uncle Bucky claims that ESSI's amazing transformation has nothing to do with him or his nephew, the president. "I don't make any calls to the 202 (DC) Area Code," Bush sneered to the *Los Angeles Times*.

Uncle Buck's characteristic modesty was swiftly undercut by statements made by top executives at ESSI, who seemed proud that their foresight in inviting Bush on board had paid off so handsomely for all concerned.

"Having a Bush certainly doesn't hurt," chuckled Dan Kreher, ESSI's vice president for industrial relations.

Uncle Bucky Bush is 16 years younger than his brother, the former president. According to Kitty Kelley's uproarious history of the Bush clan *The Family*, Bucky was raised "almost as an only child" by his aging parents Dorothy and Prescott Bush, the senator who traded with the Nazis. Bucky was a sensitive and precocious kid with a peculiar devotion to choral music. In fact, the highlight of his career at Yale University was his starring spot with Whiffenpoofs, an elite choir.

While his older brother headed to Texas to make his name in the oil patch, Bucky returned to St. Louis, the Gateway City where the original Bush fortune had been built. He settled into a modest career as an investment banker and corporate consultant. Then, with his nephew poised to seize the White House, Uncle Bucky was offered a seat on the board of ESSI, a military support and defense electronics firm. ESSI's company prospectus describes it as "a diversified supplier of high-tech, integrated military electronics, support equipment and logistics services for all branches of America's armed forces and certain foreign militaries."

Shortly after the attacks of 9/11, ESSI positioned itself to win a series of lucrative Pentagon contracts that would catapult the diminutive firm into the top ranks of defense contractors. Within a few short months, the company's shareholders were given the financial ride of their lives.

By the time of the Iraq war, ESSI was a brawny new player on the defense block. In the spring of 2003, ESSI acquired a military communications company called TAMSCO, whose prime activity was in developing military satellite terminals in the Gulf region and in US bases in Germany in anticipation of a US invasion of Iraq. After the ESSI buy-out, TAMSCO swiftly won contracts from both the Air Force and the Army for more than $90 million for the training of troops in the operation of the system and the installation of radar equipment in Kuwait.

Then Pentagon awarded ESSI a $49 million contract to remodel military trailers for use in Iraq.

In 2003, the Defense Department gave ESSI a huge deal to provide the Army with equipment to search for Iraq's non-existent chemical and biological weapons. Part of this package included a $19 million contract to provide tents designed to protect US troops from chemical bombs. The tents didn't arrive in Iraq until after it was evident to nearly everyone that the Iraqi military didn't have access to such weapons. This didn't stop the money from flowing into ESSI's coffers and it didn't stop ESSI's executives from playing along in the grand charade. "The potential threat of our troops facing a chemical or biological attack during the current conflict in Iraq remains very real," huffed Michael Shanahan, the company's former chairman.

As the invasion transformed into a military occupation of Iraq, ESSI continued to pluck off sweet deals. In late 2003, the Coalition Provisional Authority, whose contracts passed across the Pentagon desk of arch neocon Douglas Feith, awarded ESSI an $18 million deal to engineer a communications system for the CPA offices, barricaded inside Baghdad's Green Zone.

Its executives openly clucked at the likelihood for protracted war. "The increasing likelihood for a prolonged military involvement in Southwest Asia by US forces well into 2006 has created a fertile environment for the type of support products and services we offer," gloated Gerald L. Daniels, the company's Chief Executive Officer. Rarely has corporate glee over the prospects of war profiteering been expressed so brazenly.

But Daniels had a point. Even as things began to go sour for the US in Iraq, ESSI stood to make lots of money. One of its biggest no-bid contracts came in 2004 in the wake of mounting causalities in light-armored vehicles hit by roadside bombs. ESSI won a deal to upgrade the armor of thousands of vehicles in or bound for Iraq. The company's annual report for 2005 forecast that ESSI might make as much as $200 million from this bloody windfall alone.

As the flood of new contracts poured in, ESSI's stock soared. In January of 2005, it reached its all-time high of $60.39 per share. A few days before the stock hit this lofty peak, Uncle Bucky quietly exercised his option to sell 8,438 shares of ESSI stock. He walked away from that transaction with at least $450,000. The stock sale occurred a few days after ESSI announced that the Pentagon had awarded it $77 million in new contracts for the Iraq war and a few days before word leaked to the press that the company was under investigation for its handling of older Pentagon contracts. The timing of the trade was perfect.

In a February 2005 filing with the Securities Exchange Commission, ESSI discreetly disclosed to its shareholders that the inspector general of Pentagon had launched an inquiry into a series of contracts awarded to the company in 2002 for work on the Air Force's troubled automated cargo loading machine called the Tunner.

While the company's chief financial dismissed the probe as "routine" and assured investors that it would have "no effect" on ESSI's fortunes, the Pentagon held to a more restrained assessment of the potential liability. Michael Wynne, acting undersecretary of Defense, said he had referred ESSI contracts valued at $158 million to the Pentagon's inspector general because the deals "appear to have anomalies in them." Many of the contracts were awarded on a no-bid basis and much of the probe appears to focus on the role Pentagon insiders played in steering the contracts to ESSI.

Much of the thrust behind ESSI's sudden rise has been fueled by no-bid or sole-source deals with the Pentagon. These no risk deals are part of a corporate strategy cooked up in part by none other than Uncle Bucky himself. In a profitable bit of self-dealing, ESSI hired its own board member, Bucky Bush, as a consultant in 2002. Bush, who pulls in about $45,000 a year in director's fees, was paid an additional $125,000 for his advice on ESSI's buyout of other military contractors. The acquisition strategy outlined by Bush was to train the company's appetite on the gobbling up of companies that held no-bid or sole source deals with the Pentagon.

In January 2005, ESSI spent $37.6 million to buy a New York electronics testing firm called Prospective Computer Analysis, Inc. In defending the purchase to shareholders, executives at ESSI emphasized that the company held "a lot of sole-source contracts."

A few months later, ESSI acquired Spacelink, Inc, a Virginia-based defense company, for $150 million. Spacelink, which supplies parts for military satellites, is poised to cash in on the $80 billion missile defense bonanza.

ESSI isn't the only defense-oriented company to acquire the services of Uncle Bucky. The banker from St. Louis has also been retained as a trustee for the global investment firm Lord Abbott, one of the primary financial underwriters of Halliburton. Lord Abbott is both one of the top 10 shareholders in Dick Cheney's former company, as well as one of its top mutual fund holders.

Uncle Bucky didn't unload all of his ESSI stock. He still owns 45,000 shares valued at more than $2.5 million. He used the profits from the recent sale to purchase a vacation home in Florida near his other nephew nourishing presidential ambitions, Jeb Bush.

Who knows if the Bucky will stop there?

March, 2005

Twenty-Nine

Duck and Cover, Redux

Bunker Busters and City Levelers

In the fall of 2004, anti-nuclear activists won what appeared to be a stunning victory when the Republican-controlled congress eliminated funding for a new generation of nuclear weapons, the so-called bunker busting nukes. Shortly after the final vote, Rep. Ed Markey called this rare rebuke of the nuke industry the "biggest victory that arms control advocates in congress have had since 1992."

In the omnibus appropriations bill passed by Congress on December 1, 2004, all funding was zeroed-out for two favored projects of the wizards of Armageddon: the Robust Nuclear Earth Penetrator, or nuclear "bunker buster", and for the Advanced Concepts Initiative, which provided the breeding grounds for research into so-called micro nukes.

Moreover, Congress also slashed funding for grooming the Nevada Test Site for future nuclear blasts from $30 million to $22.5 million. The nuclear bomb lobby has long been lobbying for a new "pit" production facility—pits are the plutonium cores of nuclear bombs that ignite the atomic chain reaction resulting in thermonuclear explosions. The Bush administration asked Congress for $30 million to develop a new production facility, but Congress slashed the total outlay to $7 million and included language prohibiting the Department of Energy from naming a site for the facility.

All in all, these amounted to a series of devastating defeats for the nuclear-bomb making industry and its supporters in the Pentagon and on Capitol Hill. But such victories tend to have a very brief half-life.

And don't look now, but the nuclear weapons clique has launched a covert counterattack using a small provision in the very same funding bill as a kind of radioactive loophole for a new generation of nuclear weapons.

Buried in the mammoth omnibus appropriations bill was an obscure single item for something called the Reliable Replacement Warhead program. With an initial seeding of $10 million, this innocuous-sounding project will likely become the design table for the very kind of nuclear warheads that Congress tried to eliminate.

The project will fund the work of 100 nuclear weapons designers at three bomb-making laboratories: Lawrence Livermore, Los Alamos and Sandia. Proponents expect the project to start slowly, then gather budgetary momentum within the next five years. By 2015, they expect to unveil their new warhead design and inaugurate a new series of underground nuclear tests.

And guess what? Instead of the small, mini-nuke feared by anti-nuke activists, these weapons designers are moving in the opposite direction. These new nukes are likely to be bigger, bulkier and many times more potent than the current generation of weapons.

Once the project gets rolling, it becomes nearly impossible to turn off the flow of money. For one thing, the beneficiaries of these doomsday funds will soon extend beyond the weapons labs and to defense contractors, the most omnipotent lobby on the Hill. That's because the new heavier warheads will need a new generation of rockets to launch them on their path of annihilation. Here's where Lockheed and Boeing enter the picture.

All of this was sold to a gullible Congress on the grounds of reliability. The nuclear priesthood at the labs and in the Pentagon complained to congress that the current nuclear arsenal is becoming decrepit. Most of the 10,000 nuclear warheads in the US arsenal were designed to menace the world for about 15 years. The average age of a US warhead is now 20 years. And some are 30 years old and older.

The bombmakers gripe that the arsenal is getting so old that the reliability of the weapons to generate city-destroying thermonuclear blasts is now in doubt. In addition, the nuclear cohort chafes that the global test ban treaty, which outlaws underground detonations of nuclear weapons, makes it impossible for them to assess what they snidely refer to as the "health" of the US stockpile—as if regular nuclear blasts in the Nevada desert serve as a kind of treadmill to evaluate the vitality of geriatric warheads.

The only alternative, lament the weapons designers, is to redesign a new generation of warheads that are bigger and easier to certify as being reliable, that is ready to incinerate millions at the touch of a button.

Of course, a new generation of nukes will inevitably bring the US into stark conflict with the 1996 Comprehensive Test Ban Treaty, long the bane of the weapons-designers and the neo-cons in the Bush administration. And once nuclear testing begins a new arms race could follow, with Pakistan, India, China, North Korea, Israel, Russia and Iran all in the mix.

And what about those mini-nukes? Don't count them out just yet.

In January 2005, Defense Secretary Donald Rumsfeld fired-off a memo to the Department of Energy requesting that the agency quietly revive funding for a study on the design of bunker busting bombs.

"I think we should request funds in FY06 and FY07 to complete the study," Rumsfeld wrote. "Our staffs have spoken about funding the Robust Nuclear Earth Penetrator (RNEP) study to support its completion by April 2007. You can count on my support for your efforts to revitalize the nuclear weapons infrastructure and to complete the RNEP study."

The 2006 Bush budget for the Department of Energy contains $10.3 million for further work on the feasibility study, which is being conducted by weapons designers at Los Alamos and Lawrence Livermore. So much for the administration's new devotion to fiscal austerity.

Rummy's move was a brazen slap in the face to Republican congressman David Hobson of Ohio. Hobson chairs the House Appropriations subcommittee on water and energy and played the key role in eliminating funding for the bunker-buster bomb after reviewing a report from the National Nuclear Security Administration, which runs the nuclear program within the Energy Department, that estimated the Department would spend almost $500 million to produce the weapon in the budgets for fiscal years 2005 to 2009.

"Neither the Department of Defense nor the Department of Energy has ever articulated to me a specific military requirement for a nuclear earth penetrator," Hobson said in a recent speech to the Arms Control Association. "At the Pentagon's urging, I even spent an entire day at Offutt Air Force Base getting briefed by STRATCOM, but I was never told of any specific military mission requiring the nuclear bunker buster.

"The Department of Energy's nuclear weapons complex has so many fundamental management problems that have not received sufficient Federal oversight that it troubles me deeply that Congressional opposition to RNEP generate so much attention. The development of new weapons for ill-defined future requirements is not what the Nation needs at this time. What is needed, and what is absent to date, is leadership and fresh thinking for the 21st Century regarding nuclear security and the future of the U.S. stockpile."

Search across the arid vistas of the Clinton years and you're unlikely to find a more caustic indictment of the archaic and demented nuclear ambitions of the Pentagon and the nuclear labs. Indeed, the mini-nuke program was initiated and nourished by Clinton and Gore. But David Hobson is a lonely voice against an industry that has never really suffered a long-term defeat. In the absence of a real anti-nuke movement in this country, his courageous legislative victories won't amount to much.

Of course, if the demise of the Soviet Union didn't provide a rationale for the dismantling of the US nuclear arsenal, then the budgetary meddling of a fiscally conservative congressman is unlikely to provide much of an impediment. Committee chairs come and go, but the nuclear program endures forever.

So instead of witnessing the welcome abortion of a new class of nuclear warheads, the Pentagon and nuclear labs have incubated two new monsters: mini-nukes and fat nukes. Choose your poison.

Now count the months before the Bush administration invokes the "reliability" ruse as an excuse to breach the Comprehensive Test Ban Treaty. Nevada is ground zero, once again.

February, 2005

Part Five

Pie in the Sky: The Saga of Star Wars

We will bankrupt ourselves in the vain search for absolute security.

         —Dwight D. Eisenhower

Thirty

How to Restart the Arms Race
in the Name of Saving the World

The headlong rush to deploy a Missile Defense system didn't begin with George W. Bush. He is simply putting the capstone on a Pentagon program that has been in the works since the Ford Administration, nurtured by billions in annual appropriations, and sprung into the public spotlight by Ronald Reagan, who played it as a trump card against the Soviets in the mid-1980s.

Similarly, Bush didn't resurrect a dormant program. Star Wars didn't evaporate with the collapse of the Soviet Union and the dismantling of thousands of Soviet nuclear weapons targeting Europe and the United States. In fact, funding steadily increased under Bush I and through the Clinton years, bulging to $3.4 billion a year in 2000.

Let us return then to halcyon days of the 1990s, when instead of pulling the plug on the most expensive and potentially dangerous boondoogle in history, the Clinton administration nourished the Star Wars scheme, keeping the project alive, the production lines humming and its train of contractors fattened with annual disbursements of federal cash.

October 2000.

Quietly, but relentlessly, a Star Wars industry, under the new rubric of Ballistic Missile Defense, has mushroomed. The attention deficit corporate press, which had rightly heckled the plan in its infancy, soon bored of the story and left it for dead. Then in 1992 the missile shield's putative critics took over the White House and became its new masters. In the intervening years, billions of dollars poured into the Pentagon's Space and Missile Defense Command Center in Huntsville, Alabama, to production plants spread across key congressional districts and into the plump accounts of a portfolio of defense contractors and high-tech firms.

In a 1997 review of the program in *DefenseViewPoints*, an internal Pentagon newsletter, Lt. Gen Malcolm O'Neill, head of the Ballistic Missile Defense Organization, itemizes the accomplishments of his team in terms that would incite the envy of Edward Teller. Gen. Malcolm rhapsodizes about a "synergized" network of high-powered space-based lasers, satellites, radars and sea, air and ground launched "Exoatmospheric kill vehicles" that would save US cities from "theater-class ballistic missiles, advanced cruise missiles and other air-breathing threats as well." Feel safer?

Of course, there are problems. Namely, with the collapse of the Soviet Union and corporate America's coddling of China, why in the world would the US need to deploy such a system? In the coy atmosphere of DC, the why question is rarely asked. But when some outsider dares broach the subject, it prompts the most absurd frenzy of threat-inflation since the notion that the Marxist government of Grenada posed a grave threat to the western hemisphere. A coven of atomic warriors has been rolled out to fulminate about the threat of "rogue nations" and "global terrorists" that stalk what is now referred to by Pentagon brass as the "early post-cold war paradigm." Of course, if Osama Bin Laden ever decides to strike back once again at his former friends in the US government, his payload is much more likely to be delivered via FedEx in a Louis Vitton suitcase than a rocket launched from his yurt camp in the Hindu Kush. (As it turned out, Bin Laden's marauders used box cutter knives to turn commercial jetliners into the practical guerrilla's version of a V-2 rocket).

Another stumbling block was the 1972 Anti-Ballistic Missile Treaty, which flatly prohibited such a system. The architects of the ABM treaty rightly saw such as system as a de-stabilizing force that would spur proliferation and stockpiling of weapons. But the Clinton/Gore administration viewed the treaty as outmoded and, in a now customary display of hubris, on April 25, 2000, James Collins, the US ambassador to Russia, delivered to Moscow a draft copy of the US's proposed changes. The tenor of the US rewrite didn't sit well with Russian Foreign Minister Igor S. Ivanov. "These plans would inevitably undermine the whole architecture in the area of disarmament, which our countries have been building together with the world community for the last 30 years," Ivanov warned. "It could be a fatal mistake."

Some unrepentant cold warriors even chafed at this chilling dialogue. Senator Jesse Helms, who ruled the Foreign Relations Committee, vowed that any changes to the ABM Treaty agreed to by Russia would be "dead on arrival." A posture which may give new meaning to the word "treaty." The Republicans, however, had a political motive to drag their feet. They didn't want to give Al Gore a "hawkish" victory on the eve of the election or allow Clinton to add some more military luster to his legacy. "So, Mr. Clinton is in search of a legacy," Helms blustered. "La-de-da—he already has one. The Russians should not be under any illusion whatsoever that any commitments made by this lame-duck administration will be binding on the next administration."

But Helms may have met his match in new Russian president Vladimir Putin, who rose to power by engineering a brutal campaign against Chechen separatists. Putin had already upped the nuclear ante by authorizing changes in Russia's military doctrine allowing it to launch a "first strike" nuclear attack. Daniel Ellsberg suggests that may have been the bizarre intention of the Pentagon. "In order to advance a domestic political agenda, the US is encouraging the Russians to remain on and advance a launch-on-warning system," Ellsberg says.

It's the old game of escalating threats. The cheerleaders for the new Star Wars system now realize that the "rogue state" threat isn't credible. For one thing, North Korea, nearly crippled by drought and economic isolation, seems anxious to consider a rapprochement with the South. Iran, the Pentagon's other favorite stalking horse, lacks the missile-punch to strike the US. And Iraq, still smoldering from nearly 8 years of unceasing US air strikes, was barely able to maintain it's water supply system, never mind construct a fleet of transcontinental ballistic missiles. Even that normally reliable intermediary for US strategic interests Kofi Annan publicly voiced his doubts about the new Star Wars scheme, saying it could reignite a global arms race.

To top it off the system doesn't work. And isn't likely to. There have been two high-profile tests of the Interceptor missile to date. One was unmitigated failure. The other was initially touted as "a direct kill," but it later emerged that the Pentagon had fixed the test. A few months before this test, Defense Secretary William Cohen pointed to this date as a make-it-or-break-it final exam for the program. But afterwards top Pentagon officials began to show acute signs of test anxiety. "It will depend on what caused the failure," hedged Pentagon spokesman Mike Biddle. "A mechanical failure isn't necessarily terminal."

The Pentagon's Ballistic Missile Defense Organization projects the cost of the system at $36 billion, a typically modest appraisal. The Congressional Budget Office has come up with a slightly more robust number: $80 billion— a figure the government auditors admit is little more than a rough guess, since the Pentagon hadn't yet put forward details on phases II and III of the plan. But even that number was enough to stagger some of the plan's most ardent backers. "That's out of synch with anything I've seen,' gasped Rep. Curt Weldon, the Pennsylvania Republican who chairs the House Armed Services Committee's panel on Military Research and Develop. "But you can't put a price tag on protecting American cities."

"It's a case of sticker shock," says Daryl Kimball of the Coalition to Reduce Nuclear Dangers. And despite the dearth of media coverage, there is evidence that the public is beginning to sour on the plan. Popular support for Star Wars has steadily eroded since Reagantime. In 2000, less than 40 percent of Americans supported the plan, down from 55 percent in 1986.

So what *is* driving the bi-partisan push for an increasingly unpopular new missile defense system that is extravagant, inept, unnecessary and destabilizing? You don't have to dig very deep to find an answer: Raytheon, TRW, Lockheed/Martin and Boeing. Together these companies have flushed more than $2.6 million to the two political parties in soft money alone since 1996. This scenario imparts a bracing new meaning to getting more bang for the buck.

October, 2000

Thirty-One

Of SIBBERS and Penetration Aids

Nothing so clearly summarized Bill Clinton's abject surrender to the Pentagon and its congressional/industrial partners throughout his tenure than his support of the Star Wars program. Launched amid frenzied acclaim by arms profiteers by Ronald Reagan in 1983, this baroque endeavor consumed some $55 billion over the next 15 years with no discernible result. Clinton endeavored to persuade the Russians to "amend" the ABM Treaty, which explicitly forbids a Star Wars system of the type currently under development, by invoking the putative menace of North Korean and Iranian missiles raining down on North America, or Russia. The Russians rejected his proposal out of hand. [In this rationale from a Democratic President we have 2/3rds of the Axis of Evil, the missing Iraq having yet to earn its membership. Thus Bush's later frothing at the 3 was not some personality quirk but merely a continuation of Clinton's views, yet another example of how both parties stand synchronized on foreign policy.

It was a cynical ploy, for Clinton well understood that the U.S. will never produce a workable anti-missile defense system, since the technical obstacles are insuperable. But on October 14, 1999 the President brayed: " I do think it is the responsible thing to do to continue to pursue what appears to be far more promising than many had thought—including me a few years ago—in terms of missile defense."

The "promising" features of Star Wars are hard to discern, unless Clinton, like many other credulous souls, was taken in by the shrieks of triumph from the Pentagon following a National Missile Defense test on October 2 of that year. In the test, an "Exoatmospheric Kill Vehicle" (EKV) fired from Kwajalein Island in the South Pacific managed to hit a re-entry vehicle launched on an ICBM from Vandenberg AFB in California. Deferential press reports spoke of this supreme achievement in "hitting a bullet with a bullet", and even professional quotesmith John Pike of the Federation of American Scientists, who has ridden high on Star Wars critiques, agreed that the military had achieved "the equivalent of shooting a hole-in-one".

An internal assessment from inside a Pentagon agency, tells a very different story. Short of roping the interceptor and its target together, the architects of this $100 million exercise could hardly have done more to ensure the success of the operation. As the assessment notes: *"Because the ICBM was launched from California toward the mid-Pacific Ocean—an outbound trajectory instead of the inbound trajectory of an ICBM attack— the (beefed up early warning radar) in California acquired the target at close range with high signal-to-noise. In a real ICBM attack the radar would have had to detect the target at long range with low signal-to-noise."* In other words, the radar had a much better opportunity to spot the target because it was leaving from right next door instead of approaching from far over the horizon. *"The re-entry vehicle (RV—ie the target) was tracked by an on- board C-band beacon and GPS. Ground track radars were neither needed nor used to guide the EKV."*

This means that the target was conveniently broadcasting its position both via the radar beacon and the Global Positioning System, enabling the testers to guide the interceptor, as our friend puts it "into the basket". The Ballistic Missile Defense Office (BMDO) swears blind that these useful aids were not employed to steer the EKV interceptor right up to its final collision with the target. Oh no! Most certainly not! The target and its killer were merely steered "near" to each other before the $20 million EKV made whatever final adjustments were necessary using its own guidance system before closing for a 15,000 mph impact, generating a deadly shower of press releases across the northern hemisphere.

"The only penetration aid in the target suite was a large balloon. Because the large balloon had a significantly higher infrared signature than the RV, it allowed the EKV to acquire the target complex at long range and it was easy to discriminate from the RV."

A "penetration aid" is a decoy, and Star Wars critics have long postulated that such decoys, spewed out by ICBMs as they simultaneously lob off their real and deadly payloads, would totally hornswoggle the national missile defenders. Thus the fact that the October 2, 1999 test had actually incorporated a penetration aid was an item of special self-congratulation in the post test victorygrams.

However, as the internal Pentagon assessment notes, a single large balloon actually had the (intended) effect of rendering the interceptor's job much easier, since it could spot the "target complex"—target plus big, highly visible, balloon-at long range and then, when it came time to decide which to destroy, easily tell the real target from the conveniently dissimilar decoy.

"The closing velocity was lower than a typical ICBM engagement would have been"— That is, easier to hit something if it is going slowly. *"The ICBM apogee was higher than most threat ICBM apogees would be. Lower apogees would be more stressing because the NMD system would have less time to react"*. This means that they shot the target high into space, making it much easier to spot and track.

Such nit-picking doubts and caveats went unmentioned in the public analyses and it is unlikely that anyone bothered to divulge them to the Commander in Chief. Nor, in all likelihood, did anyone alert Clinton about the grave problems facing the linchpin of the entire missile defense system. In an artfully cozy phrase, the Pentagon described Star Wars, Clinton-era version, as a "family of systems," with successive layers of missile interceptors countering anything the North Koreans or the Mullahs can throw at us. However, the whole structure depends on a satellite warning and tracking system known as the Space Based Infra Red Systems-SBIRS, or, to the initiated, "Sibbers".

Sibbers, on paper at least, consists of 30 satellites, 6 in high orbit and 24 in low orbit. The six at high altitude would have the function of spotting the enemy missile as it is launched, while those lower down would have to decide whether an object is a threat (after being alerted by its higher consort), track the missile, discriminate a warhead from decoys, communicate with ground tracking stations and more. Little wonder, as John Donnelly reported in *Defense Week* in 1998, the $7.5 billion program is growing in cost at the rate of $1 billion a year and that even the Pentagon's official in charge of testing admits that it is "untestable".

Since the 1980s, the U.S. has tried and failed to develop four different warning and tracking networks. The Sibbers program was the fifth, and seasoned observers have no doubt it will follow the fate of its forbears, to be joined by the other components of ballistic missile defense on a costly junkheap. In the meantime however the ABM treaty stood in the way as the prime obstacle for the Pentagon and the host of defense companies feeding at the Star Wars trough. It would be up to George W. Bush to tear up that treaty and keep the billions flowing to the Star Wars conglomerate.

With Andrew Cockburn.

January, 2000

Thirty-Two

Star Wars Comes to the Arctic

The Kodiak Launch Complex was marketed to Alaskans as one of the nation's first commercial space ports. Many promises were made to lure public support: High-paying, year-round jobs. Better roads. A fancy cultural center. New schools with real astronauts helping out in the classrooms. Peace and prosperity.

The whole multibillion-dollar project, located on Narrow Cape, a remote tip of Kodiak Island 250 miles west of Anchorage, was supposed to be run by a state-chartered outfit called the Alaska Aerospace Development Corporation. In 1996, the state and the feds turned over 3,500 acres of public land for the project, which would house two launching pads, a space vehicle assembly plant, a radar station, a command center and other support facilities. Its backers claimed that a new age of commercial space traffic was dawning, and that Kodiak Island was one of the world's best locations for "launching telecommunications, remote sensing, and space science payloads" into orbit.

Local skeptics weren't thrilled at the prospect of their wilderness redoubt being transformed into an Alaskan Cape Canaveral. After all, Kodiak was already one of Alaska's most popular tourist destinations, with tens of thousands of people coming to fish for salmon and halibut, hike the wilderness, photograph the great grizzlies and view one of the few thriving populations of gray whales in the Pacific—people who might think twice about visiting with missiles screaming overhead. Others worried their villages might be vulnerable to misfires and toxic fallout. Some wondered how Kodiak, one of the most remote islands in North America, could possibly be the epicenter of a profitable commercial enterprise. There were suspicions that something a bit more nefarious might be in the offing.

These concerns were briskly swept aside by state and federal officials. A brief environmental analysis was slapped together, with much of the data concealed from public scrutiny, and construction began in 1998. Not long thereafter, the Alaska Aerospace Development Corporation announced it was having financial problems, and the federal government came to its rescue with a timely handout and the promise of sustained appropriations. But there was a catch: Instead of sending into orbit commercial satellites and the cremated remains of rich Trekkies, the Kodiak site was going into business with the Air Force and its legion of defense contractors.

There's some compelling evidence that this was the plan all along, starting with the man tapped to head the Alaska Aerospace Development Corporation: Pat Ladner, a former Air Force lieutenant colonel who served in the '80s as the program manager for a secretive project called the Single Stage Rocket Technology Program (SSTR). This program was a component of the initial burst of funding for Reagan's version of Star Wars. But by the early '90s, with public and congressional support lagging, the Pentagon made a decision to "privatize" much of the development and testing for many of its Star Wars projects. Ladner retired from the Air Force in 1993 and joined the Alaska Aerospace Development Corporation. The facilities at Kodiak were designed by the Defense Advanced Research Project Agency, the same shadowy wing of the Pentagon that had supervised the SSTR program on Ladner's watch.

So the launching pads at Narrow Cape turned out to be just another off-shoot of the National Missile Defense program. On November 5, 1998 the Kodiak site fired off its first rocket, an experimental Air Force missile that is part of the Pentagon's "atmospheric interceptor technology program." The rocket arced across the sky for more than 1,000 miles before slamming into the Pacific somewhere off the southern Oregon coast. A second rocket was launched from Kodiak on September 15, 1999.

Since those initial launches, a steady stream of Star Wars experiments have been ongoing at Kodiak, projects steered there by the guiding hand of Sen. Ted Stevens, the ranking member of the Appropriations Committee. Stevens is a master at manipulating the flow of federal dollars back to military projects in Alaska, often as last-minute amendments to Defense Supplemental Appropriations bills, where they receive little public scrutiny. This is how Star Wars has continued almost uninterrupted since its inception in 1983. The next round of tests at Kodiak involved a much more potent and unnerving rocket, a Polaris missile packed with a payload of simulated nuclear warheads. In August 2001, a Polaris was fired from Kodiak and streaked 4,300 miles to Kwajalein Atoll in the Marshall Islands of the South Pacific, where interceptor missiles will try to shoot it down. Over the next five years, Kodiak is slated to launch more than 20 Polaris rockets. (The other Polaris launching site is on the Hawaiian island of Kauai.)

Even though the test rockets only pack simulated nukes, they are still dangerous. The missiles' three-stage booster engines carry highly toxic materials, including magnesium, hydrazine and radioactive thorium. The boosters fall to the ocean and are not recovered. The exhaust trail itself leaves behind a poisonous plume of smoke. "Each rocket first stage releases a minimum of 8,000 pounds of aluminum oxide at lift-off," warns Brad Stevens (no relation to the senator), a biologist with the National Marine Fisheries Service in Kodiak. "Much of this will wind up in local streams that drain into Twin Lakes and the Fossil Beach tidepools and kelp beds, which provide nutrients and shelter for juvenile marine species. Documented fish kills in waterways around Cape Kennedy attest to the fact that rocket emissions can destroy aquatic life." (Also under the flight path of the missiles are rocky beaches on small islands that serve as haul-outs for Stellar sea lions, an endangered species.)

One of the launch trajectories sends missiles over the fishing villages of Akhiok and Old Harbor and across one of the world's most pristine salmon spawning grounds. The Pentagon has told the people living there not to worry: They will clear the waters of boats before each launch and build two hardened bunkers in each town. The bunkers serve as stark reminders that the townspeople not only are potential victims of an accident, but a target of Russian and Chinese defense systems designed to counter Star Wars.

Alaskans are old hands at this by now. Indeed, there's a grim irony in the fact that Alaska, the most frigid of states, has been one of the most ravaged battlegrounds of the Cold War. Over the past 55 years, Alaska has witnessed: early warning radar erected onto the fragile tundra in the early '50s; the intentional irradiation of more than 100 unwitting Alaskan native peoples in 1955 to test the acclimation of humans to sub-zero temperatures; Project Chariot, a mad scheme to excavate a naval harbor at Cape Thompson by exploding five nuclear bombs at the mouth of a coastal creek (the bombs were never detonated, but the site was left in a toxic and radioactive mess); and the Cannikin nuclear test in 1971, one of the largest ever, which permanently poisoned Amchitka Island and continues to ooze radioactive debris into the Bering Sea. Kodiak alone already suffers from 17 toxic dumps left by previous Pentagon operations on the island. Even the push to transform the Arctic National Wildlife Refuge into a forest of oil derricks has lately been justified on the grounds of national security.

So it shouldn't come as much of a surprise that Alaska seems poised to bear the brunt of Bush's revised Star Wars plan. The Kodiak site is just one of more than a dozen enclaves of assorted anti-missile paraphernalia that will be scattered across the state, from the Aleutians to the Arctic plains. In addition to Kodiak, Congress approved the construction of a $500 million radar dome on remote Shemya Island in the Aleutians. Shemya, the site of an old CIA listening post, is more than 1,500 miles from the nearest active military base. A top Pentagon official told the *Washington Post* that it posed difficult construction problems, and that when completed the site would be "very, very vulnerable" to attack.

Ted Stevens also pushed to make Fort Greely Military Reserve, an Army outpost on the Tanana River about 90 miles southeast of Fairbanks, a base for the 100 interceptor missiles once the Stars Wars scheme becomes operational. Constructed in 1945, Fort Greely already has a dark history as a kind of outdoor laboratory for some of the Army's most malign experiments. In 1953, the Army authorized the use of Fort Greely and the adjacent Gerstle River Proving Ground to test chemical and biological weapons. Of course, these operations were kept secret from the surrounding population of homesteaders, miners, trappers and the Goodpastor tribe of Athabaskan Indians.

In the early '60s one of the biological weapons tests went terribly wrong, and 21 people were infected with tularemia. After the Army stopped testing chemical and biological weapons at the site, it did a cursory cleanup and buried most of the contaminated canisters and shell-casings in shallow pits next to the river and several lakes and ponds, where the lethal detritus continues to seep out.

In 1962, the Army built a small nuclear reactor at Fort Greely, which it claimed was needed as a power station. This claim proved to be an elaborate cover. The reactor did generate some electricity, but it also produced weapons-grade plutonium. The background of this project is revealed in a startling report released in 2000 by physicist Norm Buske and Pam Miller, director of Alaska Community Action on Toxics. Among their findings: The Army dumped nuclear waste into Jarvis Creek for 10 years; disposed of liquid radioactive waste into groundwater that was used as a drinking source by the village of Clearwater; and used radioactive steam from the reactor to heat the military base. "Army leaders were more committed to producing special nuclear materials for battlefield nuclear weapons than they were to assuring the safety of the operation," Buske and Miller concluded.

Fort Greely was slated for decommissioning as part of the military's base-closure program. A convincing theory holds that Stevens and the Pentagon wanted to transform this Arctic outpost into the deployment site for 100 interceptor missiles as a convenient way to disguise the extent of the contamination and to evade accountability for what went on up there through the '60s.

What's more, Fort Greely site is a major sticking point with the Russians and Chinese. Under the Anti-Ballistic Missile Treaty, each nation is permitted only one site for missile defense. Currently, the U.S. site is in Grand Forks, North Dakota. Plans to begin pouring concrete for the new site at Fort Greely clearly violate the accord. Stevens, Alaska's senior senator, dismissed concern that these early Star Wars projects might breach the treaty, saying, "Construction of the Shemya radar in and of itself is not a violation of the ABM treaty until it is integrated into a defense system."

Why Alaska? It's not that all Alaskans welcome the Pentagon. In fact, a homegrown campaign defeated Edward Teller's nightmarish Project Chariot scenario. And in 1983, Alaskans approved the nuclear freeze initiative by an overwhelming vote. But in a state this large and sparsely populated it's relatively easy for big money to overwhelm citizen opposition, especially when those billions are backed by the lobbying might of the military, the nuclear labs and their contractors.

At present estimates, the Star Wars program will unleash a $60 billion spending spree. In Republican senators Murkowski and Stevens, Alaska sports two pitiless hoarders of Pentagon pork. Even Alaska's Clintonesque governor, Democrat Tony Knowles, got into the act, investing a chunk of state money with lobbyists to help steer as much of the Star Wars business to Alaska as possible.

It will surprise no one who is familiar with the symbiotic relationship between Stevens and the arms makers that the treasurer of his Northern Lights Leadership PAC, Richard Ladd, is also president of Robinson International, a top D.C. lobby shop that specializes in representing defense contractors. In the past two election cycles, the Northern Lights PAC has raked in more than $300,000, largely from corporate executives, many with ties to defense firms. The PAC recycled all that money back into Republican campaigns. In return, the defense companies, led by Boeing and Lockheed-Martin, have been very generous to Stevens. From 1995 to 1999, the senator received $255,650 in PAC contributions from missile defense-related firms, second only to Virginia's John Warner, who, as head of the Senate Armed

Services Committee, pulled in $330,000.

In a 2001 interview with the *Alaska Journal of Commerce*, Stevens boasted about how he almost single-handedly had steered hundreds of millions of dollars in defense contracts to Alaska, even under President Clinton. He predicted that much more federal loot was ready to flow north in the Bush regime. The money comes in, but it doesn't stay long. Most of it ends up in corporate coffers in Alabama, California and Washington State. Even Ladner, the head of the Alaska Aerospace Development Corporation, grudgingly confessed that the year-round jobs at the Kodiak launch site would only amount to a few security and maintenance positions. It's the old Cold War routine repeated once again: The money goes south, but the risk and the waste stays up in Alaska.

July, 2001

Thirty-Three

Treaty's End

I t's surely no accident that the Bush administration timed the release of the latest bin Laden tape on December 13, 2001 to coincide with the announcement later that same day of the administration's intention to unilaterally junk the once sacrosanct Anti-Ballistic Missile Treaty, the first abrogation of an arms control treaty since the end of World War II.

Of course, the Bushites' desire to withdraw from the arms accord and move forward with his revamped Star Wars scheme was an open secret. But in the nonstop spasm of coverage of the aftermath of the September 11 attacks and the ongoing war in Afghanistan, the media gave it scant attention, despite the fact that in the long run these nuclear machinations may have much more dire consequences than the war on terror. Indeed, the retreat from the ABM Treaty is just the latest act of unilateral intransigence by the Bush team.

In its first few months, the Bush administration has single-handedly brought the Biological Weapons Convention Review Conference to a halt; refused to reconsider the Comprehensive Test Ban Treaty and boycotted the CTBT review conference in New York City; rejected the International Criminal Court; walked away from the Convention on the Prohibition of Landmines; eviscerated the U.N. conference on Small Arms; and thumbed its nose at the Kyoto accord on global warming.

Even when Russian president Vladimir Putin ventured to the Bush ranch at Crawford, Texas in November 2001 for a back-slapping pow-wow with the president, the emphasis of the press coverage was on the cozy new relationship between the two leaders, eliding Putin's persistent warnings that any move by the US to abrogate the ABM Treaty risked jump starting a new nuclear arms race. Similar cautionary missives have been regularly sent out by the other nuclear states, including China, Great Britain and France. But the Bush team simply shrugged their shoulders at their international critics, ripped up the treaty and threw it in their faces.

The ABM Treaty was signed in Moscow on May 26, 1972 and was ratified by the US Senate in August of that year. For the past thirty years, the ABM Treaty has served as a hallmark of arms control measures, limiting the development of a ballistic missile system that would give one superpower a decisive nuclear advantage over the rest of the world. The treaty, which has been extensively amended over the years, required that each nation may have only two ABM deployment areas, and that those area restricted so that they cannot provide a nationwide ABM defense system or become the basis for developing one in the future.

In the end, the Russian response was curiously muted when Bush finally made the announcement that the US would abandon the treaty. Why? A top Bush official told the *New York Times's* Daniel Sanger, "It's not like Putin is going home empty handed." The implication here is that the pullback from the ABM Treaty is only the beginning of a move to unravel other arms agreements, such as START II.

"Russia may now withdraw from the START II treaty, freeing itself from the ban on the deployment of missiles with multiple warheads," said Ret. Lt. Gen. Vasily Lata, the former deputy chief of Russia's Strategic Missile Forces. "It would serve Russia's security interests well."

Under START II, signed in 1993, both countries agreed to cut in half the number of their strategic nuclear weapons from the 6,000 warheads each allowed under START I. By abandoning START II, Russia can now turn its single-warhead Topol-M missiles in MIRVed weapons, packing three nukes in each missile.

"It would have been in U.S. interests to preserve the ABM," warned Ivan Safranchuk, director of the Moscow office of the Center for Defense Information, a DC-based think tank. "By renouncing it, the United States gives Russia an opportunity to take back some of its earlier concessions."

Even though the trashing of the ABM treaty has been near the top of the Pentagon's agenda since his inauguration, Bush adorned his move in language that invoked the events of September 11. "I have concluded the ABM treaty hinders our government's ability to develop ways to protect our people from future terrorist or rogue-state missile attacks," Bush said. Typically, the president refused to answer any questions from the press about the decision.

One would have thought that the September 11 attacks, where box-cutter knives were used to transform commercial aircraft into flying bombs, would have ended all talk about the efficacy of a missile defense system—no matter how many billions are spent on it—to counter the threat from "rogue nations" or "terrorists." It's unlikely that bin Laden ever possessed even the dinkiest nuclear weapon, beyond the so-called dirty bombs that might be cobbled together by any Eagle Scout. But if he did, they weren't going to be launched from rockets, but delivered in suitcases or backpacks. And those "rogue nations", such as Iran and Pakistan, that possess primitive ballistic missile capabilities have been acting as US allies in the war on al-Qaeda and the Taliban.

It is a measure of the current Bush allure that the president was able to move with barely a whisper of protest to arrogantly kill an arms control approach that has worked, however marginally, and replace it with an unproven and provocative system geared to defend against a ballistic missile threat that doesn't exist.

On the very day the Bush administration announced it's plans to squash the ABM Treaty, the Pentagon conducted another test of its Star Wars system. It ended in a spectacular failure, with an interceptor missile veering wildly off course before it was destroyed. Of course, each failure—and there have been many—is an excuse for yet another test and a new round contracts to defense firms. And here we arrive at the crux of the matter. At $80 billion, the Bush Star Wars scheme represents the biggest Pentagon gravy train to come along in decades. And this administration let it be known that it won't allow any treaty, no matter how venerable, to stand in the way of that big of a feast at the public trough.

December, 2001

Thirty-Four

Star Wars Goes Online...Crashes

On a chilly July morning on the Alaskan tundra, the first Interceptor missile was lowered into a silo at Fort Greeley. Over the following weeks, five more missiles were planted into their silos, as the Ballistic Missile Defense System, once known as Star Wars, went on line. As part of Bush's accelerated deployment scheme, the Pentagon installed a total of 10 missiles in Alaska and 10 more at Ft. Vandenburg Air Base in California in 2004, with dozens more to follow over the next two years. The scheme is so accelerated that the Pentagon admits that they have no idea how the missiles would be launched, who would give the order to launch them and whether they will have the even the remotest chance of hitting their target.

During a 2004 campaign stop at a Boeing plant in Ridley Park, Pennsylvania, Bush lauded the missile program and chided its critics. "Opponents of missile defense are living in the past," Bush told the Boeing workers and executives. "We're living in the future. We're going to do what's necessary to protect this country. We say to those tyrants who believe they can blackmail America and the free world: You fire; we're going to shoot it down." Boeing, of course, is one of the three main contractors for the Pentagon's missile defense program, the most expensive weapons system in the federal budget.

Bush painted his pet project as a technological and military triumph. But surely even he knew better. In fact, he had just been briefed that the multi-billion dollar scheme was plagued with problems from top to bottom. According to the *Washington Post*, an internal Pentagon report presented to Bush in early August 2004 concluded that the ground based Interceptor rockets now humming in their Alaskan silos will have less than a 20 percent chance of knocking down a nuclear missile carried on a primitive North Korean rocket.

In a separate briefing, General James E. "Hoss" Cartwright, head of the US Strategic Command, the Pentagon wing responsible for nuclear war planning, told Bush that the system doesn't work and that the missile's testers don't know why. He told the president that costs were soaring; yet, little progress was being made in getting the system online in even a rudimentary way. The briefing seems to have made even less of an impression on Bush than the National Intelligence Estimates he received on the deteriorating conditions in Iraq. He refuses to admit the flaws in the technology, the incentive it gives other nations, such as China, Russia, North Korea and Pakistan, to accelerate their nuclear missiles, or to justify the staggering costs (more than the entire State Department budget) in a time of soaring budget deficits.

Even more confounding, though the missiles are poised on alert, the Pentagon has yet to develop a set of rules for spelling out who has the authority to launch the Interceptors in case of a missile attack. Such guidelines are needed because the computer software system that is meant to operate the network of Interceptors automatically isn't even close to completion. No one knows what it will look like, when it will be ready or if it will work. Moreover, the mysterious X-Band radars, which are meant to detect incoming nuclear missiles and feed their speed and location to the guidance system of the Interceptors, are not yet in place and won't be for years.

Of course, Rumseld's decision to delay issuing such a directive might be prudent, considering the fact that the Interceptors have never proven that they can hit their target in a combat situation. In testing over the past decade, the Interceptor missile's track record is far from impressive. For starters, the missile has yet to be tested when attached to its rocket booster, meant to power the missile into outer space where it is supposed to track down and destroy incoming nuclear missiles.

In eight flight tests, the Interceptors, launched without boosters, hit their target only five times. Yet in those tests, the Interceptor was travelling at less that half the speed it would need to under operational conditions.

Bush, given his academic record, might consider a 60 percent test score an impressive achievement. But it's a pretty dismal showing for a missile system that has already consumed nearly $70 billion, especially when you factor in the fact that to date all of the Interceptor tests have been fixed. For starters, the target missiles carried the equivalent of a homing beacon that "lit them up", in the words of one tester, so that the Interceptors could find them in the skies over the Pacific.

The weapons testers also knew when and where the missiles had been launched, as well as their trajectory, speed and path. In other words, they knew where they were going and when they would be there. Hitting the target only 60 percent of the time under these rigged conditions is like flunking the test even after you've stolen the exam.

The Interceptors performance didn't improve over time and the Pentagon testers had little idea about where to locate the source of the problem or how to upgrade the missile's batting average. Instead of going back to the drawing board, the Pentagon, in December 2002, simply declared that the Interceptor was ready for deployment and stopped further testing.

The decision was ridiculed by Senator Carl Levin, one of the few Democrats who have tried to put the brakes on the Missile Defense juggernaut. "The decision to field an as-yet-unproven system has been accompanied by a decision to eliminate or delay the very testing that must be conducted to show whether the system is effective."

Even when the testing demonstrates the failure of a system the Pentagon spins it as a success. A case in point. On June 18, 2003, the Navy launched a SM-3 missile from an Aegis cruiser ship off of Hawaii at a mock war warhead launched from test range on the island of Kauai. The SM-3 missile is the second layer of the Missile Defense system, designed to collide with intermediate range missiles. The collider missile missed its target by a wide margin. Another strike out for the Missile Defense team.

But hold on. That's not how the Pentagon saw it. In an interview the following day, Chris Taylor, the spokesman for the Missile Defense Agency, hailed the failure as a success. "I wouldn't call it a failure," Taylor said. "Because the intercept was not the primary objective. It's still considered a success, in that we gained engineering data. We just don't know why it didn't hit."

This is a rich vein of Orwellian doubletalk. According to the Pentagon's own records, the purpose of the Kauai test was to evaluate the performance of the solid-state engine for the guidance system of the SM-3 missile. The objective was to obliterate the mock warhead. It failed. Moreover, the data collected from the test, by Taylor's own admission, didn't help the testers to detect why it missed the target. Hard to find much solace in those results.

* * *

After 20 years and $80 billion, the Missile Defense program, hatched in a flight of cinematic fancy by Ronald Reagan and nurtured by leaders of both parties, remains little more than a science fiction fantasy. None of its dozens of components work. Many core parts of the scheme remain in an embryonic state. Others haven't even made it to the drawing board. And, after four years of fruitless work, the team assigned to develop the space-based laser system quietly disbanded

But Bush and Rumsfeld remain undeterred. From the beginning, the Bush administration promoted missile defense as its top national defense priority. Even after the attacks of September 11, the missile defense program gorges on far more money than any other weapons system. Indeed, the Bush administration has spent more than twice as much money on the failed missile defense system than on any other weapons program.

The first preemptive strike launched by Bush wasn't those cruise missiles slamming into huts in the Hindu Kush or the neighborhoods of Baghdad, but on the Anti-Ballistic Missile Treaty. And the Earth trembled.

But if the objective was to intimidate North Korea into dropping its nuclear weapons program, the gambit must be considered a staggering failure. The Korean response to the pre-emptive war on Iraq, launched on the bogus grounds that Saddam was pursuing nuclear weapons, and the mad rush to install the Interceptor missiles was entirely predictable. These provactive actions spurred Pyongyang into transferring those 8,000 fuel rods to gear up its own nuclear bomb-making capabilities. Did the plan backfire? Perhaps. But a more cynical view holds that this was the Bush administration's covert intent. They need a nuclear North Korea (and Iran and Pakistan) in order to have the requisite bogeymen to justify their imperial project and the annual disbursement of tens of billions to the weapons industry.

Damn the consequences, full speed ahead.

October, 2004

Closing Statement

Looting by Contract

"It is error only, and not truth, that shrinks from inquiry."

Tom Paine

As the summer of 2005 shuddered to a close, with Iraq tipping toward civil war and the grim toll of US casualties soaring to new heights, Bunnatine Greenhouse, the woman who blew the whistle on Halliburton's corporate thievery got demoted by the Bush administration.

Greenhouse, a black woman who was once the highest ranking civilian in the Corps of Engineers, did everything right. Her investigations and disclosures over the course of 2003 and 2004 of contractor misconduct should have saved millions of dollars and many lives. Instead, she was harassed at every turn by her superiors at the Corps of Engineers, the civilian leadership at the Pentagon, and the political hatchetmen in the White House.

Everything she said about the Halliburton contracts proved true. The no-bid contracts were awarded illegally. The subsequent alterations of the contracts violated federal regulations. Halliburton over-charged the Pentagon and manipulated its account books. Company officials lived in posh resorts and bribed local officials. Much of their work in Iraq was shoddy.

"I can unequivocally state that the abuse related to contracts awarded to Kellogg Brown and Root represents the most blatant and improper contract abuse I have witnessed during the course of my professional career," the defiant Greenhouse, a procurement veteran of more than 20 years, told congress during a June 2005 hearing on Halliburton.

Bunny Greenhouse should have been heralded as an American hero. Instead, she was forced out of her job, slimed by her bosses and slandered by the contractors she exposed. The press didn't put up much of protest on her behalf and neither did the congress.

Greenhouse's demotion was an act of casual retaliation, committed on day 32 of President Bush's vacation, as he continued to hide from Cindy Sheehan's harrowing call that he meet with her and other mothers of the fallen to explain the real reasons for the invasion and occupation of Iraq.

As Sheehan and thousands of other relatives of the slain and maimed can attest, the role of Halliburton, DynCorp, Bechtel and other US corporations in the Iraq war has not gone unnoticed by Iraqis. Call it colonialism by contract. US and British soldiers soon became viewed by Iraqi civilians, suffering from a shattered economy and three years without power or clean water, as not only an occupying force but also as a praetorian guard for US corporate interests divvying up Iraq.

The ordeal of Bunny Greenhouse is a cautionary tale for those who still believe that simple exposure of corporate and governmental malfeasance will lead to substantive changes in how the Pentagon operates.

On the very day the Pentagon demoted its most trenchant whistleblower, the waters of Lake Ponchartrain in Louisiana, swelled into a lethal maelstrom by Hurricane Katrina, breeched its levees and flooded New Orleans, one of the world's greatest cities.

By Tuesday night August 30, as the water rose to 20 feet through most of New Orleans, CNN relayed an advisory that food in refrigerators would last only four hours and would have to be thrown out. The next news item from CNN was an indignant bellow about "looters" of 7/11s and a Wal-Mart. Making no attempt to conceal the racist flavor of the coverage, the press openly described white survivors as "getting food from a flooded store," while blacks engaged in the same struggle for survival were smeared as "looters" and "thugs."

The reverence for property is now the underlying theme of many newscasts, with defense of The Gap being almost the first order of duty for the forces of law and order. But the citizens looking for clothes to wear and food to eat are made of tougher fiber and are more desperate than the polite demonstrators who guarded The Gap and kindred chains in Seattle in 1999. The police in New Orleans only patroled in large armed groups. One spoke of "meeting some resistance," as if the desperate citizens of New Orleans were Iraqi insurgents.

That same evening the newscasts were reporting that in a city whose desperate state is akin the Dacca in Bangladesh a few years ago, there were precisely seven Coast Guard helicopters in operation. Where were the National Guard helicopters? Presumably strafing Iraqi citizens on the roads outside Baghdad and Fallujah.

As the war's unpopularity soared in the summer of 2005, millions asked, Why is the National Guard in Iraq, instead of helping the afflicted along the Gulf in the first crucial hours, before New Orleans, Biloxi, and Mobile turn into toxic toilet bowls with thousands marooned on the tops of houses or crammed in the horrific bowels of the Superdome?

As thousands of trapped residents face the real prospect of perishing for lack of a way out of the flooding city, Bush's first response was to open the spigots of the Strategic Petroleum Reserve at the request of oil companies and to order the EPA to eliminate Clean Air standards at power plants and oil refineries across the nation, supposedly to increase fuel supplies--a goal long sought by his cronies at the big oil companies.

In his skittish Rose Garden press conference days after the flood, Bush told the imperiled people of the Gulf Coast not to worry, the Corps of Engineers was on the way to begin the reconstruction of the Southland. But these are the same cadre of engineers, who after three years of work, have yet to get water and electrical power running in Baghdad for more than three hours a day.

It didn't have to be this bad. The entire city of New Orleans need not have been lost. Thousands of people need not have perished. Yet, it now seems clear that the Bush administration sacrificed New Orleans to pursue its mad war on Iraq.

As the New Orleans *Times-Picayune* has reported in a devastating series of articles over the last two years, city and state officials and the Corps of Engineers had repeatedly pleaded for funding to strengthen the levees along Lake Pontchartrain that breeched in the wake of the flood. But the Bush administration rebuffed the requests repeatedly, reprogramming the funding from levee enhancement to Homeland Security and the war on Iraq.

In 2005 alone the Bush administration slashed funding for the New Orleans Corps of Engineers by $71.2 million, a stunning 44.2 percent reduction from its 2001 levels. A Corps report noted at the time that "major hurricane and flood protection projects will not be awarded to local engineering firms. . . . Also, a study to determine ways to protect the region from a Category 5 hurricane has been shelved for now."

Work on the 17th Street levee, through which much of the lethal floodwater poured, came to a halt earlier in the summer of 2005 for the lack of $2 million.

"It appears that the money has been moved in the president's budget to handle homeland security and the war in Iraq, and I suppose that's the price we pay," Walter Maestri, emergency management chief for Jefferson Parish, Louisiana told the Times-Picayune in June of last year. "Nobody locally is happy that the levees can't be finished, and we are doing everything we can to make the case that this is a security issue for us."

Too late now.

While Bush's response to hurricane relief for the people of the Crescent City was lethargic at best, his administration wasted no time in doling out multi-million dollar reconstruction contracts to his political cronies. Before the National Guard ever got their feet wet in the lethal waters of Canal Street or aimed an M-16 with shooot to kill orders at flood victims, the Navy had handed out a $30 million no bid contract to repair oil rigs in the Gulf of Mexico. The beneficiary? The name has a familiar ring: Halliburton.

There's a natural temptation among many good government types to look for easy solutions and quick fixes. But there is no longer any magic corrective wand, no simple legislative package that will turn the tide against the war profiteers. The age of liberal reformism is long gone.

Today, the roots of the two dominant political parties intertwine and are irrigated by the same freshets of corporate money, much of it coming from the weapons industry cartel. The lobbyists who prowl the halls of congress doing the bidding of war merchants earned their stripes working in that very same building or in the White House or the Pentagon itself. The revolving door is one of the main engines powering the machine.

Both parties are beholden not only to the arms makers, but more importantly are blindly wedded to the imperial project itself. Nostalgia for Carter, Clinton or even the absurd figure of John Kerry is dangerously misplaced. The Afghan war, the most expensive CIA operation in history, was launched under Carter, a secret war that gave rise to the Taliban and Osama bin Laden and his jihadis.

Instead of slashing the corpulent Pentagon budget and transferring the Cold War "surplus" into education and health care programs as he repeatedly promised in his campaigns, Bill Clinton actually increased defense spending in real dollars, began research into a new generation of nuclear weapons, ordered hundreds of air strikes and Cruise missile attacks on Iraq, kept Star Wars on life support and launched an illegal war on Serbia that killed thousands of civilians and made millions for Halliburton and DynCorp.

As for Kerry, he was up there with Bush, Rumsfeld and Blair as a huckster for all the lies that have come home to haunt Washington. "These weapons represent an unacceptable threat", he bellowed in 2003. Not just nuclear weapons of mass destruction. "Iraq has some lethal and incapacitating agents and is capable of quickly producing and weaponizing a variety of such agents, including anthrax, for delivery on a range of vehicles such as bombs, missiles, aerial sprayers, and covert operatives which could bring them to the United States homeland." Kerry's bottom line: "The President laid out a strong, comprehensive, and compelling argument why Iraq's weapons of mass destruction programs are a threat to the United States and the international community."

Not once in his sputtering campaign did Kerry mention the atrocities of Gitmo or Abu Ghraib. Not once to did he point to the civilian casualties in Iraq.

This is where the timid legions of the left, cowed by furious bluster about their treachery in deserting the Democratic standard back in 2000, might ask some serious questions, and threaten desertion again. All Kerry offered was superior management of the imperial bandwagon at home and abroad. Defense? More over, Rumsfeld and Wolfowitz! To cleanse the Augean stable, with those fragrant heaps of procurement cash handed out to Bush and Cheney's cronies Kerry called for a broom in the form of his defense adviser William Perry. Not a clean broom, mind you. Perry, a notorious shill for the avionics sector when he ran the Pentagon's R&D in the Carter years, drew deserved fire in Clinton time for being the first secretary of defense allowed to hold investments in a military contractor, Cambridge Research Associates, doing business with the Defense Department.

The War on Drugs? National Security Advice? Kerry had Rand Beers. Under Presidents Clinton and Bush, he served as Assistant Secretary of State for International Narcotics and Law Enforcement Affairs, and was one of the architects of the aerial crop fumigation program the U.S. introduced in southern Colombia when the State Department hired DynCorp, a private military contractor, to fly crop dusters at high altitudes over southern Colombia, spraying poison on all the vegetation and, often, peasants below.

Beers' has played terrible role in ongoing war in the jungles of Colombia. Beers had scant concern for peasant with their only means of subsistence, whether coca or legal yucca, wiped out. "One doesn't get a special pass for being poor," he told ABC's John Stossel, (a sentiment with which Kerry surely concurred, since he voted for Clinton's onslaught on welfare.)

Beers once gave a sworn deposition in a lawsuit filed against DynCorp in a U.S. Federal District Court by indigenous tribes in which he argued for fumigation, claiming that "It is believed that FARC terrorists have received training in Al Qaida terrorist caps in Afghanistan."

AP cited three intelligence sources in Washington expressing incredulity. "'My first reaction was that Rand must have misspoke,' said a veteran congressional staffer with extensive experience in the Colombian drug war. 'But when I saw it was a proffer signed under oath, I couldn't believe he would do that. I have no idea why he would say that.'" Beers later recanted his testimony, claiming that he had been misinformed.

How about oil and empire? Right next to Beers on Kerry's national security team was Richard Morningstar. An inside player to be sure. He ran the Overseas Private Investment Corp, a notorious swill-bin for corporate plunder, then became Clinton's oil ambassador to Central Asia where he rubbed shoulder pads with Condoleezza Rice, at that time Chevron's envoy prospecting capture of the region's vast oil reserves.

Democrats and Republicans? It's a choice between Caesar and Pompey. After all, the neocons, the masterminds of Bush's war policy, are new conservatives. That means they used to be Democrats. Indeed, many of them got their start in politics working for the late Senator Henry "Scoop" Jackson, the Washington Democrat known for years as "the Senator from Boeing."

Of course, there are things that congress can and should do. Reforms that the public should demand.

Congress should move to open up the black budget, the covert spending for big weapons systems, spy satellites and intelligence agencies. Instead, the Bush administration, with congressional complicity, has moved to dramatically to cloak much of the Pentagon's budget in secrecy, shielded from investigations by journalists, researchers and even members of congress. None of this budgetary information can be exploited by al-Qaeda, North Korea, Iran or any of the other bogeymen. The secrecy benefits only the Pentagon and its stable of contractors.

No bid contracts and cost-plus contracts should be eliminated. Both of these contracting schemes have been regularly abused by defense companies, costing the treasury tens of millions. But it must be understood that these strategies were viewed as reformist at the time they were adopted by the Pentagon. Indeed, much of the current contracting system derives from changes instituted in the Clinton years under Al Gore's Reinventing Government Program, a neoliberal project hawked as a way to trim down the bureaucracy and increase efficiency in contracting.

The big weapons systems designed for the Cold War should be unplugged from their budgetary life-support system. The B-1 and B-2 bombers should be sent to air museums. Production of the F-22 and Joint Strike Fighter should be halted. The ballistic missile defense system, aka Star Wars, should be junked.

The proposed new generation of nuclear missiles should be swiftly aborted and existing missiles should be yanked from their silos and decommissioned.

Former Pentagon employees should be prohibited from working for defense contractors for at least five years after leaving their government positions. Similar rules should apply to members of congress and congressional and White House staffers.

Contractors caught rigging bids, overcharging on contracts or submitting doctored reports on weapons systems should be barred from bidding on future Pentagon projects.

Culled of its most baroque programs, the defense budget could easily be trimmed by one-third to one-half, freeing upwards of $100 billion a year for social programs, health care and renewable energy systems.

But these transformations will not happen in a vacuum. They will need to be forced down the throats of Congress and the Pentagon by a militant and uncompromising popular movement, unaligned with either political party, whose first task must be to put an end to the wars in Afghanistan and Iraq and snuff out further imperial adventurism in Iran, Syria and North Korea.

When these wars are brought to an end, then the political and economic machinery that drove them must be dismantled and replaced by a non-interventionist posture that heeds the early warning for the Republic from Jefferson: "If there is one principle more deeply rooted in the mind of every American, it is that we should have nothing to do with conquest.

September 1, 2005

Acknowledgments

Most of these stories first appeared in CounterPunch, the newsletter and online website that I co-edit with Alexander Cockburn. As such, they've benefited greatly from Alexander's deep memory for scandal, acute editorial touch and ripe sense of humor, which has made the unsettling years of Clinton and Bush scroll by as if they were scenes from a Preston Sturges movie. It's been an exhilarating collaboration.

Alexander's brother Patrick is flat-out the best and bravest war reporter of his generation. My understanding of the bloody chaos in Iraq derives almost entirely from his vivid and often chilling dispatches for the Independent of London and CounterPunch. Similarly, Patrick and Alexander's brother Andrew Cockburn has written groundbreaking stories on the Pentagon budget and grandiose schemes such as Star Wars and the B-2 bomber. His book *The Threat*, which exposed the rusting condition of the Soviet military in the 1970s and 1980s, remains a model of its kind.

While I'm writing about CounterPunch an enormous debt of gratitude must go to our business manager Becky Grant, whose sunny disposition, accounting prowess and logistical smarts has steered us past many a dangerous shoal.

My former CounterPunch colleague Ken Silverstein now writes for the *LA Times*, *Harper's* and other lofty venues. But his reporting hasn't lost any of its punch and remains far above the standard fare. Ken's prescient book *Private Warriors* had the extreme misfortune of being released about a year too soon to receive the attention and acclaim it deserved. I wore its pages out during the writing of this book. At the major papers, Ken's only real rival is Tim Weiner at the *New York Times*. Before Weiner landed at the Times, he wrote a great book on the arms scandals of the Reagan era called *Blank Check*.

In the inner sanctum of the Whistleblower Hall of Fame there must reside a bronze statue of Ernie Fitzgerald, immortalized by Richard Nixon on one of his basement tapes as "that son of a bitch." Ernie was the original fly in the Pentagon's ointment, exposing from the inside one scandal after another—a true American hero. I've returned to Ernie's book *The Pentagonists* so many times that its pages have burned blisters on my fingers.

Win Wheeler, the man once known as Spartacus, is that rare species: a congressional whistleblower. Wheeler, a long time top senate staffer on defense matters, was chased from his position by Sen. Pete Domenici (with help from the odious John McCain and Ted Stevens) after exposing to public view the shameless and destructive porkbarrel schemes of key senators in the wake of 9/11. Thankfully, Wheeler lived to tell the gruesome tale in a great book, *The Wastrels of Defense.*

Several of the stories here, particularly the ones dealing with technical screw-ups in weapons systems, drew heavily upon the work of the Pentagon watchdogs at the Project on Government Oversight, aka POGO, which is led by the fearless and talented Danielle Brian.

When he's not sailing the oceans of the world, Chuck Spinney, who worked at the Office of the Secretary of Defense from the mid-1970s until 2003, runs the useful and informative Defense in the National Interest website (http://www.d-n-i.net/), which should be bookmarked and checked daily by all of those interested in the scandalous behavior of the Pentagon and its feeding line of contractors.

No one who cares about the fate of the planet could weather the Bush years alone without running off to the hills and these days there are fewer and fewer forested hills on which to seek sanctuary. So what's left of my sanity is attributable to a small but irreplaceable network of friends, who have offered editorial advice, internal memos, old blues, bluegrass and jazz records, jokes and recipes. I cherish you all: David Price; Ben Tripp (the SJ Perleman of Pasadena); Saul Landau and Rebecca Switzer; Michael Neumann (the Emperor of Oysters); Steve Perry (and Cecily, too); Dave Marsh; JoAnn Wypijewski; Sharon Smith and Ahmed Shawki; Oxfordian Carl Estabrook and Leigh Estabrook, who has played St. Michael to the Dragon of the Patriot Act; David Vest (the Boogie Woogie King of British Columbia); Ralph Nader; Ray McGovern; Roger Morris; Alan Maass; Gary Leupp; Peter Linebaugh; rad librarian and Christine Karatnytsky; Jason Leopold; Vijay Prashad; human rights lawyer Joanne Mariner; David Orr; Dr. Susy Block, High Priestess of Eros; Joe and Karen Paff, whose Gold Rush Coffee makes early mornings bearable and late nights possible; Ron Jacobs; Dave Lindorff; Michael Donnelly; Robert Jensen; Tariq Ali; Larry and Judy Tuttle; John Blair; Steve Higgs; Tim Hermach; Daniel Wolff; Paul Craig Roberts; Bill and Kathy Christison; Ricardo Alarcon; Roz Wolen; Badruddin Gowani; defense lawyer and civil libertarian Elaine Cassel; Niranjan Ramakrishnan; and Josh Frank (the pride of Montana).

Greg Bates and the crew at Common Courage Press are owed a special debt of gratitude for their enthusiasm, editorial insights and patience with a tardy writer who slouched far across his deadline. It's tough being a small press in the best of times, but under the wreckage of the Bush economy it's been devilishly challenging. Buy all their books and encourage your libraries to stock up on them as well.

A special thanks goes to Our Man in Istanbul, Michael Dickinson, an English teacher, artist and political agitator living in Turkey, who made the cover art for this book. Dickinson's art, which has vividly captured the grotesqueries of Bush's wars, has gotten under the skin of censorious types across the globe, prompting several timid ISPs to pull the plug on his Carnival of Chaos website. Thankfully, Dickinson's work has found a new home at the International Political Art website www.stuckism.com/. Check it out.

If this book has a soundtrack, it's to be found in the outlaw music of Texas: T-Bone Walker, Willie and Waylon, Freddie King, Lightnin' Hopkins, Alejandro Escovedo, Ornette Coleman and Kinky Friedman. Play them loud enough to rock Crawford and beyond.

My parents, Doreen and Hager, have never wavered in their love, encouragement and generosity. Those are debts I can never hope to repay.

Our children, Zen and Nat, are now marching down their own paths, both fueled by a desire for peace and social justice. I am awed by their accomplishments and sense of compassion. Their generation gives us hope.

My wife Kimberly Willson is the inspiration of my life. She is a peerless researcher, a keen editor and a member of that most valuable of professions in these senseless times, a librarian. She has sustained me through dark hours and sparked the best days of my life. "*Vedeste, al mio parere, onne valore...*"

Bibliography

Articles and Reports

"Cheney Backs Iran Investment." *Hart's Middle East Oil and Gas.* 27 June, 2000.

"FBI Searches Congressman's California Home." *Associated Press.* 1 July, 2005.

"Halliburton Ties More Than Cheney Said." *United Press International.* 23 June, 2001.

Adams, Thomas. "The New Mercenaries and the Privatization of Conflict." *Parameters.* Summer, 1999.

Alden, Diane. "Soldiers R Us: the Corporate Military." *SpinTech.* 12 September, 1999.

Ali, Tariq. "Recolonizing Iraq." *CounterPunch.* 30 May, 2003.

Arbucki, Tammy. "Building a Bosnian Army." *Jane's International Defense Review.* August, 1997.

Arieff, Irwin. "39,000 Killed in Iraq's Continuing Violence." *Reuters.* 12 July, 2005.

Arkin, William. "Nuclear Strikes: Not Just a Last Resort?" *Washington Post.* 15 May, 2005.

Arkin, William. "The Underground Military." *Washington Post.* 7 May, 2001.

Bacevich, Andrew J. "The Nation at War." *Los Angeles Times.* 20 March 2003.

Baer, Susan. "Iraq Puts Cheney in Harsh Spotlight." *Baltimore Sun.* 1 October, 2003.

Baker, David R. "Army Contract for Feinstein's Husband." *San Francisco Chronicle.* 22 April, 2003.

Baker, David R. "Bechtel Sees Record Revenue in 2004." *San Francisco Chronicle.* 29 March, 2005.

Baker, David. "Bechtel Under Siege." *San Francisco Chronicle.* 21 September 2003.

Baker, David. "SF Firm Awarded Contract in Iraq." *San Francisco Chronicle.* 12 March 2004.

Baker, David. "Short Iraqi Road is Feat for Bechtel." *San Francisco Chronicle.* 22 July, 2003.

Baker, David. "US: Bechtel's 2003 Revenue Breaks Company Record." *San Francisco Chronicle.* 20 April, 2004.

Baker, Russ. "Want to be a Patriot? Do Your Job!" *Columbia Journalism Review.* May, 2002.

Balz, Dan. "The Saudi Connection." *Washington Post.* 19 April, 1981.

Barnett, Antony. "Anger at Kosovo Mines Contract." *Observer.* 7 May, 2000.

Baum, Dan. "Nation Builders for Hire.*" New York Times Magazine.* 22 June, 2003.

Baum, Dan. "This Gun for Hire." *Wired.* February 2003.

Bedard, Paul. "A Bounty Hunt for Bin Laden Yields Ears." *US News and World Reports.* 29 July, 2002.

Bender, Bryan. "Defense Contractors Quickly Becoming Surrogate Warriors." *Defense Daily.* 28 March, 1997.

Benjamin, Daniel, and Steven Simon. "The Worst Defense." *New York Times.* 20 February, 2003.

Bishop, Sam. "Senator Stevens Defends Federal Buy Out." *Fairbanks News-Miner.* 10 July, 2004.

Bivens, Matt. "Enron's Washington." *The Nation.* 24 January, 2002.

Boles, Elson. "Iraq and Chemical Weapons: the US Connection." *CounterPunch.* 10 October, 2002.

Borenstein, Seth. "Trucks Made to Drive Without Cargo in Dangerous Areas of Iraq." *Knight Ridder.* 21 May, 2004.

Borger, Julian. "White House 'Exaggerating Iraqi Threat' Bush's Televised Address Attacked by US Intelligence." *The Guardian.* 9 October, 2002.

Branch, Taylor. "James A. Baker, III, Esq., Politician." *Texas Monthly.* May, 1982.

Brauchli, Christopher. "Halliburton Made $73 Million from Saddam." *CounterPunch.* 18 March, 2004.

Broad, William. "Private Venture Hopes for Profits in Spy Satellites." *New York Times.* 10 February, 1997.

Brooks, Douglas. "The Business End of Military Intelligence." *Military Intelligence Professional Bulletin.* September, 1999.

Brower, J. Michael. "Outland: the Vogue of DOD Outsourcing and Privatization." *Acquisition Review Quarterly*, no. 4. Fall, 1997.

Brown, Justin. "The Rise of the Private-Sector Military." *Christian Science Monitor.* 5 July, 2000.

Bryce, Robert. "The Candidate from Brown and Root." *Austin Chronicle.*

25 August, 2000.

Bumiller, Elizabeth. "Bush Aides Set Strategy to Sell Policy on Iraq." *New York Times.* 7 September, 2002.

Burkeman, Oliver, and Julian Borger. "The Ex-President's Club." *The Guardian.* 31 October, 2001.

Burkeman, Oliver. "Cheney Firm Paid Millions in Bribes to Nigerian Official." *The Guardian.* 9 May, 2003.

Burns, Margie. "Another Lucky Bush Brother." *CounterPunch.* 5 December, 2002.

Burton-Rose, Daniel, and Wayne Madsen. "Corporate Soldiers." *Multinational Monitor.* 20, no. 3. March, 1999.

Byman, Daniel. "Scoring the War on Terrorism." *National Interest,* no. 72. Summer, 2002.

Cahlink, George. "Army of Contractors.*" Government Executive.* February, 2002.

Cahlink, George. "Pentagon Faulted for Lack of Critical War Supplies." *Govexec.com.* 14 April, 2005.

Capaccio, Tony. "GAO Deflates Glossy Gulf War Weapons Claims." *Defense Week.* 22 July, 1996.

Carlson, Peter. "The USA Account." *Washington Post.* 31 December, 2001.

Carpenter, Dave. "Boeing Forces Out CEO Over Relationship." *Washington Post.* 7 March, 2005.

Cha, Ariana Eunjung. "$1.9 Billion of Iraq's Money Goes to US Contractors." *Washington Post.* 4 August, 2004.

Charbonneau, Luis. "Fake Iraq Nuke Papers Were Crude." *Reuters.* 25 March, 2003.

Cloughley, Brian. "Corruption in Bush's Iraq." *CounterPunch.* 3 May, 2005.

Cockburn, Alexander. "Crooks in the White House." *CounterPunch.* 6 July, 2002.

Cockburn, Alexander. "Running an Empire on the Cheap." *CounterPunch.* 13 December, 2004.

Cockburn, Patrick. "Dead on the 4th of July." *CounterPunch.* 11 May, 2005.

Cockburn, Patrick. "How Saddam Armed the Insurgency." *CounterPunch.* 1 December, 2004.

Cockburn, Patrick. "Iraq the Unwinnable War." *CounterPunch.* 26 July, 2005.

Cockburn, Patrick. "Iraq's Ghost Battalions." *CounterPunch.* 16 July, 2005.

Cockburn, Patrick. "Modern War in a Medieval Village." *CounterPunch.* 13 October, 2001.

Cockburn, Patrick. "The Capture of Saddam." *CounterPunch.* 15 December, 2003.

Cockburn, Patrick. "The Iraq Quagmire." *CounterPunch.* 10 May, 2003.

Cockburn, Patrick. "The True, Terrible State of Iraq." *CounterPunch.* 21 July, 2005.

Cohn, Marjorie. "Tax the War Profiteers." *CounterPunch.* 23 April, 2003.

Confessore, Nicholas. "Welcome to the Machine: How GOP Disciplined K Street and Made Bush Supreme." *Washington Monthly.* July-August, 2003.

Cooper, Pat, and Robert Holzer. "Debate Swirls Around F-117." *Defense News.* 23-29 September, 1996.

Copetas, Craig. "It's Off to War Again for Big US Contractor." *Wall Street Journal.* 4 April, 1999.

Cornwell, Rupert. "How the President's Uncle Emerged as Big Winner from Iraq War." *Independent.* 24 February, 2005.

Crain, Rance. "Charlotte Beers and the Selling of America." *Advertising Age.* 5 November, 2001.

Cummins, Chip. "US Officials May Have Steered Halliburton to Kuwaiti Supplier." *Wall Street Journal.* 15 December, 2003.

Daly, Matt. "Pentagon Probes More Air Force Contracts." *Associated Press.* 14 February, 2005.

Dawkins, Richard. "Bin Laden's Victory." *Guardian.* 22 March, 2003.

Deavel, R. Phillip. "Political Economy of Privatization for the American Military." *Air Force Journal of Logistics,* 22. Summer, 1998.

Diamond, John. "GAO Study Takes Aim at Gulf War Weapons." *Washington Post.* 1 July, 1997.

Diamond, John. "The Bribery Coast." *Chicago Tribune.* 20 February, 2000.

Dilanian, Ken. "Need for Lockheed Fighter Jets Questioned." *Miami Herald,* 17 June, 2005.

Dine, Philip. "Senate Seeks 4 More Boeing F-15 Eagle Jets." *St. Louis Post-*

Dispatch, 9 June, 1999.

Dinmore, Guy. "Bush Promotes Nuclear Hawks." *Financial Times.* 1 February, 2005.

Dobbs, Michael. "US had Key Role in Iraq Build Up." *Washington Post.* 30 December, 2002.

Dodds, Paisley. "Gitmo Soldier Details Sexual Tactics." *Associated Press.* 27 January, 2005.

Dreyfuss, Robert. "The Pentagon Muzzles the CIA." *American Prospect,* vol. 13, issue 22. 16 December, 2002.

Dugger, Ronnie. "Oil and Politics." *Atlantic.* September, 1969.

Dunn, Carroll H. "Vietnam Studies: Base Development in South Vietnam, 1965-1970." Washington, DC: Department of the Army, 1991.

Eagleton, William L. "Talking Points for Amb. Rumsfeld's Meeting with Tariq Aziz and Saddam Hussein." US Interests Section in Iraq Cable to US Embassy in Jordan. 14 December, 1983.

Eilperin, Juliet. "Plane Lease Deal to Cost US Extra." *Washington Post*, 26 December, 2001.

Escobar, Pepe. "This War Brought to You By..." *Asia Times.* 19 March, 2003.

Fairbank, Katie. "Smart Buys, Big Names Lifted Carlyle to Success." *Dallas Morning News.* 20 June, 2000.

Filkins, Dexter. "We Killed a Lot of People." *New York Times.* 29 March, 2003.

Finnegan, William. "The Economics of Empire." *Harper's.* May, 2003.

Fireman, Ken. "Bush Landing Cost $1 Million." *Newsday.* 8 May, 2002.

Fisher, Louis. "Congressional Abdication: War and Spending Powers." *St Louis University Law Journal 43*, no. 3, Summer 1999.

Floyd, Chris. "Cheney's Backdoor to Halliburton." *CounterPunch.* 29 October, 2003.

Floyd, Chris. "How the WMD Scam Put Money in Bush Family Pockets." *CounterPunch.* 5 March, 2004.

Floyd, Chris. "War is Golden for Bush Cronies." *CounterPunch.* 15 February, 2003.

Fram, Alan. "Bush Asks Congress for $82 Billion for War." *Associated Press.* 16 February, 2005.

Frank, Joshua. "CEO Bush and the Muddling of American Minds." *CounterPunch.* 10 January, 2003.

Frank, Thomas. "Hundreds of Iraqis Killed by Faulty Grenades." *Newsday.* 22 June, 2003.

Franklin, Jonathan. "US Contractor Recruits for Guards in Chile." *The Guardian.* 5 March, 2004.

Frantz, Douglas, and Murray Waas. "Bush Secret Effort Helped Iraq Build Its War Machine." *Los Angeles Times.* 23 February, 1992.

Gagnon, Bruce. "Space Warriors." *CounterPunch.* 8 August, 2003.

Galbraith, James K. "The Unbearable Costs of Empire." *The American Prospect.* 18 November, 2002.

Galbraith, Peter W. "The Wild Card in Post-Saddam Iraq." *Boston Globe Magazine.* 15 December, 2002.

Garamone, Jim. "Coalition Encouraging Private Business Growth in Iraq." *American Armed Forces Press Service.* 18 February, 2004.

Gatton, Adrian, and Clayton Hirst. "A Booty for the Barons of Baghdad." *The Independent.* 8 February 2004.

General Accounting Office. "A More Constructive Test Approach is Key to Better Weapon System Outcomes." GAO/T-NSIAD-00-137, July 2000.

General Accounting Office. "Air Force Procurement: Protests Challenging Role of Biased Official Sustained." *GAO Highlights.* 14 April 2005.

General Accounting Office. "Defense Acquisitions: Assessments of Major Weapons Systems." GAO-05-3001, March 2005.

General Accounting Office. "Missile Defense: Review of Allegationas about Early National Missile Defense Flight Test." GAO-02-125, February, 2002.

General Accounting Office. "Observations on the Air Force Plan to Lease Aerial Refueling Aircraft." GAO-03-104ST. September, 2003.

General Accounting Office. "Operation Desert Storm: Evaluation of the Air Campaign." GAO/NSIAD-97-134, June 1997.

General Accounting Office. "Report on US Construction Activities in Republic of Vietnam, 1965-1966." Report 67-11159. Washington, DC: GPO, 1967.

General Accounting Office. "Setting Requirements Differently Could Reduce Weapons Systems' Total Ownership Costs." GAO-03-57, February, 2003.

General Accounting Office. "Status of Ballistic Missile Defense in 2004." GAO-05-243, March 31, 2005.

General Accounting Office. "Use of Fiscal Year 2003 Funds for Boeing 737 Aircraft Lease Payments." Report: B-300222, March 28, 2003.

Gillan, Linda. "Brown and Root is Golden Problem Child for Halliburton." *Houston Chronicle.* 4 March, 1980.

Goff, Stan. "The Democrats and Iraq." *CounterPunch.* 19 April, 2004.

Gold, Russell, and Christopher Cooper. "Pentagon Weighs Criminal Charges of Halliburton Arm." *Wall Street Journal.* 23 January, 2004.

Gold, Russell. "Halliburton Unit Runs into Big Obstacles in Iraq." *Wall Street Journal.* 28, April, 2004.

Gold, Russell. "The Temps of War." *Wall Street Journal.* 25 February, 2003.

Golden, Tim. "In US Report, Brutal Details of 2 Afghan Detainees' Deaths." *New York Times.* 20 May, 2005.

Gompert, David C., and Jeffrey A. Isaacson. "Planning a Ballistic Missile Defense System of Systems*." Rand Issues Paper,* 1999.

Goodman, Peter. "Iraq: At Oil Plant, Bitterness and Idleness." *Washington Post.* 30 April, 2003.

Gordon, John Steele. "USS Boondoggle." *American Heritage*, February/March 1993.

Goulet, Yves. "Mixing Business with Bullets." *Jane's Intelligence Review.* September 1997.

Graham, Bradley, and Dana Priest. "Pentagon Team Told to Seek Details of Iraq—Al Qaeda Ties." *Washington Post.* 25 October, 2002.

Grant, Bruce. "US Military Expertise for Sale." National Defense University. 1998.

Gwynne, S.C. "Did Dick Cheney Sink Halliburton (and Will It Sink Him?)" *Texas Monthy.* October, 2002.

Hackworth, David. "Fire the Losers Before the Army Goes Down." *Orlando Sun-Sentinel.* 14 August 2003.

Hackworth, David. "The Bigger Threat: Osama or Saddam?" *Defense Watch.* 19 December, 2003.

Hagan, Joe. "She's Richard Perle's Oyster." *New York Observer.* 7 April, 2003.

Hallinan, Conn. "Remote Control Warriors." *CounterPunch.* 9 April, 2004.

Hallinan, Conn. "Rumsfeld's New Model Army." *CounterPunch.* 6 November, 2003.

Hanley, Charles J. "US Rejects Idea of Ban on Nuclear Attack." *Associated*

Press. 5 May, 2005.

Hartung, William D. "Iraq and the High Costs of Privatized War." *CounterPunch.* 6 March, 2004.

Hartung, William, and Frida Berrigan. "Is What's Good for Boeing and Halliburton Good for America*?" World Policy Institute.* February 2004.

Hedges, Stephen. "Out of DC, Cheney Still Carried Clout." *Chicago Tribune.* 10 August, 2000.

Helprin, Mark. "Failing the Test of September 11." *Wall Street Journal.* 16 September, 2002.

Hilsum, Lindsey. "Chaos and Denial in Baghdad." Christian Science Monitor. 7 April, 2003.

Hobsbawm, Eric. "America's Imperial Delusion." *Guardian.* 14 June, 2003.

Holzer, Robert, and Mark Walsh. "Services' Wish List Hits Hill." *Defense News.* 24-30 March, 1997.

Hossein-Zadeh, Ismael. "The Bush Military Budget." *CounterPunch.* 25 October, 2002.

House, Billy. "McCain Misses Defense Spending Vote." *Arizona Republic,* 18 October, 2002.

Howe. Jonathan T. "Iraq Use of Chemical Weapons." Memorandum to the US Secretary of State. 1 November, 1983.

Hughes, Solomon, and Jason Nisse. "How Cheney's Firm Routed $132 Million to Nigerian Lawyer." *Independent.* 3 October, 2004.

Ignatieff, Michael. "The American Empire (Get Used to It)". *New York Times Magazine.* 5 January, 2003.

Ignatius, David. "Bush's Confusion; Iraq's Mess." *Washington Post.* 23 April, 2003.

Isenberg, David. "Bush's Priceless War." *Asia Times.* 25 February, 2005.

Isenberg, David. "The Not So Friendly Reality of US Casualties." *Asia Times,* 22 October 2003.

Ivanovich, David. "Halliburton Questioning Focuses on Towels' Cost." *Houston Chronicle.* 14 February, 2004.

Ivanovich, David. "Obstacles are Many on Iraq's Oil Fields." *Houston Chronicle.* 29 April, 2003.

Jackson, Tom. "Why They Couldn't Wait to Invade Iraq." *CounterPunch.* 20 February, 2004.

Jacobs, Ron. "The Bloody Profits of General Dynamics." *CounterPunch.* 10 July, 2003.

Jaffe, Greg, and Neil King. "US General Criticizes Halliburton." *Wall Street Journal.* 15 March, 2004.

Jensen, Robert. "The Military Media." *The Progressive.* May, 2003.

Jeserich, Mitch. "Banking on Empire." *CorpWatch.* 4 February, 2004.

Johnson, Chalmers. "The War Business." *Harper's.* November, 2003.

Kamen, Al. "Sticker Shock." *Washington Post.* 31 January, 2003.

Kamen, Al. "Unearthing Democratic Roots to Halliburton Flap." *Washington Post.* 5 March, 2004.

Kaplan, Fred. "Homeland Security's Mystery Money." *Slate.* 23 February, 2004.

Kaplan, Fred. "Low-Yield Nukes: Why Spend Money on Useless Weapons?" *Slate.* 21 November, 2003.

Kaplan, Fred. "Rummy's $9 Billion Slush Fund." *Slate.* 10 October, 2003.

Kaplan, Fred. "Shooting Down Missile Defense." *Slate.* 7 August, 2003.

Kaplow, Larry. "Bechtel Criticized Over School Project in Iraq." *Palm Beach Post.* 14 December, 2003.

Karon, Tony. "Wanted: Iraqis to Run Iraq." *Time.* 15 April, 2003.

Karwash, Mohammed. "Reconstruction or Deconstruction?" *Al-Yawm.* 13 November 2003.

Keller, Bill. "Missile Defense: the Untold Story." *New York Times.* 29 December, 2001.

Kelly, Chuck. "Spiritual Patriotism." *Star Tribune.* 18 November, 2001.

Kelly, Matt. "Fewer Than 25,000 Iraqis Working on Reconstruction Funded by US." *Associated Press.* 18 May 2004.

King, Neil. "Halliburton Hits Snafu on Billing in Kuwait." *Wall Street Journal.* 2 February, 2003.

King, Neil. "Halliburton Tells Pentagon Workers Took Kickbacks to Award Projects in Iraq." *Wall Street Journal.* 23 January, 2004.

Kramer, Jerry, and Marcus Stern. "Buyer's Kin were Lenders of Cunningham Mortgage." *Copley News Service,* 5 July, 2005.

Kretzmann, Steve, and Jim Vallette. "Corporate Slush Funds for Baghdad." *CounterPunch.* 22 July, 2003.

Kromm, Chris. "The South at War." *CounterPunch.* 20 June, 2002.

Kurtz, Howard. "McCain, Rising Up Against Spartacus." *Washington Post,* 13 May 2002.

Lambro, Daniel. "Centrist Democrats Warn Liberals." *Washington Times.* 4 April, 2005.

Langman, Jimmy. "Bechtel Battles Against Dirt Poor Bolivia." *San Francisco Chronicle.* 2 February, 2002.

LeBlanc, Steve. "Natsios: It's a New Day for the Big Dig." *Associated Press.* 12 April, 2000.

Leopold, Jason. "Halliburton and Iran." *CounterPunch.* 8 June, 2005.

Leopold, Jason. "Halliburton Still Profits from Terror." *CounterPunch.* 10 May, 2003.

Leopold, Jason. "Halliburton's Secret Deal with the Pentagon." *CounterPunch.* 14 May, 2003.

Leopold, Jason. "The Bloody History of Halliburton." CounterPunch. 16 April, 2003.

Leopold, Jason. "War, Hypocrisy and Profits." *CounterPunch.* 20 March, 2003.

Leupp, Gary. "Perle's Bombshell in Iran." *CounterPunch.* 10 September, 2002.

Lieven, Anatol. "The Empire Strikes Back." *The Nation.* 7 July 2003.

Lindorff, Dave. "Fascists in the Machine." *CounterPunch.* 14 March, 2005.

Lindorff, Dave. "Inside the $40 Billion Black Budget for Spying." *CounterPunch.* 8 December, 2004.

Lindorff, Dave. "Secret Bechtel Documents Reveal: Yes, It is About Oil." *CounterPunch.* 9 April, 2003.

Lloyd, Anthony. "Fear, Vendetta and Treachery: How We Let Bin Laden Get Away." *London Times.* 3 December, 2002.

Lowe, Christopher. "What Not to Do: the Soviet's Afghanistan War." *Defense Week.* 1 October 2001.

Machines, Colin. "A Different Kind of War? September 11 and the US War." *Review of International Studies*, vol 29, no. 2. April, 2003.

Mannion, Jim. "Rumsfeld Heaps Praise on Troops for US Victory." *Agence France-Presse.* 28 April, 2003.

Margasak, Larry. "Report on Cheney, Bathrooms." *Associated Press.* 10 September, 2000.

Margolis, Eric. "Coalition of the Coerced." *American Conservative.* 30 August, 2004.

Mayer, Jane. "Contract Sport." *New Yorker.* 10 February, 2004.

Mayer, Jane. "Outsourcing Torture." *New Yorker.* 7 February, 2005.

Mayer, Jane. "The House of Bin Laden." *New Yorker.* 12 November, 2001.

McCabe, Kathy. "Veterans in Arms Over Proposed Cuts." *Boston Globe.* 24 April, 2003.

McGrory, Mary. "Mistaken Patriots." *Washington Post.* 17 October, 2002.

Melman, Seymour. "In the Grip of a Permanent War Economy." *CounterPunch.* 15 March, 2003.

Merle, Renae. "Ex-Boeing CFO to be Sentenced." *Washington Post.* 18 February, 2005.

Merle, Renae. "No Bid Contracts Said to be Common." *Washington Post.* 30 September, 2004.

Merle, Renae. "The Pentagon's Global View." *Washington Post.* 8 March, 2005.

Milbank, Dana. "For Bush, Facts are Malleable." *Washington Post.* 22 October, 2002.

Miller, Eric, and Beth Daley. "Five Weapons That Bilk the Taxpayer." *CounterPunch.* 4 February, 2002.

Miller, T. Christian. "Contract Flaws in Iraq Cited." *Los Angeles Times.* 11 March, 2004.

Miller, T. Christian. "Missing $100 Million: US Officials Suspected of Embezzlement in Iraq." *Los Angeles Times.* 5 May, 2005.

Miller, T. Christian. "U.S. went on spending spree before handover Billions handed out in June.*" Los Angeles Times.* 20 May, 2005.

Mokhiber, Russell, and Robert Weissman. "Bowling for Baghdad." *CounterPunch.* 19 October, 2002.

Montgomery, Dave. "Cheney's Halliburton Ties Draw More Scrutiny in Iraq Contracting Review." *Fort Worth Star-Telegram.* 28 September, 2003.

Morano, Lou. "Propaganda: Remember the Kuwaiti Babies?" *Universal Press International.* 26 February, 2002.

Morgan, Dan. "With Spending Bill, Credit in Advance Lawmakers Tout Projects in Measures that Congress has not Passed." *Washington Post.* 27 October, 2002.

Mowbray, Joel. "Saudis Behaving Badly." *National Review.* 20 December, 2002.

Mulvihill, Maggie, Jack Meyers and Jonathan Wells. "Bush Advisers Cashed in on Saudi Gravy Train." *Boston Herald.* 11 December, 2001.

Murphy, James. "DOD Outsources $500 Million in Spare Parts Work." PlanteGov.com. 28 September, 2000.

Nader, Ralph. "The Pentagon Connection." *CounterPunch.* 20 January, 2003.

Neubauer, Chuck, and Richard T. Cooper. "Senator Stevens' Way to Wealth Paved with Favors.*" Los Angeles Times.* 17 December, 2003.

Nimmo, Kurt. "Drones: the Militarization of Daily Life." *CounterPunch.* 21 December, 2002.

Nimmo, Kurt. "Paying Through the Nose to Kill Iraqi Kids." *CounterPunch.* 28 February, 2003.

Nordland, Rod, and Michael Hirsh. "The $87 Million Money Pit." *Newsweek.* 27 October, 2003.

Norton-Taylor, Richard. "Cluster Bombs: the Hidden Toll." *Guardian.* 2 August, 2000.

O'Harrow, Robert, and Scott Higham. "Alaska Native Corporations Cash in on Contracting Edge." *Washington Post.* 25 November, 2004.

O'Keeke, Mark. "Plans Under Way for Christianizing the Enemy." *USA Today.* 26 May, 2003.

O'Meara, Kelly. "Dyncorp Disgrace." *Insight.* 4 February, 2002.

Oppel, Richard, and Diana Henriques. "Bechtel Has Ties in Washington and Iraq." *New York Times.* 17 April, 2003.

Parry, Robert, and Norman Solomon. "Behind Colin Powell's Legend." *Consortium,* 1996.

Pastzor, Andy. "Pentagon Blasts Air Force Contract for Boeing Tankers." *Wall Street Journal.* 30 March, 2004.

Peckenpaugh, Jason. "Pentagon May Have Violated Contractor Ethics Rule." *Government Executive.* 22 June, 2001.

Perry, William J. "Defense in an Age of Hope.*" Foreign Affairs 75,* no. 6, November / December 1996.

Phillips, Michael, and Greg Jaffe. "Pentagon Rethinks Use of Cluster Bombs.*" Wall Street Journal.* 25 August, 2003.

Piatt, Gregory. "Balkans Contracts Too Costly." *European Stars and Stripes.* 14 November, 2000.

Pipes, Daniel, and Laurie Mylorie. "Back Iraq: It's Time for a US Tilt." *New Republic.* 27 April, 1987.

Pleming, Sue. "US Questions More Halliburton Bills." *Reuters.* 17 May 2004.

Priest, Dan. "Jet is an Open Secret in Terror War." *Washington Post.* 27 December, 2005.

Priest, Dana, and Robin Wright. "Scowcroft Skeptical Vote wil Stabilize Iraq; Friend of Bush Family Joins Pessimists." *Washington Post.* 7 January, 2005.

Prins, Nomi. "Making a Killing in Iraq." *Left Business Observer.* 6 August, 2003.

Prusher, Ilene. "A Year After the Taliban, Little Change." *Christian Science Monitor.* 19 November, 2002.

Quenqua, Douglas. "Guns or Butter?" *PR Week.* 11 March, 2002.

Reed, Stanley. "In Baghdad, Guns, Chaos, Enterprise." *Business Week.* 2 May, 2003.

Rich, Frank. "Torture Takes a Holiday." *New York Times.* 23 January, 2005.

Ricks, Thomas. "Army Historian Cites Lack of Post-War Plan in Iraq." *Washington Post.* 25 December, 2004.

Risen, James. "Secrets of History: the CIA in Iran." *New York Times.* 16 April, 2000.

Robbins, Carla Anne. "Spin Control." *Wall Street Journal.* 4 October, 2001.

Roberts, William. "The Struggle for Subsidies: Defense Bill Sheds Key Maritime Parts." Journal of Commerce. 29 October, 1997.

Roche, Walter. "Company's Work in Iraq Profited Bush's Uncle." *Los Angeles Times.* 23 February, 2005.

Rohd, David. "Exploited in Iraq, Indian Workers Say." *New York Times.* 7 May, 2004.

Rosenbaum, David E. "Call It Pork or Necessity, But Alaska Comes Our Far Ahead in Federal Spending." *Associated Press.* 21 November, 2004.

Rosenberg, Eric. "Despite Warnings, KBR Got Contract." *Hearst News Service.* 15 May, 2004.

Rotella, Sebastian. "Allies Find No Links Between Iraq, Al Qaeda." *Los Angeles Times.* 4 November, 2002.

Royce, Knut. "Start Up Company with Connections." *Newsday.* 15 February, 2004.

Rozen, Laura. "Strange Bedfellows: US Contractor in Iraq Helped Fund Al Qaeda." *The Nation.* 25 October, 2003.

Rubin, Elizabeth. "An Army of One's Own." *Harper's.* February, 1997.

Rudman, Warren B., and Gary Hart. "We are Still Unprepared." Washington Post. 5 November, 2002.

Said, Edward. "The Appalling Consequences of the War are Now Apparent." *CounterPunch.* 22 April, 2003.

Scaramella, Mark. "Contracts vs. Politics in Iraq." *CounterPunch.* 20 September, 2003.

Schaefer, Standard. "DARPA and the War Economy." *CounterPunch.* 13 August, 2003.

Schaefer, Standard. "Wasted at the Pentagon." *CounterPunch.* 2 June, 2003.

Schanberg, Syndey. "Senator McCain Goes Missing." *Village Voice.* 8 June, 2005.

Schor, Fran. "The Strange Career of Frank Carlucci." *CounterPunch.* 1 February, 2002.

Serrano. Richard. "Details of Marines Abusing Prisoners in Iraq are Revealed." *Los Angeles Times.* 15 December, 2004.

Sevastopulo, Demetri. "Pentagon Blamed Over Boeing Tanker Deal." *Guardian.* 7 June, 2005.

Shales, Tom. "Aboard the Lincoln, a White House Spectacular." *Washington Post.* 2 May, 2003.

Shanker, Thom. "Rumsfeld Denies Rift Exists Between Pentagon and CIA." *New York Times.* 25, October 2002.

Sharma, Amol. "US Hones in on Propaganda War." *Earth Times.* 13 October, 2001.

Shenon, Philip. "Iraq Links Germs for Weapons to US and France." *New York Times.* 6 March, 2003.

Shultz, George. "Act Now: the Danger is Immediate." *Washington Post.* 6 September, 2002.

Sieff, Martin. "Missile Defense and the Real World." *Universal Press International.* 26 July, 2005.

Singer, Peter. "Nation Builders and Low Bidders in Iraq." *New York Times.* 15 June, 2004.

Smith, R. Jeffrey, and Renae Merle. "Rules Circumvented on Huge Boeing Contract." *Washington Post.* 27 October, 2003.

Smith, R. Jeffrey. "E-mails Detail Air Force Push for Boeing Tanker Deal." *Washington Post.* 7 June, 2005.

Smith, Vicki. "Homelessness Plagues Many US Veterans." *Associated*

Press. 28 February, 2005.

Spinner, Jackie, and Mary Pat Flaherty. "Iraq: Rebuilding Plan Reviewed." *Washington Post.* 31 March, 2004.

Spinner, Jackie. "Operation Iraqi Education*." Washington Post.* 13 June, 2003.

Stanton, John, and Wayne Madsen. "America's War, Inc." *CounterPunch.* 1 April, 2002.

Stanton, John. "Arming for Armageddon." *CounterPunch.* 30 December, 2002.

State Department. "Iraq Use of Chemical Weapons." Press Statement by US Department of State. 5 March, 1984.

Stern, Jessica. "The Protean Enemy." *Foreign Affairs,* vol. 82, no. 4. July-August 2003.

Stern, Marcus. "Cunningham Defends Deal with Defense Firm's Owner." *Copley News Service*, 12 June, 2005.

Stone, Peter H. "Can We Fight Iraq and Hunt al-Qaeda?" *National Interest.* 22 February, 2003.

Strobel, Warren P., Jonathan S. Landay, and John Walcott. "Officials' Private Doubts on Iraq War*." Philadelphia Inquirer.* 8 October 2002.

Strohm, Chris. "Major defense contractors reap billions in no-bid contracts, report finds." *Govexec.com.* 30 September, 2004.

Terrall, Ben. "The Ordeal of the Lockheed 52." *CounterPunch.* 17 October, 2003.

Thompson, Estee. "Ex-CIA Contractor Facing Abuse Charges." *Associated Press.* 27, August 2004.

Thompson, Mark. "Generals for Hire." *Time.* 15 January, 1996.

Tierney, John. "Even for $25 Million, Still No Osama Bin Laden." *New York Times.* 1 December, 2002.

Towell, Pat. "Changes to Defense Bill Modest Despite Focus on Anti-Terrorism*." Congressional Quarterly Weekly*, 20 October 2001.

Traub, James. "Osama, Dead or Alive." *New York Times Magazine.* 29 December 2002.

Uchitelle, Louis, and John Markoff. "Terrorbusters, Inc." *Washington Post.* 17 October, 2004.

Unger, Craig. "Saving the Saudis." *Vanity Fair.* October, 2003.

Vallette, Jim, and Steve Kretzmann and Daphne Wysham. "Crude Visions." *Institute for Policy Studies*. March 2003.

Vallette, Jim. "Rumsfeld's Old Flame." *TomPaine.com.* 10 April, 2003.

Van Natta, Dale. "High Payments to Halliburton for Fuel in Iraq." *New York Times*. 10 December, 2003.

Vest, David. "Dubya Co." *CounterPunch.* 28 May, 2003.

Vest, David. "They Died for Halliburton." *CounterPunch.* 11 December, 2003.

Vise, David A. "Former Secretary of State James Baker Joins Carlyle Group." *Washington Post.* 11 March, 1993.

Wallace, Bruce. "Humvees Falling Prey to War." *Los Angeles Times.* 13 December, 2004.

Walsh, Elsa. "How the Saudi Ambassador Became Washington's Indispensable Operator." *New Yorker.* 24 March, 2003.

Walsh, Jim. "The Two Faces of Bush on Defense." *Los Angeles Times.* 1 May, 2001.

Walsh, Mary Williams. "Shriveling Pensions After Halliburton Deal." *New York Times*. 10 September, 2002.

Warner, Melanie. "The Big Guys Work for the Carlyle Group." *Fortune.* 18 March, 2002.

Wayne, Leslie. "Elder Bush in Big GOP Cast Toiling for Top Equity Firm." *New York Times*. 5 March, 2001.

Webb, Cynthia L. "The Pentagon's PR Play." *Washington Post.* 21 May, 2003.

Weiner, Tim. "Air Force Seeks Bush's Approval for Space Weapons." *New York Times.* 18 May, 2005.

Weiner, Tim. "Lockheed and the Future of War." *New York Times.* 28 November, 2004.

Weiner, Tim. "Selling Weapons: Stealth, Lies and Videotape." *New York Times*. 14 July, 1996.

Weiner, Tim. "Smart Weapons Were Overrated, Study Concludes." *New York Times*, 9 July, 1996.

Weisman, Jonathan, and Ariana Eunjung Cha. "Rebuilding Aid Unspent, Tapped to Pay Expenses." *Washington Post.* 30 April, 2004.

Weisskopf, Michael. "Civilian Deaths: the Bombs that Keep on Killing." *Time.* 3 May, 2003.

Wheeler, Winslow T. "Beware the Phony Defense Budget Prognosticators." *CounterPunch.* 2 February, 2004.

Wheeler, Winslow T. "How Both Parties Exploit the Defense Budget."

CounterPunch. 30 October, 2004.

Wheeler, Winslow T. "Inside the Pentagon's Pork Factory." *CounterPunch.* 4 March, 2003.

Wheeler, Winslow T. "Kill the Boeing Tanker Deal." *Defense Week.* 6 October, 2003.

Wheeler, Winslow T. "Senator McCain and the Boeing Tanker Scam." *CounterPunch.* 5 January, 2005.

White, Chris. "Is War Still a Racket?" *CounterPunch.* 9 January, 2003.

White, Griff. "Big Defense Contractor Settles Fraud Charges." *Washington Post.* 30 April, 2005.

Whittle, Richard. "Texas Star for Military.*" Dallas Morning News.* 12 January, 2003.

Wilborn, Paul. "Hummer Sales Plow Over Criticism of Gas Mileage." *Naples Daily News.* 4 February, 2003.

Wilkinson, Mariam. "Corruption Stench as Company Loses Iraq Contract." *Sydney Morning Herald.* 21 May, 2004.

Williamson, Elizabeth. "Ft. Detrich: a Lesson in No Bid Contracting." *Washington Post.* 25 November, 2004.

Wilner, Elinore. "Poetry and the Pentagon: an Unholy Alliance.*" Poetry Magainze.* October, 2004.

Withington, Thomas. "What If We Battled a Real Army?". *Newsday.* 6 August, 2003.

Wolf, Jim. "Missile Defense Test Fails.*" Associated Press.* 15 December, 2004.

Wypijewski, JoAnn. "Workers Against War." *CounterPunch.* 17 January, 2003.

Yegar, Holly. "Democrats to Back Additional War Spending." *Associated Press.* 16 February, 2005.

Yeoman, Barry. "Soldiers of Good Fortune.*" Mother Jones.* May/June 2003.

Zeese, Kevin. "Halliburton: Poster Child of the War Profiteers." *CounterPunch.* 2 April, 2005.

Books

Aburish, Said K. *The Rise, Corruption and Coming Fall of the House of Saud.* New York: St. Martin's, 1994.

Adams, James. *The Next World War.* New York: Simon and Schuster, 1998.

Ali, Tariq. *Bush in Babylon.* New York: Verso, 2003.

Anonymous. *Imperial Hubris.* Dulles, VA: Brassey's, 2004.

Arkin, William, and Richard W. Fieldhouse. *Nuclear Battlefields: Global Links in the Arms Race.* Cambridge, MA: Ballinger, 1985.

Arnold, Guy. *Mercenaries.* London: St. Martin's Press, 1999.

Baer, Robert, *Sleeping with the Devil,* New York: Crown Publishers, 2003.

Bamford, James. *Body of Secrets.* New York: Anchor Books, 2002.

Bamford, James. *The Puzzle Palace.* New York: Penguin, 1983.

Beschloss, Michael R., ed. *Taking Charge: the Johnson White House Tapes, 1963-1964.* New York: Simon and Schuster, 1997.

Betts, Richard K. *Nuclear Balance and Nuclear Blackmail.* Washington, DC: the Brookings Institution, 1987.

Biddle, Stephen. *Afghanistan and the Future of Warfare: Implications for Army and Defense Policy.* Carlisle, PA: Strategic Studies Institute, US Army War College, 2002.

Blum, William. *Killing Hope, the updated edition.* Monroe, Maine: Common Courage, 2004.]

Bovard, James. *The Bush Betrayal.* New York: Palgrave-MacMillan, 2004.

Boyne, Walter J. *Beyond the Horizons: the Lockheed Story.* New York: St. Martin's, 1998.

Brasch, Walter M. *America's Unpatriotic Acts.* New York: Peter Lang, 2005.

Brewton, Pete. *The Mafia, CIA & George Bush.* New York: SPI Books, 1992.

Briody, Dan. *The Halliburton Agenda.* New York: Wiley and Sons, 2004.

Briody, Dan. *The Iron Triangle.* Hoboken, NJ: John Wiley and Sons, 2003.

Brown, Anthony Cave. *Oil, God and Gold: the Story of Aramaco and the Saudi Kings.* Boston: Houghton Mifflin, 1999.

Bruni, Frank. *Ambling Into History.* New York: HarperCollins, 2002.

Bryce, Robert. *Cronies.* New York: Public Affairs, 2004.

Bryce, Robert. *Pipedreams.* New York: Public Affairs, 2002.

Burton, James G. *The Pentagon Wars.* Annapolis: Naval Institute Press, 1993.

Bush, Barbara. *Barbara Bush: a Memoir.* New York: Touchstone, 1999.

Bush, George W. *A Charge to Keep.* New York: William Morrow, 1999.

Bush, George. *All the Best, George Bush.* New York: Touchstone, 1999.

Butler, Gen. Smedley D. *War is a Racket.* Los Angeles: Feral House, 2003.

Cannon, Lou. *President Reagan: the Role of a Lifetime.* New York: Simon and Schuster, 1991.

Caro, Robert A. *LBJ: Means of Ascent.* New York: Vintage, 1990.

Caro, Robert. *LBJ: Master of the Senate.* New York: Knopf, 2002.

Caro, Robert. *LBJ: the Path to Power.* New York: Alfred Knopf, 1982.

Chatterjee, Pratap. *Iraq, Inc.: a Profitable Occupation.* New York: Seven Stories Press, 2004.

Choate, Pat. *Agents of Influence.* New York: Knopf, 1990.

Chomsky, Noam. *Hegemony or Survival.* New York: Henry Holt, 2003.

Clarke, Richard. *Against All Enemies.* New York: Free Press, 2004.

Cockburn, Alexander, and Jeffrey St. Clair. *Al Gore: a User's Manual.* New York: Verso, 2000.

Cockburn, Alexander, and Jeffrey St. Clair. *Imperial Crusades: Iraq, Afghanistan and Yugoslavia.* New York: Verso, 2004.

Cockburn, Alexander, and Ken Silverstein. *Washington Babylon.* New York: Verso, 1996.

Cockburn, Andrew, and Patrick Cockburn. *Out of the Ashes: the Resurrection of Saddam Hussein.* New York: HarperColllins, 1999.

Cockburn, Andrew. *The Threat: Inside the Soviet Military Machine.* New York: Random House, 1983.

Connally, John with Mickey Herskowitz. *In History's Shadow.* New York: Hyperion, 1993.

Crevald, Martin. *The Rise and Decline of the State.* New York: Cambridge University Press, 1999.

Crile, George. *Charlie Wilson's War.* New York: Atlantic Monthly Press, 2003.

Dean, John. *Worse Than Watergate.* New York: Little, Brown, 2004.

Devlin, John F. *The Ba'ath Party.* Stanford, CA: Hoover Institute Press, 1976.

Domke, David. *God Willing.* London: Pluto Press, 2004.

Drew, Elizabeth. *Citizen McCain.* New York: Simon and Schuster, 2004.

DuBose, Lou, Jan Reid and Carl M. Cannon. *Boy Genius.* New York: Public Affairs, 2003.

Dugger, Ronnie. *The Politician.* New York: Norton, 1982.

Ehrlichman, John. *Witness to Power.* New York: Simon and Schuster,

1987.

Engler, Robert. *The Brotherhood of Oil.* Chicago: University of Chicago Press, 1977.

Fallows, James. *National Defense.* New York: Random House, 1981.

Ferrell, Robert H. *The Eisenhower Diaries.* New York: Norton, 1981.

Fitzgerald, A. Ernest. *The Pentagonists.* Boston: Houghton Mifflin, 1989.

Fitzgerald, Frances. *Way Out There in the Blue: Reagan, Star Wars and the End of the Cold War.* New York: Touchstone, 2000.

Flanders, Laura. *Bushwomen: Tales of a Cynical Species.* New York: Verso, 2004.

Fox, J. Ronald. *Arming America: How the United States Buys Weapons.* Cambridge, MA: Harvard Business School, 1974.

Frank, Joshua. *Left Out.* Monroe, ME: Common Courage Press, 2005.

Frank, Justin A. *Bush on the Couch.* New York: ReganBooks, 2004.

Gerhart, Ann. *The Perfect Wife.* New York: Simon and Schuster, 2004.

Goff, Stan. *Full Spectrum Disorder.* Brooklyn: Softskull, 2004.

Green, Fitzhugh. *George Bush: an Intimate Portrait.* New York: Hippocrene Books, 1989.

Green, Mark, and Gail MacColl. *Reagan's Reign of Error.* New York: Pantheon, 1987.

Greenberg, Karen J., and Joshua L. Dratel, eds. *The Torture Papers.* New York: Cambridge University Press, 2005.

Greene, John Robert. *The Presidency of George Bush.* Lawrence: University of Kansas, 2000.

Greider, William. *Fortress America.* New York: Public Affairs, 1998.

Hanrahan, John. *Government By Contract.* New York: Norton, 1983.

Hartung, William D. *And Weapons For All.* New York: HarperCollins, 1994.

Hartung, William D. *How Much Are You Making on the War, Daddy?* New York: Nation Books, 2004.

Hatfield, J.H. *Fortunate Son.* New York: Softskull Press, 2000.

Hedges, Chris. *War is a Force that Gives Us Meaning.* New York: Anchor Books, 2002.

Herken, Gregg. *Counsels of War.* New York: Knopf, 1985.

Hersh, Seymour. *Chain of Command.* New York: HarperCollins: 2004.

Herskowitz, Mickey. *Duty, Honor, Country.* Nashville: Rutledge Hill Press, 2003.

Higgs, Robert. *Against Leviathan*. Oakland: Independent Institute, 2004.

Higham, Charles. *Trading with the Enemy*. New York: Delacorte Press, 1983.

Hoopes, Townsend. *The Devil and John Foster Dulles*. Boston: Little Brown, 1973.

Hughes, Emmet Johh. *The Ordeal of Power: a Political Memoir of the Eisenhower Years*. New York: Atheneum, 1963.

Hunt, Gaillard, ed. *The Writings of James Madison*. New York: G.P. Putnam's Sons, 1906.

Isaacson, Walter and Evan Thomas. *The Wise Men*. New York: Touchstone, 1986.

Ivins, Molly and Lou DuBose. *Bushwhacked*. New York: Random House, 2003.

Janos, Lee, and Ben R. Rich. *Skunkworks: a Personal Memoir of My Years at Lockheed*. Back Bay Books, 1994.

Jensen, Robert. *Citizens of Empire*. San Francisco: City Lights Books, 2004.

Jettleson, Bruce W. *With Friends Like These: Reagan, Bush and Saddam, 1982-1990*. New York: Norton, 1994.

Johnson, Chalmers, *The Sorrows of Empire: Militarism, Secrecy and the End of the Republic*. New York: Henry Holt, 2004.

Kaplan, Fred. *The Wizards of Armageddon*. Stanford, CA: Stanford University Press, 1983.

Kelley, Kitty. *The Family: the Real Story of the Bush Dynasty*. New York: Random House, 2004.

Kilian, Pamela. *Barbara Bush*. New York: St. Martin's Press, 1992.

King, Nicholas. *George Bush: a Biography*. New York: Dodd, Mead. 1980.

Kinzer, Stephen. *All the Shah's Men: an American Coup and the Roots of Middle East Terror*. New York: Wiley and Sons, 2003.

Knaggs, John R. *Two-Party Texas*. Austin: Eakin Press, 1986.

Kolko, Gabriel. *Another Century of War*. New York: New Press, 2002.

Kotz, Nick. *Wild Blue Yonder: Money, Politics and the B-1 Bomber*. Princeton: Princeton University Press, 1988.

Landau, Saul. *The Preemptive Empire: a Guide to Bush's Kingdom*. London: Pluto Press, 2003.

Lewis, Charles and the Center for Public Integrity. *The Buying of the*

President 2000. New York: Avon Books, 2000.

Lewis, Charles, and the Center for Responsive Politics. *The Buying of the President: 2004.* New York: HarperCollins, 2004.

Lind, Michael. *Made in Texas.* New York: Basic Books, 2003.

Lindquist, Sven. *A History of Bombing.* New York: New Press, 2001.

Liske, Craig and Barry Rundquist. *The Politics of Weapons Procurement.* Denver: Unversity of Denver, 1974.

Loftus, John and Mark Aarons. *The Secret War Against the Jews.* New York: St. Martin's Press, 1994.

Mahajan, Rahul. *Full Spectrum Dominance: US Power in Iraq and Beyond.* New York: Seven Stories, 2003.

Mahajan, Rahul. *The New Crusade.* New York: Monthly Review Press, 2002.

Mansfield, Steven. *The Faith of George W. Bush.* New York: Jeremy P. Tarcher, 2003.

Marton, Kati. *Hidden Power.* New York: Pantheon, 2001.

Mayer, Kenneth R. *The Political Economy of Defense Contracting.* New Haven: Yale University Press, 1991.

McCain, John, with Mark Salter. *Worth the Fighting For.* New York: Random House, 2002.

McCartney, Laton. *Friends in High Places: the Bechtel Story.* New York: Ballatine, 1989.

McGrath, James, ed. *Heartbeat: George Bush in His Own Words.* New York: Scribner, 2001.

McMaster, H.R. *Dereliction of Duty: Lyndon Johnson, Robert McNamara, the Joint Chiefs of Staff and the Lies that Led to Vietnam.* New York: Harper Perennial, 1997.

Milbank, Dana. *Smashmouth.* New York: Basic Books, 2001.

Miller, Mark Crispin. *The Bush Dyslexicon.* New York: Bantam Books, 2001.

Minutaglio, Bill. *First Son.* New York: Times Books, 1999.

Moore, James, and Wayne Slater. *Bush's Brain.* New York: John Wiley and Sons, 2003.

Napoleoni, Loretta. *Terror Incorporated.* New York: Seven Stories Press, 2005.

Newhouse, John. *Imperial America.* New York: Knopf, 2003.

Norris, Guy. *Boeing.* Osceola, WI: MB Publishing, 1998.

Pamet, Herbert S. *George Bush: the Life of a Lone Star Yankee*. New York: Scribner, 1997.

Phillips, Kevin. *American Dynasty*. New York: Viking, 2004.

Pilger, John. *The New Rulers of the World*. London: Verso, 2002.

Pollin, Robert. *Contours of Descent*. New York: Verso, 2003.

Pool, James, and Suzanne Pool. *Who Financed Hitler: the Secret Funding of Hitler's Rise to Power, 1919-1933*. New York: Dial Press, 1978.

Pratt, Joseph A. and Christopher J. Casteneda. *Builders: Herman and George Brown*. College Station, TX: Texas A & M Press, 1999.

Priest, Dana. *The Mission: Waging War and Keeping Peace with America's Military*. New York: Norton, 2003.

Proxmire, William. *Uncle Sam: Last of the Big Time Spenders*. New York: Simon and Schuster, 1972.

Radcliffe, Donnie. *Simply Barbara Bush*. New York: Warner Books, 1989.

Rai, Milan. *War Plan Iraq*. New York: Verso, 2002.

Rampton, Sheldon, and John Stauber. *Weapons of Mass Deception*. New York: Penguin, 2003.

Ranelagh, John. *The Agency: the Rise and Decline of the CIA*. New York: Touchstone, 1986.

Rasor, Dina. *The Pentagon Underground*. New York: Times Books, 1985.

Reagan, Ronald. *An American Life*. New York: Simon and Schuster, 1990.

Redding, Robert, and Bill Yenne. *Boeing: Planemaker to the World*. San Diego: Thunder Bay Press, 1997.

Robbins, Alexandra. *Secrets of the Tomb*. Boston: Little, Brown, 2002.

Rodengen, Jeffrey. *The Legend of Halliburton*. Ft. Lauderdale: Write Stuff Press, 1996.

Scheer, Robert. *With Enough Shovels: Reagan, Bush and Nuclear War*. New York: Vintage Books, 1983.

Schweizer, Peter, and Rochelle Schweizer. *The Bushes*. New York: Doubleday, 2004.

Sherrill, Robert. *LBJ: the Accidental President*. New York: Grossman, 1967.

Sherrill, Robert. *Why They Call It Politics*. New York: Harcourt, Brace, Jovanovich, 1990.

Sherry, Michael S. *The Rise of American Air Power: the Creation of Armageddon*. New Haven: Yale University Press, 1987.

Shultz, George P. *Turmoil and Triumph*. New York: Scribner, 1993.

Silverstein, Ken. *Private Warriors*. New York: Verso, 2000.

Simpson, Christopher. *The Splendid Blond Beast: Money, Law and Genocide in the Twentieth Century*. New York: Grove Press, 1993.

Singer, P.W. *Corporate Warriors*. Ithaca, NY: Cornell University Press, 2003.

Smith, Hedrick. *The Power Game: How Washington Works*. New York: Random House, 1988.

Stares, Paul B. *Space and National Security*. Washington, DC: Brookings Institution, 1987.

Stevens, Stuart. *The Big Enchilada*. New York: Free Press, 2001.

Stone, I.F. *The War Years*. Boston: Little, Brown, 1988.

Stubbing, Richard A., and Richard A. Mendel. *The Defense Game: an Insider Explores the Astonishing Realities of America's Defense Establishment*. New York: Harper and Row, 1986.

Trento, Susan B. *The Power House*. New York: St. Martin's Press, 1992.

Tsipis, Kosta. *Arsenal: Understanding Weapons in the Nuclear Age*. New York: Touchstone, 1983.

Unger, Craig. *House of Bush, House of Saud*. New York: Scribner, 2004.

Union of Concerned Scientists. *Empty Promise: the Growing Case Against Star Wars*. Boston: Beacon, 1986.

Vidal, Gore. *Dreaming War*. New York: Nation Books, 2002.

Vidal, Gore. *Perpetual War for Perpetual Peace*. New York: Nation Books, 2002.

Walsh, Lawrence. *Firewall*. New York: Norton, 1997.

Wead, Doug. *All the President's Children*. New York: Atria Books, 2003.

Weiner, Tim. *Blank Check: the Pentagon's Black Budget*. New York: Warner Books, 1990.

Wicker, Tom. *George Herbert Walker Bush*. New York: Viking, 2004.

Williams, Ian. *Deserter*. New York: Nation Books, 2004.

Winslow T. Wheeler. *The Wastrels of Defense: How Congress Sabotages U.S. Security*. Annapolis: Naval Institute Press, 2004.

Wise, David. *The Politics of Lying: Government Deception, Secrecy and Power*. New York: Random House, 1973.

Woodward, Bob. *Bush at War*. New York: Simon and Schuster, 2002.

Woodward, Bob. *Veil: the Secret Wars of the CIA*. New York: Simon and Schuster, 1987.

Woodward, Bob. *Plan of Attack*. New York: Simon and Schuster, 2004.

Woodward, Bob. *The Commanders*. New York: Scribner, 2001.

Yergin, Daniel. *The Prize*. New York: Simon and Schuster, 1991.

Young, Marylin B. *The Vietnam Wars: 1945-1990*. New York: HarperCollins, 1991.

Zunes, Stephen. *Tinderbox: US Foreign Policy and the Roots of Terrorism*. Monroe, Maine: Common Courage, 2003.

Resources

CounterPunch
www.counterpunch.org

Center for Public Integrity
Windfalls of War Report
http://www.publicintegrity.org/wow/report.aspx?aid=334

CPI
Making a Killing Report
http://www.publicintegrity.org/bow/

DefenseLink
http://www.defenselink.mil/search/

Defense in the National Interest
http://www.d-n-i.net/

Iraq Coalition Casualties Count
http://icasualties.org/oif/

Open Secrets
Rebuilding Iraq: the Contractors
http://www.opensecrets.org/news/rebuilding_iraq/index.asp

International Relations Center
The Right Web
http://rightweb.irc-online.org/index.php

Project on Government Oversight
http://www.pogo.org/

Committee on Government Reform (Waxman)
Iraq Contracting and Reconstruction
http://www.democrats.reform.house.gov/investigations.asp?Issue=Iraq+Contracting+and+Reconstruction

World Policy Institute
Arms Trade Resource Center
http://www.worldpolicy.org/projects/arms/index.html

Global Security
Iraq Reconstruction and Occupation
http://www.globalsecurity.org/military/ops/iraq_reconstruction.htm

Halliburton Watch
http://halliburtonwatch.org/

CorpWatch
http://www.corpwatch.org/

Sustainable Energy and Economy Network
http://www.seen.org/pages/about.shtml

Taxpayers for Common Sense
http://www.taxpayer.net/

Federation of American Scientists
http://www.fas.org

Arms Control Association
http://www.armscontrol.org/assorted/dkbio.asp

Institute for Policy Studies
www.i-p-s.org

Transnational Institute
www.tni.org

Index

T

U

About the Author

J effrey St. Clair edits, along with Alexander Cockburn, the investigative newsletter and website CounterPunch.org, which has been called "the best political newsletter in America." He is a contributing editor of *In These Times* and writes the weekly Nature and Politics column for the *Anderson Valley Advertiser*. His reporting has appeared in *The Washington Post, San Francisco Examiner, The Nation, The Progressive, New Left Review* and many other publications. His books include *Whiteout: The CIA, Drugs and the Press, Al Gore: A User's Manual, Five Days That Shook the World: The WTO, Seattle and Beyond, The Politics of Anti-Semitism* (all with Cockburn), *A Guide to Environmental Bad Guys* with James Ridgeway, and *Been Brown So Long It Looked Like Green To Me* and *Imperial Crusades*. A native of Indiana, he now lives in Oregon with his wife Kimberly, daughter Zen and son Nat.